Cambridge English Prose Texts

ictorian Criti
of the Novel

ed by Edwin M. Eigner and George J. Worth

OE;

NCE.

WAVERLEY," &c.

ow traversed the cart,
but seem'd loth to depart !
PRIOR.

E VOLUMES.

OL. I.

DINBURGH:
.D CONSTABLE AND CO. EDINBURGH;
N, AND CO. 90, CHEAPSIDE, LONDON.
1820.

IDDLEMARCH

A

UDY OF PROVINCIAL LIFE

BY

GEORGE ELIOT

VOL. I.

M BLACKWOOD AND SONS
NBURGH AND LONDON
MDCCCLXXI

CAMBRIDGE ENGLISH PROSE TEXTS

Victorian Criticism of the Novel

CAMBRIDGE ENGLISH PROSE TEXTS

General editor: GRAHAM STOREY

OTHER BOOKS IN THE SERIES
The Evangelical and Oxford Movements, edited by Elisabeth Jay
Science and Religion in the Nineteenth Century, edited by Tess Cosslett
Burke, Paine, Godwin and the Revolution Controversy, edited by
Marilyn Butler
Revolutionary Prose of the English Civil War, edited by
Howard Erskine-Hill and Graham Storey
American Colonial Prose: John Smith to Thomas Jefferson,
edited by Mary Ann Radzinowicz

FORTHCOMING
Romantic Critical Essays, edited by David Bromwich

Victorian Criticism of the Novel

edited by

EDWIN M. EIGNER

Professor of English
University of California, Riverside

and

GEORGE J. WORTH

Professor of English
University of Kansas

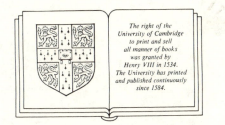

The right of the
University of Cambridge
to print and sell
all manner of books
was granted by
Henry VIII in 1534.
The University has printed
and published continuously
since 1584.

CAMBRIDGE UNIVERSITY PRESS

Cambridge
London   New York   New Rochelle
Melbourne   Sydney

Published by the Press Syndicate of the University of Cambridge
The Pitt Building, Trumpington Street, Cambridge CB2 1RP
32 East 57th Street, New York, NY 10022, USA
10 Stamford Road, Oakleigh, Melbourne 3166, Australia

First published 1985

Printed in Great Britain at
the University Press, Cambridge

Library of Congress catalogue card number: 84-28572

British Library Cataloguing in Publication Data
Victorian criticism of the novel. – (Cambridge
English prose texts)
1. English fiction – 18th century – History
and criticism 2. English fiction – 19th
century – History and criticism
I. Eigner, Edwin M.   II. Worth, George J.
809.3   PR851
ISBN 0 521 25515 5 hard covers
ISBN 0 521 27520 2 paperback

PR872
V5
1985

CE

Contents

Acknowledgements

We wish to acknowledge the help of some of the many scholars who have given of their time and knowledge: Professors Ruth apRoberts, George Haggerty, and Thomas Scanlon of the University of California at Riverside; Frank Baron, Michael Henderson, Stanley Lombardo, Harold Orel, Oliver Phillips, Robert Rankin, Michael Shaw, and Donald Warders of the University of Kansas. Many librarians have provided valuable assistance. Among them are Ruth Halman, Elizabeth Lang, and Clifford Wurfel of the University of California; James Helyar, Sally Hocker, and Eleanor Symons of the University of Kansas; Mildred Abraham of the University of Virginia; and M. A. Begg of the National Library of Scotland. Dr Andrew Brown of Cambridge University Press has been a helpful, a patient, and a creative editor.

Introductory essay

It has become usual to begin such discussions as this by contesting the traditional view that there was no valuable theoretical criticism of British fiction before Henry James. Both commonplaces, the usual *and* the traditional, are valid. Throughout the nineteenth century there was a great deal of novel criticism published in Britain, and a fair amount of it was written by highly intelligent reviewers and essayists, who were well paid for their efforts and were passionate about their subject. It is also true, however, that most of these critics rather prided themselves on the non-theoretical character of their intellects. For example, only a year before the celebrated James–Stevenson debate on the art of fiction, a less brilliant but more representative critic, Henry Norman, could write with Podsnappian complacency, 'The truth is that theory in such matters is alien to the English mind, and that to find it we must pass to other nations whose authors are always critical, even to the sacrifice of their creative powers' (*Fortnightly Review*, 1883). From such a point of view, of course, since James was himself a foreigner whose creative powers were frequently understood to suffer because of his penchant for theories, there were, as Edith Simcox had written in *Academy* in 1871, 'no general principles of criticism recognized at once in the production and the appreciation of works of fiction', and no nineteenth-century theory of English fiction at all.

Obviously we do not agree with this view; although we do concede that because of the national prejudice against abstract thinking, especially in regard to so down-to-earth an item as a story, it is necessary frequently to read between the lines and to find English theory almost reluctantly put forth in arguments whose avowed purpose was to protect the English novel from theoretical foreigners and their misguided native disciples. Thus the ideas which informed English realism at the beginning of the Victorian period developed out of the defense against the theorists of German and French romantic fiction, and at the end of the century what the romancer Hall Caine was to call 'The New Watchwords of Fiction' (*Contemporary Review*, 1890) were spoken in opposition to the realistic manifestos of Zola and Howells. Indeed, the title of Stevenson's response to James,

'A Humble Remonstrance', could serve ironically for an entire history of Victorian criticism of prose fiction.

The period began, if we take 1832 as a starting point, with the death of Walter Scott, who had transformed the novel into the most profitable art form in England and who was perhaps the first Briton since Shakespeare who had achieved both popularity and distinction throughout Europe. It was also the year of Goethe's death, and British Germanophiles did not hesitate to compare the two masters, concluding usually that mass popularity was not enough. 'Literature *has* other aims than that of harmlessly amusing indolent, languid men', Carlyle wrote in his review of Lockhart's *Life of Scott*, 'or if literature have them not, then literature is a very poor affair; and something else must have them, and must accomplish them, with thanks or without thanks' (*London and Westminster Review*, 1838). Bulwer Lytton, who was never willing to admit that literature, and especially the writing of fiction, was or could be anything less than man's highest calling, is similarly hard on Scott, but what both critics were really challenging was the whole tradition of the English novel which Scott represented, with its emphasis on the description of external reality and manners. Bulwer Lytton especially professed himself unable to see how a genre which consciously divorced itself from philosophical interests and made virtues of its languid lack of aesthetic principles and its *ad hoc* mode of construction could fulfil the traditional functions of a leading art form.

Thackeray and some of the more doctrinaire realists responded at first simply by ridiculing Bulwer Lytton's pretensions, but gradually main-line critics forged a coherent, if not a systematic aesthetic of realism. Not that domestic realism ever felt itself seriously threatened. 'The only semblance of a principle which presided at the birth of the British novel', according to Edith Simcox, once again, 'was the principle of realistic probability', and the genre was well-enough entrenched in the nineteenth century easily to outlast the Newgate Novel of the 1830s, with its criminal heroes, and to survive the Brontës, Dickens, the vogue of the sensational novel, and even the aesthetic movement. Moreover, the great majority of the criticism published during the first half of the period seemed to call for realism of the most simple sort – mere verisimilitude and historical accuracy. As late as 1901 Arnold Bennett could say, with the complacency of a Dr Johnson kicking the stone, 'By the term "realistic novel" I simply mean, of course, one whose aim is to be *real*, regardless of any conventions which would involve a divergence from life itself' (*Fame and Fiction*). Nevertheless, the undercurrent of romantic criticism, represented in this volume by the contributions of Bulwer Lytton, George Moir, and Archibald Alison, provoked a majority rationale, put forth by thoughtful realists like G. H. Lewes and George Eliot and Henry James, who wished also to argue the case for fiction as a fully serious art form.

A critic writing in 1843 in *Fraser's Magazine*, the early bastion of realism, based the propensities of the English novel on principles derived from Baconian induction, whereas the French novel, he argued, grew out of theory and fancy. 'From the moment Frenchmen become candidates for literary popularity, they abandon themselves to visions and ecstasies, and renounce realities.' An important *Athenaeum* review of Mrs Trollope's *Charles Chesterfield* maintained in 1841 that the novel, as opposed to the romance, which 'addresses itself to the imagination alone', was in keeping with the spirit of the present age because it 'appeals to the observant and reasoning faculties also'. And R. H. Hutton wrote that 'the empire of the novel ... is really based on the desire of a self-conscious race to look at itself in the glass, and to see itself, as it were, under analysis, – to study itself either clothed, as with [Anthony] Trollope; or nude, as with Thackeray; or under the anatomist's knife, as with the author of *Romola*' (*Spectator*, 1869).

Lewes himself always maintained that fiction, if it is to have any value, must be based on experiential reality and that it should present a convincing picture of life, yet his is always an intelligent modification of the position held by the more doctrinaire realists, one which takes seriously into account many of the points the apologists for romance had been making. Art, he felt, should present 'a selection of typical elements from life', rather than a transcript or a mirror reflection (*Leader*, 1853). He ranked Jane Austen as the greatest craftsman among English novelists and called her his favourite; yet he worried that her work might not be significant or deep or passionate enough to warrant the highest praise. 'Her place is among great artists, but it is not high among them' (*Blackwood's*, 1859). Lewes's admiration for Goethe was so great that, rather than reject his novels, he dismissed the usual distinction between realism and idealism in favour of a contrast between realism and falsism, thus rendering meaningless the novel-versus-romance controversy that the former set of terms had traditionally informed. With this change of language, even Raphael, who had symbolized the idealizing artist in almost all nineteenth-century discussions of aesthetics, but who was another favourite of Lewes, could be claimed as a realist. But by the same token, realism became a genre capable of bearing a considerable intellectual burden.

And, of course, Lewes's was the criticism which, to a large extent, informed and enabled the fiction of George Eliot.

In one respect, however, Lewes refused to modify the realist position in response to the theorists of romance criticism. He maintained that unity in a novel is no different from unity in the drama (*Blackwood's*, 1860). This was in contrast to William Henry Smith, whose important article 'The Novel and the Drama', which had appeared in *Blackwood's* fifteen years earlier, argued for a clear distinction between the two genres. So had William Godwin in the 'Preface' to *Cloudesley* (1830), and so, indeed, had Bulwer Lytton in 'On the Different Kinds of Prose Fiction' (1835). Smith, Godwin, and Bulwer were trying to define fiction as a genre with rules particular to itself. James Philip Runzo, who is the best historian of early Victorian criticism of fiction, writes that 'The most striking feature ... between 1830 and 1850 is the explicit recognition and valuation of the novel as a genre distinct from other forms, particularly the drama.'[1] To establish this distinction some romance critics were specifically trying to establish unity of theme rather than unity of action as appropriate to those art forms, a position Bulwer Lytton would amplify in still another *Blackwood's* article (May 1863). The basis for this preference is to be found in the romancers' primary and immediate interest in the philosophy they had all along been insisting fiction must express. Unity of action, dramatic unity, it was felt, swept the reader off his intellectual feet and made him captive to induced passions rather than master of encouraged thought. Thus George Moir complains about Dick Turpin's exciting ride in Ainsworth's *Rookwood* because it is so effective: 'the truth is, the reader is never allowed to pause for an instant to think at all' (*Edinburgh Review*, 1837), and R. H. Hutton was somewhat dubious about Trollope because his imagination did not seem ever

to brood long over visions that task its full power ... There is nothing, apparently, of the agony of meditated travail about his mind ... In short, Mr Trollope does not give us so much the impression of conceiving his own conceptions, as of very accurately observing them as they pass along the screen of some interior faculty. In this respect he differs from almost all his greater brother artists. (*Spectator*, 1862)

Critics hospitable to realism were sometimes keenly aware of this problem of the apparent non-intellectuality of the genre. We have already noted Lewes's reservations about Jane Austen, the most dramatic and least meditative of important novelists to that date. W. C. Roscoe in his article on Defoe (*National Review*, 1856) was concerned that the realist's essential interest in the external nature of things and events might be at the expense of his powers of analysis.

Roscoe could be stern about Bulwer Lytton's claims to be a philosopher (*National Review*, 1859); yet, when he turned his attention to the realist Thackeray, he regretted 'the absence from his books of what we are accustomed to call ideas', and he suggested in a troubled manner that Thackeray might just be 'the better observer of manners *because* he never cares to penetrate below them' (*National Review*, 1856. Our emphasis). Like Roscoe, Leslie Stephen was concerned that Defoe's technique of photographic realism, which more or less dictated a go-ahead dramatic mode of narration, worked against authorial interpretation (*Hours in a Library*, vol. 1). He also wished there might have been more theme and more thought in Charlotte Brontë's *Villette* so that the hero, Paul Emanuel, whom Stephen greatly admired as a realistic portrait, might have been seen also from 'an intellectual point of view, placed in his due relation to the great currents of thought and feeling of the time' (*Hours in a Library*, vol. 3). And in his essay on Hawthorne (*Cornhill Magazine*, 1872), Stephen posited that 'some central truth should be embodied in every work of fiction, which cannot be compressed into a definite formula, but which acts as the animating and informing principle, determining the main lines of the structure and affecting even its most trivial details'.

As this last quotation indicates, a concern for unity was common to critics of all stripes. It is apparent even in the formats of the book reviews, which beginning in the late 1840s were becoming self-conscious about the time-honoured practice of filling out the bulk of the articles with passages extracted from the novels under discussion. By the late 1850s most reviewers had enough respect for the integrity of a work of fiction to resist representing it through snippets. This respect is also apparent in the very frequent objections one hears about the novel's serial mode of publication, a method 'unprincipled in the artistic sense', according to Harriet Martineau (*Autobiography*, vol. 1, p. 416) and, as another critic pointed out, 'destructive of the regular development of the tale [because it] subordinates the natural march of events to the necessity of producing a *coup de théâtre* for each distinct issue' (*Athenaeum*, 1841). Moreover, critics throughout the period complained bitterly about the arbitrary three-volume structure, imposed on the novel by the marketing needs of the circulating library.

Lewes, who criticized even *Tom Jones* for its want of unity, was also aware of this current of Victorian criticism of the novel. 'The object of construction', he wrote, 'is to free the story from all superfluity' (*Blackwood's*, 1869). But Lewes's objection, in so far as the question of unity was concerned, had to do with episodic digressions from the central *action* rather than with the absence of a controlling *thought*. Indeed, although the novel was being taken more and more seriously in these years as a vehicle for the expression of significant ideas, the concept of a theme controlling its action was in some ways adverse to the developing aesthetic of realism. One of the most underrated of the critics of the earlier part of the period, Thomas Lister, had argued that 'although the "purpose" of the novel – the evaluation of the materials – is implicit in the work, it must seem "casual", [because] the reader demands the illusion that the novel generates itself' (*Edinburgh Review*, 1839). Even earlier, Lister had anticipated Henry James by recommending a point of view – he actually uses the term – as a means of producing this illusion of self-generation. Some novelists fail, he wrote, 'because they present to us objects as they are, rather than as they appear ... Others, though they in part describe objects as they appear to the spectator, yet mix them confusedly with circumstances of which the eye could not have taken cognisance at all, – or could not have seen from the same point of view' (*Edinburgh Review*, 1832). In the same year, Lockhart had explained how it was possible simultaneously to achieve both unity and real self-generation, rather than merely the illusion of it, simply by focusing dramatically on a given character and permitting the action to develop naturally out of his nature and the circumstances surrounding him. The key to this technique was to avoid introducing anything arbitrary, such as a moral position or a controlling thought (*Blackwood's*). A writer for the *North British Review* (1856) argued that when a novelist tries to prove a point, he loses the chance of showing how the destinies of his characters are 'influenced by one another and by circumstances in accordance with the natural course of events as presented to us by experience ... By aiming at the two incompatible objects', the review concludes, 'the author does not succeed in either.'

This insistence on dramatic as opposed to thematic unity was of course intended as much as a defence against the demands of the moralists as of the philosophical romancers and, indeed, sometimes it is difficult to keep the two schools of critics apart. Presumably the romancers wanted to elevate fiction to the status of philosophy, and the only way some of them believed this could be done was to make the story illustrative of a preconceived intellectual position. The moralists insisted that fiction should induce good behaviour in the reader and provide him with healthy models to emulate, or at the very least not seduce him to evil actions by glorifying sick thoughts and wicked characters. All of these aims also required considerable pre-conception. When Carlyle is taking Scott to task it is hard to decide whether he thinks the Waverley Novels fall short of greatness because their author is too little like Goethe or not enough like John Knox, or whether Carlyle really sees a significant difference between the two:

> In the nineteenth century, our highest literary man, who immeasurably beyond all others commanded the world's ear, had, as it were, no message whatever to deliver to the world; wished not the world to elevate itself, to amend itself, to do this or to do that, except simply pay him for the books he kept writing.
>
> (*London and Westminster Review*, 1838)

One difference between the romancers and the moralists was that the latter certainly did not represent only an undercurrent in the flow of criticism. The demand that a novel be moral was at least as frequently made as the requirement that it be real, and even though the majority of the better critics were against direct exhortation, morally improving fiction was popular throughout the period. As Havelock Ellis wrote as late as 1896, 'whereas children can only take their powders in jam, the strenuous British public cannot be induced to devour their jam unless convinced that it contains some strange and nauseous powder' (*Savoy*).

This demand for didactic fiction worked against the romancers, especially in the 1830s and the 1870s when romance writers were interested in exploring the criminal psyche. A review of one of Bulwer Lytton's criminal novels admired the 'eloquence, natural and fervent feeling, and vigorous delineation of human character in this work', and yet 'sincerely' wished that he 'had left it unwritten. We think the principle on which it is constructed is unnatural. Genius can do much, but not all: she cannot, with propriety, clothe a treacherous murderer in the garments of beauty' (*Athenaeum*, 1832). Thomas Cleghorn wrote that since the main interest of *Oliver Twist* 'is made to depend on the most debased and villainous agents ... the work had done much towards creating in the public a morbid interest in such heroes and their mode of life, [and] a relish for such writing', he warned ominously, 'soon becomes a craving' (*North British Review*, 1845). Dickens had already expressed himself as having no respect for the 'opinion, good or bad of people of so refined and delicate a nature that they cannot bear the contemplation of these horrors' (Preface to the 1841 edition of *Oliver Twist*), and Bulwer Lytton, after his novel *Lucretia* (1846) had been almost universally condemned as a wicked book, replied in a pamphlet that 'Crime, in fact, is the essential material of Tragic Drama' (*A Word to the Public*, 1847). 'If so,' replied one moral critic who refused to be put off, 'we should be disposed to assert that the decline of the drama, as far as tragedy is concerned, is not a subject for lamentation; and the fact that many tragedies formerly popular, and still considered classic, have been driven from the stage, we trace to the tendencies of a growing civilisation' (*Westminster and Foreign Quarterly Review*, 1847).

But the realistic novel of ordinary life was certainly not exempt from the strictures of these same critics. Indeed, Clara Reeve in *The Progress of Romance* (1785) had argued that the realistic novel (she had *Tom Jones* especially in mind) was unfit as a vehicle for moral instruction because it was bound to reality and compelled, as the romance was not, to present men as they really are. In the nineteenth century some critics felt that the fallible protagonist of the everyday novel was even more dangerous than the pernicious hero of glamourous romance because the ordinary reader would find it the easier to identify with him. According to some moralists it was spiritually unprofitable for the reader to empathize even with morally good characters for, as Elizabeth Jay has recently written, evangelicals believed that this exercise would 'dissipate love for one's fellow creatures upon imaginary figures'.[2]

It was this last charge that George Eliot may have been responding to in the famous digression in chapter 17 of *Adam Bede*. There she argues that the reader's identification with a character, at least when the latter is of the sort the reader must encounter in his own life, exercises and builds an empathic muscle, so to speak, making it possible for the reader to identify with his real neighbours and to feel charitably towards them. Some of the other objections of the moralists could also be dealt with. Although attorneys from the 1840s to the present have found it at least worth a try in the defence of obviously guilty clients, critics were becoming less and less impressed with the argument that readers imitate the wicked or illegal behaviour of fictional characters. 'It will take many Aurora Floyds [bigamist title character of M. E. Braddon's novel, 1863] to make one interesting bigamist', a writer for the *Saturday Review* remarked in 1866. The same critic warned, it is true, that novels might work more subtly on the reader, inculcating in them an 'epicurism' and an 'absolute indifference to all that appertains to the higher life of a rational being'. Moreover, Leslie Stephen insisted that 'cynicism, prurience, and voluptuous delight in cruelty' are abominable, and 'he who keeps them alive is doing harm, and more harm if he has the talent of a Shakespeare, a Mozart, or a Raphael' (*Cornhill Magazine*, 1875). But such concerns, serious though they were, did not require preconception on the part of the author. All that was needed was that, unlike such writers as Laurence Sterne, as Thackeray and Stephen saw him, and unlike most French novelists, the author be of a healthy and sensibly moral character and that, following the model of Scott, he permit his basic decency to shine through and become naturally embodied in the work. This sort of thing could be overdone, as Thackeray thought was the case with L.E.L.'s *Ethel Churchill* – 'she has no idea of a dramatic character; and it is Miss Landon who speaks and feels throughout' (*Fraser's*, 1838) – but it could certainly be managed by a skilful artist, as it was to be managed by Thackeray himself, by Trollope, and by others, both with and without intrusive narrators.

What could not be so easily accommodated within the growing aesthetic of the realistic novel were the demands by moralists that the novel improve the world in some very specific way. The curate novel of the 1840s, one critic recalled nostalgically,

produced, on the whole, a very healthy excitement in the female bosom. It developed the missionary zeal which is strong in women. It stimulated young ladies to unprecedented feats of parochial activity. They lectured the poor, they visited the sick, they taught in schools, they carved poppy-heads, they worked altar-clothes, they scrubbed brasses, they even went so far as to dabble in theology, and could speak fluently of the points of difference between Romish and Anglican communities.

(*Saturday Review*, 1866)

A novel intended to move the pious reader to such exertions needed careful planning. Dickens, who would have found little to admire and much to satirize in such activities, was frequently praised for the moral aims of his novels. His works, wrote Richard Ford in his review of *Oliver Twist*, 'like good sermons, contribute to our moral health' (*Quarterly Review*, 1839). And, of course, novels which sought to improve social conditions, as written by Dickens, Kingsley, Reade and others, absolutely required considerable preconception.

This last topic brings up an interesting side question which bears ultimately, as do all these considerations, on the problem of unity. In his review of Disraeli's *Sybil*, Thackeray criticized the very practice of airing social problems in fiction. 'You can't have a question fairly debated in this way. You can't allow an author to invent incidents, motives, and characters, in order that he may attack them sub-sequently. How many Puseyite novels, Evangelical novels, Roman Catholic novels have we had, and how absurd and unsatisfactory are they' (*Morning Chronicle*, 1845). This was precisely the position James Fitzjames Stephen was to take in his several anonymous *Spectator* and *Edinburgh Review* articles on *Little Dorrit*, especially regarding Dickens's invention in that novel of the Circumlocution Office, which Stephen read as a veiled attack on his own father. A novelist, Stephen complained, could simply make up any evidence he pleased and use it to lead his readers to false conclusions which might have serious consequences in the real world. Dickens's response, 'A Curious Misprint in the *Edinburgh Review*' (*Household Words*, 1857), showed clearly that essayists, Stephen in particular, could also falsify evidence for their own purposes, but the problem was not so easily disposed of. Dickens's article discredited Stephen's because an essay is required to be accurate in its facts. Veracity is essential to the discipline of persuasive writing. But, as the exasperated Stephen points out, no one ever desires the novel, where fiction and invention are the names of the game, to be factual. There is no accountability because, presumably, there is no discipline. The novelist can do just as he pleases, and honest men, like Stephen's father, are at his mercy.

What infuriated Dickens more than the charge of inaccuracy was the implication, not only in Stephen, but more frequently in Thackeray, that imaginative literature of whatever sort ought not to attempt to provide its readers with anything beyond simple amusement. Neither of them professed a high opinion of the social or moral value of fiction, and poets, for them, were certainly not the unacknowledged legislators of the world. Thackeray, indeed, liked to compare his own writing to pastry-making. Theirs was very much a minority position in the middle of the nineteenth century, but the two critics suggest perhaps a more interesting question than they may have intended, albeit a question as old as Socrates: Since poets do not seem, as judged from their behaviour, to be the wisest of men outside their poetry, what can be the authority for their wisdom within it? In the nineteenth century, and especially in the nineteenth-century novel, the muse is seldom invoked. Is fiction writing, therefore, anything better than soft journalism, or does it have a discipline unsuspected by Thackeray and Stephen, and even an epistemology?

The realists continued to regard as anathema the philosophical novel, where, as William Henry Smith described it, 'some theory or some dogma is expressly taught, where a vein of scholastic, or political, or ethical matter alternated with a vein of narrative and fictitious matter' (*Blackwood's*, 1845). But the same critic allows that 'every work of art of a high order will, in one sense of the word be philosophical'. How is this possible? The answer which the English realists seemed to be approaching was that a discipline could be found in fiction and new knowledge actually generated in the novel if the writer was prepared to trust his material absolutely, to recognize, as Lewes did, that 'the primary object' in fiction 'is character' (*The Life of Goethe*, 1855), and to be willing to get out of the way, so to speak, of the character's development, to be content simply and modestly to follow it as it unfolds. Such an aesthetic was related to

Keats's concept of negative capability, expressed shortly before the beginning of our period, and to Conrad's plea, near the end of it, that the reader (and the writer) forget to ask for the glimpse of truth which it is the business of the novel nevertheless to supply. The aesthetic required not only that a novelist abstain from incorporating raw hunks of his own philosophy and politics into his fiction, but that he himself be, as far as is possible, free from any philosophical or political conviction. Thackeray, writes William Caldwell Roscoe,

has no interest in intellectual conclusions. He would never have felt sufficient interest to ask with Pilate, 'What is truth?' Always occupied with moral symptoms, intently observing men, and deeply interested in their various modes of meeting the perplexities of life, he never attempts to decide a moral question ... Elsewhere ready enough to show in his proper person, he here shrinks anxiously out of sight.

(*National Review*, 1856)

The novelist, as Smith writes, must not be 'preoccupied with some engrossing idea which so besets the man that he can see nothing clearly in the world around him' (*Blackwood's*, 1845).

Indeed, the novelist is scarcely permitted even to direct his plot. 'The true medium', according to the author of 'A Novel or Two' (*National Review*, 1855), 'is to give so much agitating movement to the story as will justify a higher than ordinary tint of colouring in the delineation of external life; so that this again, in its turn, may justify subsidiary description of inward emotion.' Critics of the early part of the period, as James Phillip Runzo has written, believed that 'the novel renders an illusion of life, and any betrayal of the novelist–audience relationship, at least in the action proper of the work, where the characters and events, as in real life, work on their own without any *deus ex machina*, is a violation of its aesthetics'.[3] Runzo accurately paraphrases the critic George L. Craik (*Sketches of the History of Literature and Learning in England*, 1844–5) to the effect that 'the author must efface himself in spirit ... in order to live within the beings of his imagination ... must imagine himself as not possessing the knowledge he in fact must have to write the work'.[4] Sometimes, as W. C. Roscoe points out, Thackeray 'warns you expressly [that] he will not be responsible for what he is putting into the mouth of one of his characters' (*National Review*, 1856). At the end of the period, according to another modern commentator, Lynn C. Bartlett, the novelist's task is perceived as an attempt 'to present life as objectively as possible; he should avoid making explicit moral judgments; he ought not to take sides with or against his characters; he should conceal his own feelings and not try openly to influence the feelings of his readers'.[5] And, of course, the novelist must not enter the story in his own person and break the illusion. Scott felt that such intrusions indicated a lack of confidence of the author in his 'own powers' (*Ballantyne's Novelist's Library*, vol. 2, 1821). G. H. Lewes thought that Thackeray's interruptions called into question his 'respect for his art' (*The Leader*, 1850). And Henry James, as is well known, found that Trollope's authorial digressions, his 'little slaps at credulity', were 'very discouraging' (*Century Magazine*, 1883).

Poor Trollope got it from both sides. 'No great novelist', complained R. H. Hutton, 'probably ever drew so little from the resources of his own visionary life, – so much from impromptu variations of the forms given by experience' (*Spectator*, 1862). The fact is that in spite of his intrusions, Trollope was committed, perhaps more than any other English realist, to the aesthetic of following the characters to the conclusions, both dramatic and intellectual, which they chose for themselves. 'I have been impregnated with my own creations', he wrote in his *Autobiography*, 'till it has been my only excitement to sit with the pen in my hand, and drive my team before me at as quick a pace as I could make them travel.' As to the author's relationship to the reader, Trollope saw it not as one between teacher and pupil or puppet-master and childish audience, but as a companionship of travellers, each with respect for the other. 'Our doctrine is that the author and the reader should move along together in full confidence with each other. Let the personages of the drama undergo ever so complete a comedy of errors among themselves, but let the spectator never mistake the Syracusan for the Euphesan. Otherwise he is one of the dupes, and the part of a dupe is never dignified' (*Barchester Towers*, 1859). This is a position as far removed as possible from the aesthetic implicit in the novels of Dickens, where the reader is constantly being deceived for his own good, like the hero of *David Copperfield* or the heroine of *Our Mutual Friend*, by a Prospero-like author with an *a priori* vision. It is easy, especially when one is trying to find a theory of fiction, to pay the most attention and the most respect to the romancers and the romance apologists who are not shy about theorizing, and it is not surprising therefore to find even so excellent a historian as Richard Stang concluding that Trollope's *Autobiography* is 'not very intelligent critically'.[6] Indeed, our own selections in this volume include a larger number of romance critics than are warranted by the relative importance of romantic fiction in the period, and we have been forced, by space considerations, to exclude an excellent piece by Trollope. It remains, nevertheless, that the scraps of criticism Trollope let fall from the overcrowded table of his literary output, though many of them lack the savour of originality, may have provided the best nourishment towards the growth of a theory of English realism. Trollope, like most of the realists since Scott, did not set himself up as a thinker: quite the contrary, for he held indeed that preconceived intellectual purpose, like preconceived social purpose, destroyed the discipline of fiction. He believed that the best wisdom which might come out of fiction was psychological insight and that such wisdom could be achieved only by identifying with the characters. So long as one refrained from complicating the narrative with digressions, episodes, or sub-plots, such characters could be trusted to reveal themselves. If romance, as has often been stated, was the Tory genre, realism was the Whig, and its motto was *laissez-faire*.

Trollope's thoughts about realism, however, put forth modestly in bits and pieces as descriptions of his own working habits, stop short, as does English realism in general, of presenting anything so grandiose as an ideology. And when the more theoretical French and Americans go the final step in this direction, the best English critics use their considerable powers of argument to deflate them. After steadfastly calling for realism throughout the first four-and-a-half decades of the period, they found themselves, more times than not in the last twenty years of the century, when realism seemed indeed to have triumphed, either hostile to it or disposed at least to limit its scope severely.

Sometimes, ironically, these refutations go indirectly to develop the English theory of realism further, or at least to define it more clearly. The arguments against the school of Zola are cases in point. George Moore originally had been attracted to Zolaesque realism because he saw it as 'a new art based upon science in opposition to the art of the old world that was based upon imagination' (*Confessions of a Young Man*, 1888). The Philistine government officer at Gradgrind's school in *Hard Times* hardly could have spoken more forthrightly. But Moore and others turned away from Zola ultimately because they concluded that his claims of scientific objectivity were absurd. Realists, they recognized, must, like all novelists, be selective and must tend, consciously or unconsciously, to choose incidents and thoughts which express their own preconceived views of the world. 'Any work of art', wrote Hubert Crackanthorpe, 'can never be more than a corner of Nature, seen through the temperament of a single man. Thus all literature is, must be, essentially subjective' (*Yellow Book*, 1894). Arthur Symons went further in his essay, 'A Note on Zola's Method': 'This professed realist is a man of theories who studies life with a conviction that he will find there such things which he has read about in scientific books ... He observes in support of preconceived ideas ...

[and thus] his realism is a distorted realism' (1893). And so realism, carried too far, could be dismissed as another kind of romance.

Another objection to Zolaesque realism is stated by Garnet Smith, who objects to the 'utter indifference' towards, and the 'lack of sympathy' for, the characters observed according to the French method (*Gentlemen's Magazine*, 1888). Some English naturalists – Arthur Morrison, for example – resented this requirement for sympathy, objecting to the great-hearted Dickensian version of it as a hypocritical 'parade of sympathy' which the readers demand so that 'they can keep their own sympathies to themselves and gain comfort from the belief that they are eased of their just responsibility by vicarious snivelling' (*New Review*, 1897). But the concept of sympathetic identification was deeply imbedded in the realist aesthetic and did not apply merely to the strategies of social melodrama. In 1869 G. H. Lewes had alleged lack of sympathy as the principal failing which kept Henry Fielding from being a profound thinker. 'Knowledge of human nature is not to be obtained through observation, but through sympathy. Where the sympathy is extensive and profound, the knowledge may be various and deep; where the sympathy is narrow, the knowledge will necessarily be superficial' (*Blackwood's*, 1869). Thus, sympathy was essential to the epistemology of realism.

It was because they recognized this point and stated it more clearly than it was usually stated by Englishmen that the American realists, Howells and James, were more difficult to dispose of than were the French. Here were critics and practising novelists of reputation and considerable popularity who seemed, although they frequently gave the credit to Daudet and Turgenev, to be carrying the tendencies of English realism to their logical conclusions, arguing in favour of an absolute identification of author (and consequently of reader) with character, and speaking against all invention of plot which does not develop from the simple interaction of character and situation. 'What is plot but the illustration of character?' James asked, and he wrote with obvious condescension about the ordinary reader's 'weakness for a plot' (*Century Magazine*, 1883).

Some English critics welcomed this extreme position. A writer for *The Speaker* (1891) stated, for instance, that such great novelists as Cervantes, Thackeray, Balzac, Fielding, Dickens, and Turgenev, were to be praised for neglecting plot, and he believed that most of them began their stories without a notion of how they would end. On the other hand, the larger number of critics felt that Howells and James had gone too far. The Americans, in fact, had always gone too far, according to some English critics. Kenneth Graham finds that before the issue of American realism had come up, it was Hawthorne's romanticism which had provided a major battleground for the debate over the novel and the romance.[7] In 1862, a critic writing in *Macmillans* had complained that American romancers were simply 'unable to look ordinary life steadily in the face'. Now, Howells's passionate defence of the depiction of ordinary life, together with the statement in his essay on Henry James that character must become the centre of fiction because all the plots have anyway been used up (*Century Magazine*, 1882), became the provocations for attack in a surprising number of essays.

It is not accurate to say that suddenly there was a debate between character and plot. Such an opposition had been shaping up in English criticism since a reviewer for *Fraser's* noted in 1835 that by changing the title of Victor Hugo's romance from *Notre Dame de Paris* to *The Hunchback of Notre Dame* the English translator had changed the nature of the work. Similarly, Bulwer Lytton makes a distinction between the novel of character and the novel of incident in an early section of 'On Art and Fiction'. More than one reviewer of the 1850s, moreover, noted the difference between the novel of action and the novel of character. Nevertheless, the conflict began shaping up in earnest during the 1870s as part of the defence of and the attack on the sensational novel. Trollope tried to quiet the warfare. 'Among English novels of the present day,' he wrote,

a great division is made. There are sensational novels, and anti-sensational; sensational novelists and anti-sensational; sensational readers and anti-sensational. The novelists who are considered to be anti-sensational are generally called realists. The readers who prefer the one are supposed to delight in the elucidation of character. They who hold by the other are charmed by the construction and gradual development of a plot. All this we think is a mistake, – which mistake arises from the inability of inferior artists to be at the same time realistic and sensational. A good novel should be both, – and both in the highest degree. (*Nineteenth-Century*, 1879)

How serious the conflict became, nevertheless, may be indicated by noting that George Saintsbury, arguing on the plot side, brought out Homer as his champion to set against the then still underrated Jane Austen, whom he regarded as the only English novelist 'who obtains the first rank with something like a defiance of interest in story' (*Fortnightly Review*, 1887). James's *The Portrait of a Lady* was seen by a hostile *Quarterly Review*er as a work carrying out 'unflinchingly the theories of his school. There is no story ... and there is not a single incident in it from beginning to end ... The characters are described at enormous length ... but nothing can relieve their inborn tediousness' (1883).

Robert Louis Stevenson, who, as we shall see, became the elected spokesman for romance, went so far as to argue that character can be omitted or at least subordinated in the novel of action (*Longman's Magazine*, 1882), and while he admired Henry James greatly he could not help wishing, as he mentioned in a letter of 1884, and in a style playfully parodying his correspondent, that 'in one novel, to oblige a sincere admirer', James might be willing to cast his 'characters in a mould a little more abstract and academic . . . and pitch the incidents, I do not say in any stronger, but in a slightly more emphatic key – as it were an episode from one of the old (so-called) novels of adventure'. And as for Howells, Robert Louis Stevenson feared, as he stated in another letter of 1884, that his precepts would create an art 'like mahogany and horsehair furniture, solid, true, serious, and as dead as Caesar'. The danger, he wrote, 'is lest, in seeking to draw the normal, a man should draw the null, and write the novel of society instead of the romance of man' ('A Humble Remonstrance', p. xi).

By 1890, the romancers, the exponents of story, appeared to have triumphed. 'The innings of realism is over', wrote Hall Caine in *The Contemporary Review*; 'It has scored badly or not at all, and is going out disgraced. The reign of mere fact in imaginative literature was very short . . . and . . . is making its exit rapidly with a sorry retinue of either teacup-and-saucer nonentities or of harlots at its heels.' Even in America 'the first champions of such Realism, who have said that there is sufficient incident in "the lifting up of a chair", and that "all the stories are told", are themselves turning their backs on their own manifesto, and coming as near to Romanticism as their genius will let them'.

This news of the victory of incident over character was, of course, premature, and while adventurous, psychological, and/or visionary romantic fiction enjoyed a hectic popularity in the last decade of the century, the stable, English interest in character, sympathetically, lovingly identified with, was to reassert itself. In the same year as Caine's pronouncement, Grant Allen, another novelist-critic, but of the other school, asserted that 'characters predetermine the plot, instead of plot predetermining the characters' (*Speaker*, 1890), and five years later, in an article significantly entitled 'On Literary Construction', and which begins with elaborate praise for Stevenson's *Catriona*, Vernon Lee gives pride of place to the novelist's 'absolutely sympathetic, unanalytic, subjective creation of characters', whereby 'our experience of the [fictional] person, and our increasing experience of ourselves are united, and the person who is not ourselves comes to live, somehow, for our consciousness, with the same reality, the same intimate warmth, that we do' (*The Contemporary Review*,

1895). This almost mystical and certainly non-intellectual process of empathy, the article goes on to say, controls point of view in the novel, and ultimately, therefore, governs both plot and incident. This is the direction toward which the mainstream of English fiction and criticism had been tending since Scott – actually since Defoe – and it was clearly the direction in which Henry James was encouraging it to flow. It was the direction which even Bulwer Lytton, for whom Scott was inadequate because of his lack of skill in metaphysical analysis, had conceded, when he ended his essay 'On Art in Fiction', by saying, 'perhaps, if we were to search for the true secret of creative genius, we should find that secret in the intenseness of its sympathies'.

Since this general overview was intended, among other things, to supplement the essays which follow, relatively few of those selections have been cited to this point. Moreover, many famous and infamous essays are unrepresented both in this introductory essay and the text because the editors felt they were primarily works of practical criticism or concerned with problems of the book trade or else interesting largely as social documents. The essays, articles, reviews, and prefaces represented in this book were chosen because they were perceived as being chiefly theoretical and as illustrating the developments in the history of novel criticism which we have just been tracing.

Bulwer Lytton's essay, 'On Art in Fiction' (1838), which modern commentators regard as the most significant if not the most influential piece of early Victorian criticism of prose fiction, sets in motion many of the concerns the other essays engage. Most importantly, perhaps, it insists on the seriousness of fiction as an art form and seeks to differentiate it not only from other kinds of literature, specifically from the drama, but to formulate critical theories relevant to its uniqueness.

George Moir's *Encyclopaedia Britannica* article of 1842 picks up on the subject of the special quality of fiction as opposed to drama. It emphasizes also the distinction, a very important one at the time and throughout the period, between the novel and the romance. In his treatment of Defoe, moreover, Moir develops another theme of Bulwer Lytton's – the propriety of portraying the criminal hero in works of polite literature. This essay is perhaps most useful for the canon of eighteenth-century novels it establishes. Of historical interest in light of the development and popularity of the young Dickens is the relative importance Moir gives to the works of Smollett.

In Archibald Alison's 'The Historical Romance' (1845) we encounter a sensibility formed chiefly by eighteenth-century influences of a different nature, especially those of Johnson and Reynolds, but directed now at an essentially nineteenth-century sub-genre of fiction. Alison finds himself opposed both to the sensationalism of the modern romancers, with their criminal heroes, and to the particularizing, the tulip-streaking, of the middle-class realists. On the other hand, he sees that the historical romance, as practised by Scott and Bulwer Lytton in their English and Scottish novels, provides what Hawthorne was later to call 'a suitable remoteness', a distancing of the reader from the material in time but not in interest, which would permit the depiction, as Alison writes, of recognizable human nature, 'common to all ages and centuries, not its peculiarities in a particular circle or society'. Alison also looks forward to another critic, R. L. Stevenson, when he calls for a narrative structure built out of simplified plot materials.

The next item, an anonymous review of Mrs Gaskell's *Ruth* (1853), is significant for a number of reasons. It picks up a central point of the earlier essays when it argues that there is at least a potential difference between fiction and the drama and that some novels are best judged according to the rules of epic. The reviewer also enters the growing debate between realistic and idealistic fiction by insisting that the novel 'conjures up an ideal world in the midst of our prosaic realities', making it 'the idealized transcript of actual experience'. This stance permits the essay to make two controversial points on the subject of the next essay, 'The Relation of Novels to Life'. Novels, writes the anonymous reviewer of *Ruth*, have an obligation to make moral statements, albeit unobtrusively, and such works have become in the nineteenth century 'the chosen medium for the discussion of the vexed and difficult questions, moral, religious, social and political, which agitate the minds of men'.

James Fitzjames Stephen, the author of 'The Relation of Novels to Life' (1855), takes a contrary view. Most of his essay is dedicated to showing that while fiction has an obligation to be as realistic as it possibly can, its other obligation, to be interesting, prevents it from having any truly meaningful relation to life at all. This is a formula which, as we shall see, Vernon Lee precisely reverses later on in the century. But Stephen believes that when novels influence our lives, it is generally for the bad, because fiction necessarily presents us with an incomplete picture of reality. When writers of fiction set out consciously to influence us, they do not produce novels at all, according to Stephen, because a novel ought to be nothing more or less than an imaginary biography. When writers like Dickens and Mrs Gaskell use fiction to 'ventilate opinions', they are writing party pamphlets. Stephen's essay gives an example of the realist position at its narrowest, but while it is easy to see him, from one point of view, as a Gradgrindian Philistine, it is also possible to hear in his demand for the separation of art and social action the more tolerant tones of his famous brother, Leslie Stephen, and the uncompromising voice of his still more famous niece, Virginia Woolf, insisting, as she does in 'Mr Bennett and Mrs Brown', that 'it is to express character, not to preach doctrine, sing songs, or celebrate the glories of the British Empire that the form of the novels … has been evolved'.

The next essay, 'W. M. Thackeray, Artist and Moralist' (1856), takes an entirely different line. Its author, W. C. Roscoe, is representative of, although he rises far above, a large body of critics who find themselves in general agreement with the aims of English realism, but find these aims insufficient. Roscoe appreciates Thackeray as 'the greatest painter of manners that ever lived', but regrets that 'he never penetrates into the interior, secret, *real* life that every man leads'. Thackeray is for Roscoe the greatest writer since Fielding, but 'it is curious how independent he is of thought'. His view of English society is a 'true but strictly one-sided representation', and it is 'bad for us to be constantly rubbed against vice and sin of any kind'. Roscoe gives Thackeray his full due as a great artist who has depicted characters as real as those we meet with in our lives, and Roscoe obviously does enjoy meeting with them, but he misses a truly creative rather than merely a marshalling power in Thackeray; a power which would, he believes, have permitted a higher conception of mankind, and a more helpful, finally, a more moral sort of fiction.

In 'British Novelists Since Scott' (1859), David Masson values Thackeray even more highly than Roscoe does, and he understands that the roles of the novelist and the moralist must necessarily differ. But he is equally removed from the position of James Fitzjames Stephen. Whether it is intended or not, 'there is a latent doctrine', writes Masson, in every choice the novelist makes. As might be expected from the great biographer of Milton, Masson maintains that 'no artist will be found greater as an artist than he was as a thinker', and that no novels 'can rank in the first class of literature' unless their authors are 'at least abreast of the best speculation of their time'. He does not assume that novels of social reality, such as he believed Thackeray wrote, are incapable of expressing such thought, but he is concerned lest the exclusive valuing of realistic works might lead his contemporaries to neglect novels of the poetic or ideal school, such as Dickens wrote, and thus prevent the development of 'the full theoretical capabilities of the Novel, as being the prose counterpart of the Epic'. Masson's is a balanced but a strong plea for romance in an age of growing realism, and it is an insistence that fiction be granted the same scope and treated with the same seriousness as the greatest poetry.

The next selection, George Eliot's 'Silly Novels by Lady Novelists' (1856), is presented out of strict chronological order so that it can be read along with the succeeding piece by George Henry Lewes, 'Criticism in Relation to Novels' (1865), for the two articles can be regarded almost as a single essay. They make a point similar to that of Masson, although they choose to do it largely with negative examples of weak novels which they insist must be subjected to the most rigorous criteria of the best criticism. To do otherwise, to make exception for the works of women, writes George Eliot, would be to encourage a kind of fiction bound to strengthen male prejudices about the pointlessness of female education. According to Lewes, to judge fiction by less demanding standards than are generally applied to 'a history, an article, or a pamphlet', would be to ensure the mediocrity of the novel as a genre. The implication of both writers is that the writing of novels is a significant activity of the human mind, one which deserves to be judged by the highest standards.

The next two pieces, Henry James's 'The Art of Fiction' and Robert Louis Stevenson's 'A Humble Remonstrance', belong together for a contrary reason: they represent the opposing sides of an 1884 skirmish begun by the lecture of still another novelist, Walter Besant. They represent also the forces of a major critical battle of the last quarter of the century between the novel of character and that of incident. James, along with his compatriot William Dean Howells, was associated in the minds of virtually every British reviewer with the character novel, but here he denies the distinction altogether, as well as the distinction between the novel and the romance. 'What is character', he asks, 'but the determination of incident? What is incident but the illustration of character?' Stevenson begins his attack by erasing even more distinctions, those between prose and verse and between the fictitious and the historical. He is interested, he insists, only in the art of narrative. Yet he finds it necessary to talk about different kinds of 'novels': those of adventure, of character, and of passion. His own works belong in the first category; those of James, he argues, in the second. The bases for the distinctions each author makes, or for the absence of them, are the assumptions they make about the primary nature of narrative, assumptions with which the reader of the present volume will be familiar from a reading of Stephen's 'The Relation of Novels to Life' and the surrounding essays. Stevenson believes that fiction, like all art, can and must be a significant simplification of life; whereas James insists that art can compete with life and can represent both its fullness and its complexity. In other words, what James calls 'the celebrated distinction between the novel and the romance', but which he felt answered 'little to any reality', was still very much alive, at least in the minds of those new romancers, like Stevenson, whose brief innings were about to begin.

But in one respect, James and Stevenson were in agreement, an agreement which formed the basis of their life-long friendship: they both felt certain of the status of the novel as a work of art. James rubs his eyes at the very notion of anyone's ever having doubted such a proposition, and on this point, at least, Stevenson does not remonstrate. Vernon Lee, however, argues a contrary position in her 'A Dialogue on Novels' (1885). She feels that 'psychological, sympathetic interest' has become dominant in the novel, and that as a result fiction must be regarded now as only a 'half-art', owing at least as great an allegiance to the laws of ethics as to those of aesthetics. Thus 'the novel has less value in art, but more importance in life'; and not only more importance than the other arts but more importance than all other ethical activities, for it is principally the novel that has guided that development in moral sensibility which seemed apparent towards the end of the nineteenth century.

The final selection, Joseph Conrad's 'Preface' to *The Nigger of the Narcissus* (1897), restores fiction as a full art. Not that it abandons truth as an aim. On the contrary, the first paragraph of the essay proclaims that 'the artist . . . like the thinker or the scientist, seeks the truth and makes his appeal'. However, it is by refusing to be bound by 'the modern formulas of his craft', such as Realism and Romanticism, which are, after all, the products of discursive thinkers, and by descending into himself, into his own psyche, that the novelist is able to discover the universal meanings underlying human experience. And by making his appeal to the senses rather than to the intellect, the novelist communicates, temperament to temperament, truths more profound, more stirring, and more enduring than those discovered and expressed by philosophers and scientists. Thus meaning is both the aim and the product of narrative fiction; but, like the tentative framers of the developing aesthetic we have been tracing in this essay, Conrad makes it a condition of the search for a glimpse of the truth that we, the readers, as well as he, the artist, forget specifically to ask for it.

Edward Bulwer Lytton
(1803–1873)
From 'On Art in Fiction', 1838

Edward Bulwer Lytton was the most complete man of letters of the Victorian period. He was successful in his own time as a poet, an essayist, an historian, a translator, a playwright, a social commentator, an editor, a political writer, and of course the author of popular, controversial, but generally respected novels. A majority of critics during his almost half-century career in fiction, including some of the critics represented in this volume, regarded him as the major novelist of the period. This reputation has diminished in our own century to the extent that most non-specialists think of him only as the author of *The Last Days of Pompeii* and as the man who persuaded Dickens to change the ending of *Great Expectations*.

Bulwer Lytton's literary criticism, especially his criticism of fiction, is the one area of his writing which has more than held its own. All scholars in this field rank him as the most compelling spokesman for the idealist position in early and mid-Victorian criticism of the novel, and 'On Art in Fiction' is generally regarded as the most thoroughgoing and important single English work of its sort before Henry James. It is only one of many such ventures by Bulwer Lytton which would deserve place in this volume if it could have been larger. He wrote numerous prefaces addressed to the generic problems raised by the novels to which they are attached, and since he attempted so many different kinds of novels, a collection of these introductions would provide an excellent survey of the varieties of Victorian fiction. Indeed, his contemporary David Masson speculated that he may have been so versatile as a novelist because he wished to illustrate his various critical theories.[1]

But even if, as seems more likely from their polemic tone, the theories were intended rather to serve the fiction they seem to have outlasted, Bulwer Lytton's criticism remains valuable. The pamphlet *A Word to the Public* (1847) represents the best Victorian apology for the use of sensational action and subject matter, and some of the essays he published in *Blackwood's* in the early 1860s and then collected under the title of *Caxtoniana* provide evidence of a remarkably matured vision of the capabilities of fiction. One recent scholar[2] has written that Bulwer Lytton's many and not unregarded comments on his craft seemed to instil a self-consciousness in novelists and critics alike which, if it did nothing else – and it seems to have done a great deal – established the novel on a very wide scale as a work of art worthy of the best critical effort.

'On Art in Fiction' originally appeared in two instalments in *The Monthly*

Chronicle of March and April, 1838. Our selection presents the second part only. The first is somewhat more practical than theoretical, apparently intended as advice to aspiring novelists on such subjects as characterization and the proper and effective use of historical material, of the passions, and of sentiment. The discussion of 'The Conception', with which our selection begins, expresses Bulwer Lytton's conviction of the importance of fiction as a serious art form, and much of the rest of the essay seeks to define that form as one peculiar to itself and not, as many critics seemed content to believe, merely an expanded form of the drama. This discussion, as we shall see from the succeeding essays in this volume, repeats itself with variations throughout the Victorian period.

The conception

A STORY may be well constructed, yet devoid of interest; on the other hand, the construction may be faulty and the interest vivid. This is the case even with the drama. Hamlet is not so well constructed a story as the Don Carlos of Alfieri;[3] but there is no comparison in the degree of interest excited in either tragedy. Still, though we ought not to consider that excellence in the technical arrangement of incidents as a certain proof of the highest order of art, it is a merit capable of the most brilliant effects, when possessed by a master. An exquisite mechanism in the construction of the mere story, not only gives pleasure in itself, but it displays other and loftier beauties to the best advantage. It is the setting of the jewels.

It is common to many novelists to commence a work without any distinct chart of the country which they intend to traverse – to suffer one chapter to grow out of another, and invention to warm as the creation grows. Scott has confessed to this mode of novel-writing but Scott, with all his genius, was rather a great mechanist than a great artist. His execution was infinitely superior to his conception. It may be observed, indeed, that his conceptions are often singularly poor and barren, compared with the vigour with which they are worked out. He conceives a story with the design of telling it as well as he can, but is wholly insensible to the high and true aim of art, which is rather to consider for what objects the story should be told. Scott never appears to say to himself, "Such a tale will throw a new light upon human passions, or add fresh stores to human wisdom: for that reason I select it." He seems rather to consider what picturesque effects it will produce, what striking scenes, what illustrations of mere manners. He regards the story with the eye of the *property man*, though he tells it with the fervour of the poet. It is not thus that the greatest authorities in fiction have composed. It is clear to us that Shakspeare, when he selected the tale which he proposed to render Χτῆμά ἐζ ἀεὶ,[a] – the everlasting possession of mankind – made it his first and paramount object to work out certain passions, or affections of the mind, in the most complete and profound form. He did not so much consider how the incidents might be made most striking, as how the truths of the human heart might be made most clear. And it is a remarkable proof of his consummate art, that though in his best plays we may find instances in which the mere incidents might be made more probable, and the theatrical effects more vivid, we can never see one instance in such plays where the passion he desired to represent, could have been placed in a broader light, or the character he designed to investigate, could have been submitted to a minuter analysis. We are quite sure that Othello and Macbeth were not written without the clear and deep and premeditated CONCEPTION of the story to be told us. For with Shakspeare the conception itself is visible and gigantic from the first line to the last. So in the greatest works of Fielding a very obtuse critic may perceive that the author sat down to write in order to embody a design previously formed. The perception of moral truths urged him to the composition of his fictions. In Jonathan Wild, the finest prose satire in the English language, Fielding, before he set pen to paper, had resolved to tear the mask from False Greatness. In his conception of the characters and histories of Blifil and Jones, he was bent on dethroning that popular idol – False Virtue. The scorn of hypocrisy in all grades, all places, was the intellectual passion of Fielding; and his masterpieces are the results of intense convictions. That many incidents never contemplated would suggest themselves as he proceeded – that the technical plan of events might deviate and vary, according as he saw new modes of enforcing his aims, is unquestionable. But still Fielding always commenced *with* a plan – with a conception – with a moral end, to be achieved by definitive agencies, and through the medium of certain characters pre-formed in his mind. If Scott had no preconcerted story when he commenced Chapter the First of one of his delightful tales, it was because he was deficient in the highest attributes of art, viz., its philosophy and its ethics. He never seems to have imagined that the loftiest merit of a tale rests upon the effect it produces, not on the fancy, but on the intellect and the passions. He had no grandeur of conception, for he had no strong desire to render palpable and immortal some definite and abstract truth.[4]

It is a sign of the low state of criticism in this country that Scott has

---

[a] This phrase from Thucydides I, xxii, 4, although mis-spelt, is correctly translated in the text immediately following.

been compared to Shakspeare. No two writers can be more entirely opposed to each other in the qualities of their genius, or the sources to which they applied. Shakspeare ever aiming at the development of the secret man, and half disdaining the mechanism of external incidents; Scott painting the ruffles and the dress, and the features and the gestures – avoiding the movements of the heart, elaborate in the progress of the incident. Scott never caught the mantle of Shakspeare, but he improved on the dresses of his wardrobe, and threw artificial effects into the scenes of his theatres.

Let us take an example: we will select one of the finest passages in Sir Walter Scott: a passage unsurpassed for its mastery over the PICTURESQUE. It is that chapter in "Kenilworth," where Elizabeth has discovered Amy, and formed her first suspicions of Leicester.

Leicester was at this moment the centre of a splendid group of lords and ladies, assembled together under an arcade or portico, which closed the alley. The company had drawn together in that place, to attend the commands of her majesty when the hunting party should go forward, and their astonishment may be imagined, when instead of seeing Elizabeth advance towards them with her usual measured dignity of motion, they beheld her walking so rapidly, that she was in the midst of them ere they were aware; and then observed with fear and surprise, that her features were flushed betwixt anger and agitation, that her hair was loosened by her haste of motion, and that her eyes sparkled as they were wont when the spirit of Henry VIII mounted highest in his daughter. Nor were they less astonished at the appearance of the pale, extenuated, half-dead, yet still lovely female, whom the queen upheld by main strength with one hand, while with the other she waved aside the ladies and nobles, who pressed towards her, under the idea that she was taken suddenly ill. "Where is my Lord of Leicester?" she said, in a tone that thrilled with astonishment all the courtiers who stood around – "Stand forth, my Lord of Leicester!"

If, in the midst of the most serene day of summer, when all is light and laughing around, a thunderbolt were to fall from the clear blue vault of heaven, and rend the earth at the very feet of some careless traveller, he could not gaze upon the smouldering chasm which so unexpectedly yawned before him, with half the astonishment and fear which Leicester felt at the sight that so suddenly presented itself. He had that instant been receiving, with a political affectation of disavowing and misunderstanding their meaning, the half-uttered, half-intimated congratulations of the courtiers upon the favour of the queen, carried apparently to its highest pitch during the interview of that morning; from which most of them seemed to augur, that he might soon arise from their equal in rank to become their master. And now, while the subdued yet proud smile with which he disclaimed those inferences was yet curling his cheek, the queen shot into the circle, her passions excited to the uttermost; and, supporting with one hand, and apparently without an effort, the pale and sinking form of his almost expiring wife, and pointing with the finger of the other to her half-dead features, demanded in a voice that sounded to the ears of the astounded statesman like the last dread trumpet-call, that is to summon body and spirit to the judgment seat, "Knowest thou this woman?"

The reader will observe that the whole of this splendid passage is devoted to external effects: the loosened hair and sparkling eyes of

Elizabeth – the grouping of the courtiers – the proud smile yet on the cheek of Leicester – the pale and sinking form of the wife. Only by external effects do we guess at the emotions of the agents. Scott is thinking of the costume and postures of the actors, not the passions they represent. Let us take a parallel passage in Shakspeare; parallel, for, in each, a mind disturbed with jealousy is the real object placed before the reader. It is thus that Iago describes Othello, after the latter has conceived *his* first suspicions:

> Look where he comes! Not poppy, nor mandragora,
> Nor all the drowsy syrups of the world,
> Shall ever medicine thee to that sweet sleep
> Which thou ow'dst yesterday.
> *Othello.*   Ha! ha! false to me?

Here the reader will observe that there is no attempt at the Picturesque – no sketch of the outward man. It is only by a reference to the woe that kills sleep that we can form any notion of the haggard aspect of the Moor. So, if we compare the ensuing dialogue in the romance with that in the tragedy, we shall remark that Elizabeth utters only bursts of shallow passion, which convey none of the deep effects of the philosophy of jealousy; none of the sentiments that "inform us what we are." But every sentence uttered by Othello penetrates to the very root of the passion described: the farewell to fame and pomp, with comes from a heart that, finding falsehood in the prop it leaned on, sees the world itself, and all its quality and circumstance, crumbled away; the burst of vehement incredulity; the sudden return to doubt; the intense revenge proportioned to the intense love; the human weakness that must seek faith somewhere, and, with the loss of Desdemona, casts itself upon her denouncer; the mighty knowledge of the heart exhibited in those simple words to Iago, "I greet *thy* love;" – compare all this with the mere words of Elizabeth, which have no force in themselves, but are made effective by the picturesque grouping of the scene, and you will detect at once the astonishing distinction between Shakspeare and Scott. Shakspeare could have composed the most wonderful plays from the stories in Scott; Scott could have written the most excellent stage directions to the plays of Shakspeare.

If the novelist be contented with the secondary order of Art in Fiction, and satisfied if his incidents be varied, animating, and striking, he may write from chapter to chapter, and grope his way to a catastrophe in the dark; but if he aim at loftier and more permanent effects, he will remember that to execute grandly we must conceive nobly. He will suffer the subject he selects to lie long in his mind, to be revolved, meditated, brooded over, until from the chaos breaks the light, and he sees distinctly the highest end for which his materials can be used, and the best process by which they can be reduced to harmony and order.

If, for instance, he found his tale upon some legend, the author, inspired with a great ambition, will consider what will be, not the most vivid interest, but the loftiest and most durable *order* of interest he can extract from the incidents. Sometimes it will be in a great truth elicited by the catastrophe; sometimes by the delineation of one or more characters; sometimes by the mastery over, and development of, some complicated passion. Having decided what it is that he designs to work out, he will mould his story accordingly; but before he begin to execute, he will have clearly informed his mind of the conception that induces the work itself.

Interest

No fiction can be first-rate if it fail to create INTEREST. But the merit of the fiction is not, by any means, proportioned to the *degree* of excitement it produces, but to the *quality* of the excitement. It is certainly some merit to make us weep; but the great artist will consider from what sources our tears are to be drawn. We may weep as much at the sufferings of a beggar as at the agonies of Lear; but from what sublime sympathies arise our tears for the last! what commonplace pity will produce the first! We may have our interest much more acutely excited by the "Castle of Udolpho"[5] than by "Anastasius;"[6] but in the one, it is a melo-dramatic arrangement of hair-breadth escapes and a technical skill in the arrangement of vulgar mysteries – in the other; it is the consummate knowledge of actual life, that fascinates the eye to the page. It is necessary, then, that every novel should excite interest; but one novel may produce a much more gradual, gentle, and subdued interest than another, and yet have infinitely more merit in the *quality* of the interest it excites.[7]

Terror and horror

True art never disgusts. If, in descriptions intended to harrow us, we feel sickened and revolted by the very power with which the description is drawn, the author has passed the boundary of his province; he does not appal – he shocks. Thus, nothing is more easy than to produce a feeling of intense pain by a portrait of great bodily suffering. The vulgarest mind can do this, and the mistaken populace of readers will cry, "See the power of this author!" But all sympathy with bodily torture is drawn from our basest infirmities; all sympathy with mental torture from our deepest passions and our most spiritual nature. HORROR is generally produced by the one, TERROR by the other. If you describe a man hanging by a breaking bough over a precipice – if you paint his starting eyeballs, his erect hair, the death-sweat on his brow, the cracking of the bough, the depth of the abyss, the sharpness of the rock, the roar of the cataract below, you may make us dizzy and sick with sympathy; but you operate on the physical nerves, and our sensation is that of coarse and revolting pain. But take a *moral* abyss: Œdipus, for instance, on the brink of learning the awful secret which proclaims him an incestuous parricide. Show the splendour of his power, the depth of his wisdom, the loftiness of his pride, and then gradually, step by step, reveal the precipice on which he stands – and you work not on the body but the mind; you produce the true tragic emotion, *terror*. Even in this, you must stop short of all that could make terror revolt while it thrills us. This, Sophocles has done by one of those fine perceptions of nature which opens the sublimest mysteries of art; we are not allowed time to suffer our thoughts to dwell upon the incest and self-assault of Œdipus, or upon the suicide of Jocasta, before, by the introduction of the Children, terror melts into pity, and the parricide son assumes the new aspect of the broken-hearted father. A modern French writer, if he had taken this subject, would have disgusted us by details of the incest itself, or forced us from the riven heart to gaze on the bloody and eyeless sockets of the blind king; and the more he disgusted us the more he would have thought that he excelled the tragedian of Colonos. Such of the Germans, on the contrary, as follow the School of Schiller, will often stop as far short of the true boundaries of Terror as the French romanticists would go beyond it. Schiller held it a principle of art never to leave the complete and entire effects of a work of art one of pain.[8] According to him, the pleasure of the art should exceed the sympathy with the suffering. He sought to vindicate this principle by a reference to the Greek drama, but in this he confounded the sentiments with which we, moderns, read the works of Æschylus and Sophocles, with the sentiments with which a *Greek* would have read them. No doubt, to a Greek religiously impressed with the truth and reality of the woes or the terror depicted, the "Agamemnon" of Æschylus, the "Œdipus Tyrannus" of Sophocles, and the "Medea" of Euripides, would have left a far more unqualified and over-powering sentiment of awe and painful sympathy than we now can entertain for victims, whom we believe to be shadows, to deities and destinies that we know to be chimeras. Were Schiller's rule universally adopted, we should condemn Othello and Lear.

Terror may then be carried up to its full extent, provided that it work upon us through the mind, not the body, and stop short of the reaction of recoil and disgust.

Description

One of the greatest and most peculiar arts of the Novelist is DESCRIPTION. It is in this that he has a manifest advantage over the dramatic poet. The latter will rarely describe scenery, costume, *personals*, for they ought to be placed before the eyes of the audience by the theatre and the actors. When he does do so, it is generally understood by an intelligent critic, to be an episode introduced for the sake of some poetical beauty, which, without absolutely carrying on the plot, increases the agreeable and artistical effect of the whole performance. This is the case with the description of Dover cliff, in "Lear," or with that of the chasm which adorns, by so splendid a passage, the monstrous tragedy of "The Cenci." In the classical French theatre, as in the Greek, Description, it is true, becomes an essential part of the play itself, since the catastrophe is thrown into description. Hence the celebrated picture of the death of Hippolyte, in the "Phedre" of Racine – of the suicide of Hæmon in the "Antigone" of Sophocles. But it may be doubted whether both Sophocles and his French imitator did not, in this transfer of action to words, strike at the very core of dramatic art, whether ancient or modern; for it may be remarked – and we are surprised that it has not been remarked before, that Æschylus preferred placing the catastrophe before the eyes of the reader; and he who remembers the sublime close of the Prometheus, the storm, the lightning, the bolt, the shivered rock, and the mingled groans and threats of the Titan himself, must acknowledge that the effect is infinitely more purely tragical than it would have been if we had been told how it all happened by the Aggelos or Messenger. So in the "Agamemnon" of the same sublime poet, though we do not see the blow given, the scene itself, opening, places before us the murderess and the corpse. No messenger intervenes – no description is required for the action. "I stand where I struck him," says Clytæmnestra. "The deed is done!"

But without recurring farther to the Drama of other nations, we may admit at once that in our own it is the received and approved rule that Action, as much as possible, should dispense with Description. With Narrative Fiction it is otherwise: the novel writer is his own scene painter; description is as essential to him as canvass is to the actor – description of the most various character.

In this art, none ever equalled Scott. In the comparison we made between him and Shakspeare, we meant not to censure the former for indulging in what the latter shunned; each did that which his art required. We only lament that Scott did not combine with external description an equal, or, at least, not very inferior, skill in metaphysical analysis. Had he done so, he would have achieved all of which the novelist is capable.

In the description of natural scenery, the author will devote the greatest care to such landscapes as are meant for the localities of his principal events. There is nothing, for instance, very attractive in the general features of a common; but if the author lead us through a common, on which, in a later portion of his work, a deed of murder is to be done, he will strive to fix deeply in our remembrance the character of the landscape, the stunted tree, or the mantling pool, which he means to associate in our minds with an act of terror.

If the duration of time in a fiction be limited to a year, the author may be enabled artfully to show us the progress of time by minute descriptions of the gradual change in the seasons. This is attempted to be done in the tale of "Eugene Aram:"[9] instead of telling us when it is July, and when it is October, the author of that fiction describes the signs and characteristics of the month, and seeks to identify our interest in the natural phenomena, with the approaching fate of the hero, himself an observer and an artist of the "clouds that pass to and fro," and the "herbs that wither and are renewed." Again, in description, if there be any natural objects that will bear upon the catastrophe, if, for instance, the earthquake or the inundation be intended as an agent in the fate of those whose history the narrative relates, incidental descriptions of the state of the soil, frequent references to the river or the sea, will serve to make the elements themselves minister to the interest of the plot; and the final catastrophe will be made at once more familiar, yet more sublime, if we have been prepared and led to believe that you have from the first designed to invoke to your aid the awful agencies of Nature herself. Thus, in the Œdipus at Colonos, the Poet, at the very opening of the tragedy, indulges in the celebrated description of the seats of the Dread Goddesses, because the place, and the deities themselves, though invisible, belong yet more essentially to the crowning doom of the wanderer than any of the characters introduced.

The description of *feelings* is also the property of the novelist. The dramatist throws the feelings into dialogue, – the novelist goes at once to the human heart, and calmly scrutinises, assorts, and dissects them. Few, indeed, are the writers who have hitherto attempted this – the master mystery of the hierophant! Godwin[10] has done so the most elaborately; Goethe the most skilfully. The first writer is, indeed, so minute, that he is often frivolous – so lengthened, that he is generally tedious; but the cultivator of the art, and not the art itself, is to be blamed for such defects. A few words will often paint the precise state of emotion as faithfully as the most voluminous essay; and in this department condensation and brevity are to be carefully studied. Conduct us to the cavern, light the torch, and startle and awe us by what you reveal; but if you keep us all day in the cavern, the effect is lost, and our only feeling is that of impatience and desire to get away.

Arrangement of incidents

Distinctions between the Novel and the Drama

In the arrangements of incidents, the reader will carefully study the distinctions between the novel and the drama – distinctions the more important, because they are not, at the first glance, very perceptible.

In the first place, the incidents of a play must grow, progressively, out of each other. Each scene should appear the necessary consequence of the one that precedes it. This is far from being the case with the novel; in the last, it is often desirable to go back instead of forward – to wind, to vary, to shift the interest from person to person – to keep even your principal hero, your principal actor, in the background.[11] In the novel, you see more of Frank Osbaldistone than you do of Rob Roy; but bring Rob Roy on the stage, and Frank Osbaldistone must recede at once into a fifth-rate personage.

In our closets we should be fatigued with the incessant rush of events that we desire when we make one of a multitude. Oratory and the drama in this resemble each other – that the things best to hear are not always the best to read. In the novel, we address ourselves to the one person – on the stage we address ourselves to a crowd: more rapid effects, broader and more popular sentiments, more condensed grasp of the universal passions are required for the last. The calm advice which persuades our friend would only tire out the patience of the crowd. The man who writes a play for Covent Garden ought to remember that the Theatre is but a few paces distant from the Hustings: success at either place, the Hustings or the Theatre, will depend upon a mastery over feelings, not perhaps the most common-place, but the most commonly felt. If with his strong effects on the stage, the dramatic poet can, like Shakspeare, unite the most delicate and subtle refinement, like Shakspeare he will be a consummate artist. But the refinement will not do without the effects. In the novel it is different: the most enchanting and permanent kind of interest, in the latter, is often gentle, tranquillising, and subdued. The novelist can appeal to those delicate and subtle emotions, which are easily awakened when we are alone, but which are torpid and unfelt in the electric contagion of popular sympathies. The most refining amongst us will cease to refine when placed in the midst of a multitude.

There is a great distinction between the plot of a novel and that of a play; a distinction which has been indicated by Goethe in the "Wilhelm Meister." The novel allows *accident,* the drama never. In the former, your principal character may be thrown from his horse, and break his neck; in the latter, this would be a gross burlesque on the first laws of the drama; for in the drama the incidents must bring about the catastrophe; in the novel, there is no such necessity. Don Quixote at the last falls ill and dies in his bed; but in order that he should fall ill and die in his bed, there was no necessity that he should fight windmills, or mistake an inn for a castle. If a novelist had taken for his theme the conspiracy of Fiesco, he might have adhered to history with the most perfect consistency to his art. In the history, as Fiesco, after realising his ambitious projects, is about to step into the ship, he slips from the plank, and the weight of his armour drowns him. This is accident, and this catastrophe would not only have been admissible in the novel, but would have conveyed, perhaps, a sublimer moral than any that fiction could invent. But when Schiller adapted Fiesco for the stage, he felt that accident was not admissible,[12] and his Fiesco falls by the hand of the patriot Verrina. The whole dialogue preceding the fatal blow is one of the most masterly adaptations of moral truth to the necessity of historical infidelity, in European literature.

In the "Bride of Lammermoor," Ravenswood is swallowed up by a quicksand. This catastrophe is singularly grand in romance; it could not be allowable on the stage; for this again is *accident*, and not *result*.

The distinctions, then, between the novel and the drama, so far as the management of incidents is concerned, are principally these: that in the one the interest must always progress – that in the other, it must often go back and often halt; that dealing with human nature in a much larger scale in the novel, you will often introduce events and incidents, not necessarily growing one out of the other, though all conducing to the completeness of the whole; that in the drama you have more impatience to guard against – you are addressing men in numbers, not the individual man; your effects must be more rapid and more startling; that in the novel you may artistically have recourse to accident for the working out of your design – in the drama, never.

The ordinary faults of a play by the novelist,[13] and of a novel by the play-writer, will serve as an illustration of the principles which have insensibly regulated each. The novelist will be too diffuse, too narrative, and too refined in his effects for the stage; the play-writer will be too condensed, abrupt, and, above all, too exaggerated, for our notions of the Natural when we are in the closet. Stage effect is a vice in the novel; but, how can we expect a man trained to write for the stage to avoid what on the stage is a merit? A certain exaggeration of sentiment is natural, and necessary, for sublime and truthful effects when we address numbers; it would be ludicrous uttered to our friend in his easy chair. If Demosthenes, urging a young Athenian to conduct himself properly, had thundered out[14] that sublime appeal to the shades of Marathon, Platea, and Salamis, which thrilled the popular assembly, the young Athenian would have laughed in his face. If the dialogue of "Macbeth" were the dialogue of a romance on the same subject, it would be equally good in itself, but it would seem detestable bombast. If the dialogue in "Ivanhoe," which is matchless of its kind for spirit and fire, were shaped into blank verse, and cut up into a five-act play, it would be bald and pointless. As the difference between the effective oration and the eloquent essay – between Pitt so great to hear, and Burke so great to read, so is the difference between the writing for the eye of one man, and the writing for the ears of three thousand.

Mechanism and conduct

THE MECHANISM AND CONDUCT OF THE STORY ought to depend upon the nature of the preconceived design. Do you desire to work out some definite end, through the passions or through the characters you employ? Do you desire to carry on the interest less through character and passion than through incident? Or, do you rather desire to entertain and instruct by a general and wide knowledge of living manners or human nature? or, lastly, would you seek to incorporate all these objects? As you are faithful to your conception, will you be attentive to, and precise in, the machinery you use? In other words, your *progress* must depend upon the order of interest you mean to be predominant. It is by not considering this rule that critics have often called that episodical or extraneous, which is in fact a part of the design. Thus, in "Gil Blas,"[15] the object is to convey to the reader a complete picture of the surface of society; the manners, foibles, and pecularities of the time; elevated by a general, though not very profound, knowledge of the more durable and universal elements of human nature in the abstract. Hence, the numerous tales and nouvelletes scattered throughout the work, though episodical to the adventures of Gil Blas, are not episodical to the design of Le Sage. They all serve to complete and furnish out the conception, and the whole would be less rich and consummate in its effect without them. They are not passages which lead to nothing, but conduce to many purposes we can never comprehend, unless we consider well for what end the building was planned. So if you wish to bring out all the peculiarities of a certain character, you will often seem to digress into adventures which have no palpable bearing on the external plot of incident and catastrophe. This is constantly the case with Cervantes and Fielding; and the critic who blames you for it, is committing the gross blunder of judging the novel by the laws of the drama.

But as an ordinary rule, it may be observed that, since, both in the novel and the play, human life is represented by an epitome, so in both it is desirable that all your characters should more or less be brought to bear on the conclusions you have in view. It is not necessary in the novel that they should bear on the physical events; they may sometimes bear on the mental and interior changes in the minds and characters of the persons you introduce. For instance, if you design in the life of your hero to illustrate the Passion of Jealousy upon a peculiar conformation of mind, you may introduce several characters and several incidents, which will serve to ripen his tendencies, but not have the least bearing on the actual catastrophe in which those tendencies are confirmed into deeds. This is but fidelity to real life, in which it seldom happens that they who foster the passion are the witnesses or sufferers of the effects. This distinction between interior and external agencies will be made apparent by a close study of the admirable novel of Zeluco.[16]

In the mechanism of external incidents, Scott is the greatest model that fiction possesses; and if we select from his works that in which this mechanism is most artistical, we instance not one of his most brilliant and popular, but one in which he combined all the advantages of his multiform and matured experience in the craft: we mean the "Fair Maid of Perth." By noting well the manner in which, in this tale, the scene is ever varied at the right moment, and the exact medium preserved between abruptness and *longueur*; how all the incidents are complicated, so as to appear inextricable, yet the solution obtained by the simplest and shortest process, the reader will learn more of the art of *mechanical* construction, than by all the rules that Aristotle himself, were he living, could lay down.

Divisions of the work

In the Drama, the DIVISIONS of the plot into *Acts* are of infinite service in condensing and simplifying the design of the author. The novelist will find it convenient to himself to establish analogous divisions in the conduct of his story. The division into volumes is but the affair of the printer, and affords little help to the intellectual purposes of the author. Hence, most of our greatest novelists have had recourse to the more definite sub-partition of the work into *Books*; and if the student use this mode of division, not from capricious or arbitrary pleasure, but with the same purposes of art, for which, in the drama, recourse is had to the division into Acts, he will find it of the greatest service. Properly speaking, each Book should be complete in itself, working out the exact and whole purpose that the author meditates in that portion of his work. It is clear, therefore, that the number of his Books will vary according to the nature of his design. Where you have shaped your story after a dramatic fashion, you will often be surprised to find how greatly you serve to keep your construction faithful to your design by the mere arrangement of the work into the same number of sub-divisions as are adopted in the drama, viz., five books instead of five acts. Where, on the other hand, you avoid the dramatic construction, and lead the reader through great varieties of life and action, meaning, in each portion of the history of your hero, to illustrate separate views of society or human nature, you will probably find a much greater number of sub-divisions requisite. This must depend upon your design. Another advantage in these divisions consists in the rules that your own common sense will suggest to you with respect to the introduction of Characters. It is seldom advisable to admit any new character of importance, after the interest has arrived at a certain point of maturity. As you would not introduce a new character of consequence to the catastrophe, in the fifth act of a play, so, though with more qualification and reserve, it will be inartistical to make a similar introduction in the corresponding portion of a novel. The most illustrious exception to this general rule is in "Clarissa," in which the Avenger, the brother of the heroine, and the executioner of Lovelace, only appears at the close of the story, and for the single purpose of revenge; and here the effect is heightened by the lateness and suddenness of the introduction of the very person to whom the catastrophe is confided.

The catastrophe

The distinction between the novel and the drama is usually very visible in the Catastrophe. The stage effect of bringing all the characters together in the closing chapter, to be married or stabbed as the thing may require, is, to a fine taste, eminently displeasing in a novel. It introduces into the very place where we most desire verisimilitude, a clap-trap and theatrical effect. For it must be always remembered, that in prose fiction we require more of the Real than we do in the drama (which belongs, of right, to the regions of pure poetry), and if the very last effect bequeathed to us be that of palpable delusion and trick, the charm of the whole work is greatly impaired. Some of Scott's romances may be justly charged with this defect.

Usually, the author is so far aware of the inartist-like effect of a final grouping of all the characters before the fall of the curtain, that he brings but few of the agents he has employed to be *present* at the catastrophe, and follows what may be called the wind-up of the main interest, by one or more epilogical chapters, in which we are told how Sir Thomas married and settled at his country seat, how Miss Lucy died an old maid, and how the miser Grub was found dead on his money chest; disposing in a few sentences of the lives and deaths of all to whom we have been presented – a custom that we think might now give place to less hacknied inventions.

The drama will bear but one catastrophe; the novel will admit of more. Thus, in "Ivanhoe," the more vehement and apparent catastrophe is the death of Bois Guilbert; but the marriage of Ivanhoe, the visit of Rebecca to Rowena, and the solemn and touching farewell of the Jewess, constitute, properly speaking, a catastrophe no less capital in itself, and no less essential to the completion of the incidents. So also there is often a moral catastrophe, as well as a physical one, sometimes identified each with the other, sometimes distinct. If you have been desirous to work out some conception of a principle or a truth, the design may not be completed till after the more violent effects which form the physical catastrophe. In the recent novel of "Alice, or the Mysteries,"[17] the external catastrophe is in the vengeance of Cæsarini and the death of Vargrave, but the complete *denouement* and completion of the more typical meanings and ethical results of the fiction are reserved to the moment when Maltravers recognises the Natural to be the true Ideal, and is brought, by the faith and beauty of simple goodness, to affection and respect for mankind, itself. In the drama, it would be necessary to incorporate in one scene all the crowning results of the preceding events. We could not bear a new interest after the death of Bois Guilbert; and a new act of mere dialogue between Alice and Maltravers, after the death of Vargrave, would be unsufferably tame and frigid. The perfection of a catastrophe is not so much in the power with which it is told, as in the feeling of completeness which it should leave on the mind. On closing the work, we ought to feel that we have read a *whole* – that there is an harmonious unity in all its parts – that its close, whether it be pleasing or painful, is that which is essentially appropriate to all that has gone before; and not only the mere isolated thoughts in the work, but the unity of the work itself, ought to leave its single and deep impression on the mind. The book itself should be a thought.

There is another distinction between the catastrophe of a novel and that of a play. In the last, it ought to be the most permanent and striking events that lead to the catastrophe; in the former, it will often be highly artistical to revive for the consummating effect, many slight details – incidents the author had but dimly shadowed out – mysteries, that you had judged, till then, he had forgotten to clear up; and to bring a thousand rivulets, that had seemed merely introduced to relieve or adorn the way, into the rapid gulf which closes over all. The effect of this has a charm not derived from mere trick, but from its fidelity to the natural and lifelike order of events. What more common in the actual world than that the great crises of our fate are influenced and coloured, not so much by the incidents and persons we have deemed most important, but by many things of remote date, or of seeming insignificance. The feather the eagle carelessly sheds by the way-side plumes the shaft that transfixes him. In this management and combination of incidents towards the grand end, knowledge of Human Nature can alone lead the student to the knowledge of Ideal Art.

These remarks form the summary of the hints and suggestions that, after a careful study of books, we submit to the consideration of the student in a class of literature now so widely cultivated, and hitherto almost wholly unexamined by the critic. We presume not to say that they form an entire code of laws for the art. Even Aristotle's immortal treatise on Poetry, were it bequeathed to us complete, would still be but a skeleton; and though no poet could read that treatise without advantage, the most glorious poetry might be, and has been, written in defiance of nearly all its laws. Genius will arrive at fame by the light of its own star; but Criticism can often serve as a sign-post to save many an unnecessary winding, and indicate many a short way. He who aspires to excel in that fiction which is the glass of truth, may learn much from books and rules, from the lecturer and the critic; but he must be also the Imaginer, the Observer. He will be ever examining human life in its most catholic and comprehensive aspects. Nor is it enough to observe, – it is necessary to feel. We must let the heart be a student as well as the head. No man who is a passionless and cold spectator, will ever be an accurate analyst, of all the motives and springs of action. Perhaps, if we were to search for the true secret of CREATIVE GENIUS, we should find that secret in the intenseness of its SYMPATHIES.[18]

George Moir
(1800–1870)
From 'Modern Romance and Novel',
1842

Like a number of his gifted contemporaries, George Moir managed to combine a strong inclination toward literature with a professional commitment to the law. Born in Aberdeen, he pursued his legal studies in Edinburgh; by the time he was admitted to the Faculty of Advocates (the Scottish equivalent of being called to the bar) in 1825, he had already begun writing for the *Edinburgh Review*. For more than three decades he continued to contribute criticism, translations, political essays, and some rather feeble fiction to that distinguished quarterly and its great rival, *Blackwood's Edinburgh Magazine*, as well as to the *Foreign Quarterly Review*, the *Quarterly Review*, and the *New Monthly Magazine*. Moir's interest in German literature was especially keen: his publications include English versions of Schiller's *Wallenstein* (1827) and *Historical Works* (1828). Between 1825 and 1840, Moir was Professor of Rhetoric and Belles Lettres at the University of Edinburgh.

Throughout his life, however, George Moir was also active in the law, lecturing and writing about it as well as practising it. He served as sheriff first of Ross and Cromarty (1855–9) and then of Stirlingshire (1859–68) and briefly held the position of Professor of Scots Law at the University of Edinburgh (1864–5) until forced to resign because of poor health. His legal scholarship appears in such books as *The Appellate Jurisdiction of Scotch Appeals* (1851) and *Principles of the Law of Scotland* (1870).

'Modern Romance and Novel' was written for and published in the seventh edition (1842) of the *Encyclopaedia Britannica* (vol. 19, pp. 334–59). Presumably the essay had come out earlier than that in one of the monthly parts of this edition that were sold separately between March 1830 and January 1842; at any rate, its first appearance in book form was in *Treatises on Poetry, Modern Romance, and Rhetoric; Being the Articles on Those Heads, Contributed to the Encyclopaedia Britannica, Seventh Edition* (1839; pp. 157–271). For the eighth edition of the *Encyclopaedia Britannica* it was revised by William Edmondstoune Aytoun. The text of the following selection, representing about a third of Moir's 35,000-word original, is taken from the seventh edition: pp. 334–41 and 347–9. We have omitted his discussions of minor English novelists of the late eighteenth and early nineteenth centuries – including 'Miss [Jane] Austin' [*sic*] – and his extensive treatment of Italian,

Spanish, French, and German fiction, as well as numerous examples that add little to his argument.

One reason why 'Modern Romance and Novel' remains of interest is that in it Moir attempts to transcend the traditional classification of fiction into two chief kinds. Though he accepts the distinction between the novel ('in which the events are accommodated to the ordinary train of human events, and the modern state of society') and the romance ('in which the interest of the narrative turns chiefly on marvellous and uncommon interests'), and though he shows a strong bias in favour of realism and what he calls *vraisemblance* (probability or truth to life), Moir is prepared to admit passion, mystery, and even the supernatural into modern fiction, provided that these elements are skilfully integrated into the over-all design of a particular work. Moreover, though he recognizes that the novelist enjoys greater freedom in the construction of his plots than does the playwright, Moir nevertheless insists that a piece of prose fiction needs to observe certain structural principles of coherence and that the mutual interrelationships among its parts and between its parts and the whole must be clear. Finally, in Moir's view there is a close connection between literature on the one hand and manners and morals on the other. But for him this is more than a question of the effect of novels on character and behaviour, important as that undeniably is; rather, the kind of literature written and savoured during a particular age is itself a sign and a consequence of the spirit of that age. So, for example, changing social conditions at the beginning of the eighteenth century brought about the rise of the novel along with the concomitant decline of the drama; and toward the end of that century, the revolutionary ethos of the time – 'that spirit of restlessness and discontent with political institutions' – led novelists 'to dress up moral paradoxes in the shape of narrative, and to employ their eloquence in attacking those principles of society which tend to make men happy, or which keep them so'. (These quotations are from Moir's discussion of fiction before Scott, which is not included in our selection.)

In his knowledgeable and intelligent approach to the eighteenth- and nineteenth-century novel, George Moir joins a firm adherence to principle with a refreshing flexibility and willingness to grant exceptions to general rules.

We alluded in the commencement of this essay, to the division of fictitious narratives in prose, into two classes; the *romance*, in which the interest of the narrative turns chiefly on marvellous and uncommon incidents; and the *novel*, in which the events are accommodated to the ordinary train of human events, and the modern state of society.[1]

The rise of this last department of fictitious composition in England, takes place about the commencement of the eighteenth century; and its coincidence with the decline of the drama is remarkable. The novel aspired, in fact, to perform for a reading and refined age, what the drama had done for a ruder and more excitable period; to embody the spirit of the times in pictures at once amusing and accurate, and in the form best calculated to awaken attention and interest in those to whom they are addressed. In the earlier periods of a national literature, while the poetical and imaginative spirit of the time takes the direction of the long prose romance, the task of painting manners, and satirizing follies, and displaying the comic oddities of character, is most efficiently performed by the drama. Its strength, terseness, and brevity, with the aid of action and scenery, present the manners living as they rise, with abundance of force at least, and probably, for a time, with sufficient fidelity. But as society becomes more decorous, and peculiarities of manners less marked, the pictures exhibited by the stage are apt to become less true; for dramatic effect appears to demand something more stimulating than reality affords; and hence the drama, with a pardonable leaning to the principle of stage effect, often continues to reproduce the manners, vices, and humours of a preceding age, long after they have ceased to exist, merely because they are found better adapted to that broad and strongly-coloured delineation in which it chiefly deals ... It is in the works of our novelists, therefore, rather than our dramatists, and in those passages in our essayists of Queen Anne's time, in which they treat of past fashions, manners, whims, and humours, that we must look for the changes which society has undergone, and from which we must try to realize to ourselves the features which it exhibited at any particular period.

The novel, then, affords a wider field for accurate and complete delineation of passions and feelings than the drama, and certainly one more in harmony with the dispositions of a modern public. In powerful effects no doubt it cannot compete with the stage. The whole range of novel or romance contains nothing, for instance, which in its tremendous impression, can be compared with the explosion of passion in the third act of Othello; but, on the other hand, it has greatly the advantage in the impression of verisimilitude which it leaves behind, produced by the accumulation of many particulars and minute traits of character; in pleasing interchanges of action and repose; in the delineation of emotions, which the drama, speaking only to the eye and the ear, cannot lay before us; in the descriptions of external scenery, which, in the hand of a writer of genius, are far more effective, when presented in words to the imagination, than when counterfeited to the eye upon the stage, even by all the united resources of the scene-painter and the mechanist; and which, from the strong connection which exists between the state of our feelings and external influences, are found in the hands of a judicious novelist, to afford powerful materials for deepening the pervading tone of sentiment which he aims to produce; just as in painting relief and effect are obtained by the tone and character of the background against which the figures are opposed. Another advantage obtained by the substitution of narrative fiction for the drama, was, that a much wider licence was obtained in the conduct of the plot. A good plot is no doubt as essential to the novel as the drama; but the kind of plot which may be used with effect in each, and the manner in which the incidents are to be conducted, differ materially. A play in which every scene does not grow out of the preceding, and lead directly into the next, with the visible progress of plot, is in that respect faulty. On the contrary, in the novel and romance, as in real life, much is admissible which is episodical, which does not directly help forward nor produce the catastrophe, but merely tends to bring out some point of character in the personages represented, or to increase the air of verisimilitude in the main story, by the appearance of minute and literal correctness in the details. In the novel or romance, too, it has been generally remarked that the catastrophe may be made to turn upon accident, but that this is inadmissible in the drama.[2] Thus the catastrophe in the *Bride of Lammermoor*, where Ravenswood is swallowed up by a quicksand, is singularly grand in romance, but would be inadmissible in a drama. And on the same principle, Schiller has, in his *Fiesco*, thought himself compelled to deviate from the actual truth of history, and to ascribe the Count's death, not to an accidental stumble from a plank, but to the hand of the republican Verrina. In a novel, the real catastrophe would have been far more impressive in its moral effect than the imaginary one; but Schiller held, and we think rightly, that in the drama nothing must be *accident*, but every thing *result*.

Although, as compared with the romance, the term novel may be said to indicate a class of fictions dealing more with calm feelings, and with manners and humours, than with strong passions, and deriving its interest more from the probability than the marvellous nature of its incidents, this definition is not to be taken too literally; for there are many works which we might call novels, in as much as the scene is laid in modern times, and the general course of the incidents is that of every-day life, but in which the even tenor of the story is occasionally broken by scenes of powerful passion, or incidents of a mysterious and terrible character, elevating the composition for the time into the sphere of the romantic; so that perhaps the word tale, as a middle term between the others, would most appropriately describe them. It has been doubted whether, although such a union of the common-place with the extraordinary, be not unfrequently met with in the course of real life, a more cautious separation of these elements would not, on the whole, be most favourable to the effect of a narrative as a work of art; and whether the attempt to blend them, does not produce in fiction, something of that illegitimate effect which is the result of the melo-drama on the stage. It is certain, however, that the tendency for some time past, and particularly since the school of fiction introduced by Sir Walter Scott, has been towards a mixture of the novel and romance in the same composition, so that broad comedy is often found alternating with the pathetic, the gaiety of a ball-room with midnight murders upon lonely heaths, and the disclosure of some piece of fashionable scandal standing side by side with the discovery of some secret and fearful crime. . . .

Defoe, (1661–1731) without high imagination, with no power of raising the passions, with little pathos and no eloquence, had yet that peculiar genius which enabled him to excel within the peculiar department which he chose for himself; that of counterfeiting homely truth by fiction, and forging, as it were, the handwriting of nature herself, with a dexterity which defied detection. Whether Defoe was led to the selection of his peculiar themes, by a real sympathy with roguery, (and his conduct in regard to the well-known imposture of Mrs. Veal's Ghost[3] would justify us in believing him to be like Gil Blas, "tant soi peu fripon;"[a]) or by the influence of the Spanish romances of roguery, such as Lazaro de Tormes, Marcos de Obregon, and Gusman d'Alfarache,[4] with some of which it is highly probable that he was acquainted through translations; or whether his strong vulgar likenesses of seafaring personages, half privateer, half mariner, and his fondness for the delineation of equivocal characters of all kinds, arose from his familiarity with the one class, through his residence at Limehouse,[5] and his acquaintance with Dampier,[6] – and with the other, from his long and frequent imprisonments; – it is certain that though he had no intention of favouring immorality, he yet enters upon the delineation of personages, and scenes of roguery, low profligacy and vice, with a degree of curiosity and complacency, and dwells upon them with a fondness and minuteness of detail, altogether uncommon, and not a little unaccountable in a person who in his opinions savoured of the puritan. This strange labour of love, and study of the morbid anatomy of society, has resulted in a series of night pieces from the haunts of crime, which, though sombre and

[a] A bit of a rascal.

gloomy in a high degree, and little suited to a cultivated taste, nay, indeed, frequently producing on the mind the painful effect of a real chapter from the *Newgate Calendar*,[7] yet display the most wonderful invention and keeping in all their parts, and a coherence and dexterity of adaptation to each other, which render the ordinary tests by which we endeavour to discriminate a fictitious from a real narrative, inadequate or altogether inapplicable to these singular compositions of Defoe....

There can be but one opinion, however, as to the wonderful air of veracity, resembling that of a deposition upon oath, which Defoe has imparted to his fictitious creations, and which his genius effects, mainly by accumulation of details, *non vi sed sæpe cadendo*;[a] often even by the introduction of a multitude of irrelevant particulars and repetitions, just as in the conversation of uneducated persons in real life. Accordingly the result, as a simulacrum of reality, is one of magical deception....

But notwithstanding this peculiar power of stamping the impression of reality upon the coinage of his imagination, which, to say the truth, was seldom of the finest metals, it may be safely affirmed, that but for his *Robinson Crusoe* Defoe would scarcely now be remembered as a writer of fiction. The charm of that work, the first part of which appeared in 1719, is, that it emancipates us from those low haunts and questionable society with which his other novels make us acquainted. We escape from the fumes of tobacco and strong waters, to breathe a purer air on that lone island placed far amidst the melancholy main, where he has imprisoned his shipwrecked mariner; and while Defoe's unrivalled power of inventing a series of probable minutiæ, both in the way of reflexion and incident, enables him to conduct with consummate skill, what we may call the self-education of Crusoe in his solitude, – the process by which he adapts himself to his situation, and the gradual triumphs which, by his ingenuity and patience, he obtains over the difficulties and privations by which he is surrounded, till he changes desolation into comfort; – the imagination of the writer is visibly raised beyond its usual grovelling level by the romance of the situation which he describes. His genius imbibes the spirit of the place; it imparts to the cave of the sailor, something of the seclusion and purity of a hermitage; till the simple train of reflections which he puts into the mouth of his uneducated mariner, upon the sublimity and awfulness of solitude, impress the mind more than the most eloquent declamation....

[a] [The drop of rain maketh a hole in the stone] not by violence, but by oft falling. (Hugh Latimer, Seventh Sermon Before Edward VI, 19 April 1549.)

That *Robinson Crusoe* may be considered in a great measure as a fortunate accident, and that its main charm arises from the more poetical and refined character which the nature of the story and its locality almost necessarily impressed upon it, is indeed evident from the visible inferiority of the second part, where the seclusion of the scene is broken in upon, and Defoe peoples the island with his usual retinue of planters and ship's captains; a production which scarcely rises above the level of his *Captain Singleton*.

The application of the same principle of producing effect by minuteness of detail rather than by grasp, or the selection of a few marking traits, is visible in our next great novelist, Richardson (1689–1761), but the principle is applied in a different and higher way. Defoe was satisfied with weaving chains of probable incidents, which might be fitted to any character, or at least any character of a given class, such as a mariner or a merchant, a planter or a pickpocket. He did not care, at all events he did *not* labour, to individualize character. Crusoe, his most finished portrait, is still only the average representative of all shipwrecked mariners; his reflections and his struggles, embody the hopes, fears, and efforts, of all men left to maintain a solitary warfare with difficulties. So his Captain Jack, born a gentleman and bred a pickpocket, has nothing to separate him from other *enfants perdus*[a] of the same class. But Richardson aspired to the creation rather of probable character than probable incident; and to this he applied the same system of accumulating minute traits of words, thoughts, and actions, and reiterating small touches, and minute lights and shadings, which Defoe had done to the creation of masses of coherent and plausible events. In the latter department, indeed, he is probably neither remarkable for success nor failure. Occasionally, and particularly in his *Sir Charles Grandison*, he outrages both patience and probability in no inconsiderable degree; and so little progress does the narrative make, that as Johnson remarked to Erskine; "Were you to read Richardson for the story, your impatience would be so fretted, you would go hang yourself."[8] But even in the most successful portion of his plots, there is no chance of our mistaking fiction for fact; the artist does not disappear behind his creations as in the case of Defoe. The very form, too, in which his novels are cast, that of a series of correspondence, however favourable to the display of traits of character, and minute dissection of sentiment, is almost in itself fatal to the vraisemblance of incident. The affairs of private life we cannot help recollecting, are seldom managed to any great extent through the post-office, while in many cases it

_____
[a] Stray children.

45

remains a mystery how such matters came to be committed to paper at all, and least of all under the circumstances in which they are supposed to be recorded by these persevering, and, in the existing state of the revenue laws, formidable correspondents.

There is in the mind of Richardson a very remarkable union of feminine tastes with masculine vigour. Early accustomed peculiarly to court the society of females; the depository of their gossip, the confident of their love secrets, the complete letter-writer of a little knot of young ladies when only thirteen years of age, the deference which he thus acquired for their tastes, and the insight he obtained into their habits of thinking, though probably springing, as Johnson believed, very much from his own vanity and love of praise, appear to have been of the utmost use to him in his novels, in which so much of the interest rests upon the female characters, and in the minute dissection and study of emotions and sentiments in which women are either the chief actors or sufferers. The traces of this influence appear constantly, and sometimes in excess, in the minute accuracy with which he dwells, in description, upon those little particulars of looks, and voice, and gesture, and turns of speech, which men in their correspondence generally overlook, but which women note with such care, and interpret with such sagacity; in the complacency with which he dwells on the details of robes and wedding dresses, which are conceived in the spirit of a waiting-woman, and executed with the learning of a man-milliner; and which, as in the minute description given by Lovelace of Clarissas' dress at the time of her elopement, are occasionally introduced in the worst place.

The more favourable results of these tastes are exhibited in the wonderful familiarity he evinces with the feelings and sympathies of women; for though, in his notions of perfection, either in manners or morals, we of another age often see cause to depart from Richardson's standard, we may trust implicitly to his accuracy, when he is delineating the movements of passion in the female breast, the revolutions of feeling, or the struggle between feeling and delicacy. In his female portraits even more than in his corresponding delineations of male character, we acknowledge the justice of the remark which Sir Walter Scott applies to his portraits generally, that 'in his survey of the heart, he left neither head, bay, nor inlet behind him, until he had traced its soundings, and laid it down in his chart with all its minute sinuosities, its depths, and its shallows.'[9] This accuracy, indeed, constitutes at once his strength and his weakness; for not content with having surveyed the coast and taken its bearings, he still, from the very pride of discovery, insists on following the windings of the shore, and pointing out its landmarks, when those on board would have gladly seen him make his passage by the shortest course. It was the misfortune of Richardson, that, like nervous men in company, or like painters who go on retouching till the picture becomes loaded, he never knew when to have done, either with a character or a conversation. . . .

It is not often that with this feminine character of intellect, a masculine vigour in painting scenes of a passionate and terrible cast is found united, and yet Richardson has proved his mastery over the higher passions, not less than his minute study of sentiment and manners, in the conclusion of *Clarissa Harlowe*. To apply to him the epithet of the Shakspeare of prose fiction, which has been done by D'Israeli,[10] is extravagant. A solitary creation of this kind, highly pathetic and morally impressive as it is, is but a narrow basis on which to rest the claims of the novelist to such a title. But the conceptions of the noble character of Clarissa Harlowe, set off by such a foil as is afforded by that of Lovelace, perhaps the most finished picture of the self-possessed and insinuating libertine ever drawn, (and certainly as great an improvement on that of the Lothario[11] from which it was drawn, as Rowes' hero had been on the vulgar rake of Massinger[12]), and the closing scenes of that novel, are at all events sufficient to place Richardson *among* the great writers of fiction; among the few who have formed a striking and original conception, which they have wrought out with a corresponding felicity and power. It is not the common-place idea of a woman of virtue foiling the schemes of a seducer, which Richardson has undertaken to illustrate: in the case of a lady like Clarissa, of birth, education, and good feelings, Mrs. Barbauld says truly, that would have been no triumph worthy of being recorded by such a pen;[13] but it is the dignity, the deep interest, he has lent to the character, even in that situation of personal dishonour, with which, from whatever cause it has arisen, we are apt to connect the idea of degradation. . . .

A strong contrast to the subtlety, the fine perception, and the power over the passions evinced by Richardson, is presented by his rival Fielding, (1707–1754,) who, with no command of the pathetic, no great share of wit, and no taste for that minute analysis of sentiment and wire-drawing of description in which our English Marivaux[14] indulges, has yet maintained a more general and permanent popularity, by a combination of qualities well suited for the purpose. His grasp of observation led him to select with unerring sagacity, the leading traits of ordinary character, and to epitomize nature with skill, instead of transcribing her at full length. His field of delineation admits of such variety and contrast, that in fact it excludes none but the highest and most poetical elements, in which Fielding had neither power of observation or conception. His flow of animal spirits and healthy vivacity of manner, contrast strangely with the Dutch finishing[15] of Richardson's pencilling, but are as well suited to the active, out-of-door scenes which Fielding loved to draw, in his pictures of imbroglios at ale-houses, and the stirring life of the road, as the pains-taking inventories of Richardson were to his still-life interiors, and the drowsy monotony of the occupations of their inhabitants. To these he added, at least in his great work, *Tom Jones*, the charm of a plot of unrivalled skill, in which the complex threads of interest are all brought to bear upon the catastrophe in a manner equally unexpected and simple, a grave humour, and power of quiet satire unmixed with caricature, in which he is equally superior to Richardson and to Smollett. And with his other requisites he combined a knowledge of English life, both in its better features and its deformities, by which we mean, of the essential qualities of men, as modified at that time by the accidents of situation, education, and pursuits, – the result, perhaps, of a long, and not always reputable experience, – to which Richardson, surrounded by a circle of female gossips, and weaving out his materials in his quiet back shop, purely from the stores of his imagination, can make but slender pretension. . . .

The name of Fielding always suggests that of his rival Smollett (1721–1724,) though, as writers of fiction, they rather admit of being contrasted than compared. They have, in fact, very few, if any, points in common; agreeing only perhaps in a preference for the delineation of the comic, or the common, over the impassioned and poetical. They chose different departments in novel writing, and they cultivated them by different means. As Fielding was the faithful and graphic painter of all the common features of character, so the extraordinary and the eccentric were the peculiar appanage of Smollett. He either did not feel sufficiently the charm of the natural in character, and its power of endless recombination in the hands of a great artist, or he doubted his own powers, at least in comparison with Fielding, of extracting novelty from such simple materials. But the sphere of humourous exaggeration appeared to be open to him, without the awe of a predecessor, or the dread of a rival; on that, therefore, he concentrated his powers of mind, neglecting in a great measure the other requisites of fiction; and undoubtedly with a success, which leaves him, within the province which he was the first to occupy, and with the occupation of which he was content, still the undisputed sovereign. No one has ever yet equalled him in the observation, or where that does not serve his purpose, the creation of oddities and exceptional characters which never did or could exist, but still with just enough of humanity about them, to give us an interest in their eccentric movements, or in the invention of combinations of burlesque incidents not always of the best odour, which his fertile fancy showers forth spontaneously as from a cornucopia; mistakes, rencounters, equivoques,[a] whimsicalities of speech or action, all generally the best calculated to bring out in high raised and ludicrous relief the comic aberrations of the character represented, and to develope its latent madness; and never failing, at all events, to produce that result which Smollett seemed far more studious to attain than that of 'purging the passions by pity or terror;'[16] namely, the excitement of a broad-grin mirth, and 'laughter holding both his sides.'[17] That the characters, where they have any decided features at all, are generally caricatures; for instance, that such commodores and lieutenants as Trunnion and Hatchway,[18] never floated even under the primitive flag of Benbow;[19] that the absurdities of Pallet[20] are painted an inch thick; that by no human possibility could such an accumulation of comic disasters have befallen the characters of the tale, may, and indeed must be granted, even by Smollett's warmest admirers. But if, following Smollett's own example, we throw nature mainly out of the question, and look to what seems to have been his real aim, the objection of want of verisimilitude, while it may retain its truth, seems to lose half its force, and, we may add, wholly its power of conviction. It is in vain to point out the extravagance of the scene where Jolter, in an agony of terror, on hearing the direction given to put on the dead lights in the storm off Calais, goes through the steps of a mathematical proposition with infinite fervour, instead of a prayer, or to criticise the manœuvres of Trunnion, tacking his way to church on his wedding day in consequence of a head wind; – when the reader cannot see the force of the objection, through tears of laughter. In that consummation which he chiefly aimed at, and in which he rarely fails, Smollett has gained his end; – *solvuntur risu tabulæ;*[b] the sense of the improbability of the conceptions is lost in the irrepressible merriment which they occasion.

Humour, then, was the quality in which Smollett felt himself strongest; character, incident, the excitement of the feelings, were obviously with him minor considerations. There is no difficulty in discriminating his style of humour from that of Fielding. Fielding's is

---

[a] Double meanings.
[b] In a tempest of laughter, The Tables will go to pieces. (Horace, *Satires* II, i, 86.)

calmer, chaster, perhaps of a higher kind than Smollett's, but it certainly has not its breadth, force, and felicity. As Smollett could hardly have created in its main features so gentle a humourist as Parson Adams,[21] so he probably could have scarcely imagined a stroke of humour so delicate and appropriate to the character, as when the Parson offers to walk ten miles to fetch his sermon against Vanity, in order to convince his auditor of his total freedom from that vice. But neither, on the other hand, could he have imagined the feast after the manner of the ancients, the apparition of Pipes to the Commodore, the terrors of Pallet on learning the supposed conditions of his emancipation from the Bastille, or the ludicrous concatenation of mischances which beset the luckless inmates of the Inn in Flanders 'doing or suffering.'[22] Some scenes of this sort, in which Fielding enters into competition with Smollett, such as those at the Inn at Upton,[23] are among the least successful in his novels. The effort to raise the waters, the malice prepense in the preparation of the comic machinery, is too obvious; and after all, though he creates abundance of confusion, he raises but few smiles.

In another quality, though he has but rarely availed himself of his powers in this respect, Smollett far surpassed Fielding; we mean in his power of exciting the emotions of terror, or the sublime. From scenes of this kind, Fielding, knowing the prosaic turn of his own mind, and the limits of his invention, kept at a respectful distance; Smollett, who felt within himself the spirit of a poet, has occasionally ventured upon them, and with complete success. The robber scene in the old woman's hut in *Count Fathom*,[24] though often imitated since, still remains one of the most impressive and agitating night pieces of its kind; and the sublimity of the situation on ship board, where Random sits chained to the poop during an engagement, covered with the blood and brains of the wounded, and screaming in delirium,[25] has been often pointed out.

The morality of Smollett and Fielding is nearly on a par; with this difference, that the slight dash of generosity which is infused into the blackguardism of Tom Jones, while it renders him more natural, makes him at the same time more dangerous than the selfish and often ruffianly heroes of Smollett; whom we despise or dislike, even while laughing at the cruel frolics in which they indulge. The heroes of the latter are mere animals, good-natured or savage, as the fit strikes them; the heroines, with the exception perhaps of Aurelia Darnel in *Sir Lancelot Greaves*, the weakest of Smollett's works, have been justly described as objects rather of appetite than affection. In regard, indeed, to anything like purity of morals, or gentlemanly feeling, the inferiority both of Smollett and Fielding to Richardson is obvious. Richardson sometimes mistook his means, but his aim was certainly always moral. On the contrary, both the theory and the practice of the justice were latitudinarian; and Smollett, though in real life a man of pure morals, had a boundless toleration in fiction for certain vices; for most, indeed, which did not imply want of spirit, courage, or pecuniary generosity.

In the unity of conception and coherence of incident which the plot of the novel, though more pliable than that of the drama demands, Fielding, in his two principal works (for *Joseph Andrews* was merely a parody on Richardson's *Pamela*) has a great advantage over Smollett, whose plots indeed in general scarcely deserve the name, being simply a series of strange accidents, odd rencontres, tricks and frolics, making little or no progress towards the only catastrophe which Smollett seems to have in view, namely, the marriage of his hero. In his *Roderick Random*, *Peregrine Pickle*, and *Count Fathom*, Smollett adopted the easy inartificial plan of *Gil Blas*, in which we are carried through a succession of scenes where the personages are constantly changing, and those who take part in the close of the story, are quite different from those by whom we are surrounded at its commencement. Fielding, on the contrary, both in his *Tom Jones* and *Amelia*, is singularly attentive to regularity of plan, and to the dexterous evolution and winding up of his plot, which he regarded as of vital importance. From the very commencement we perceive that he keeps his conclusion clearly in view, "and sees as from a tower the end of all." From this attention to symmetry, and tendency of all the incidents towards the catastrophe, his best work has been not inaptly termed a prose epic; it is at all events a happy accommodation of the principles of the epic, so far as they could be rendered applicable, to the manner of the novel. One exception ought perhaps to be made from this remark on the imperfection of Smollett's plots, in favour of that of *Humphrey Clinker*, in which the plot, though not of much art, is naturally evolved, and a quiet little family romance is gracefully combined with the usual gallery of oddities which Smollett never fails to lay before us. In all respects, this is the most pleasing of his performances. While Lesmahago may rank with the very best of his extravagances, there is more of character and less of caricature in the testy, yet kind-hearted, Matthew Bramble "frosty but kindly," than in any personage he has painted; and though the humour, as usual, is dashed with filth, without a *soupçon* of which indeed Smollett seems always to have thought it wanted pungency, the tale is entirely free from that indecency which deforms both *Roderick Random* and

Perigrine Pickle. We rather think, too, that Smollett had the merit of originating in this novel that species of the humourous which arises from bad spelling, and which Sheridan afterwards applied to mistakes of words in his Mrs. Malaprop; a humble kind of humour no doubt in itself, yet capable, as Smollett has proved, of powerfully aiding the ludicrous effect.

Equal genius, though far more deformed by affectation, is visible in Sterne, (1713–1768) the first two volumes of whose *Tristram Shandy* appeared in 1759. If a regular progress of incidents towards a catastrophe, were an essential requisite in a novel, it would be difficult to bring the works of Sterne within the protection of that definition. Story he has none to tell; at all events he tells it not. But, "what is a plot good for," says Bayes, "except to bring in good things,"[26] and Sterne adopted the theory of the dramatist in its full license. At the conclusion of the eighth volume, Tristram is not emancipated from the nursery, and had Sterne lived to fulfil his threat of carrying on his work, by the aid of a vegetable diet, through as many more, the Tristrapædia,[a] we fear, would still have made no material progress. Sterne's singular work owes its interest, as every one knows, not to the narrative, which is broken and interrupted by cross currents of the most wayward and whimsical description, far exceeding all the fair license of digression, but to his power of seizing on and bringing forward into distinct consciousness, as Coleridge says, some of those points on which every man is a humorist, and to the masterly manner in which he has brought out the characteristics of two beings of the most opposite natures, the elder Shandy and Toby, and surrounded them with a group of followers sketched with equal life and individuality: in the Corporal, the obstetric Doctor Slop; Yorick, the lively and careless parson; the widow Wadman, and Susannah.

The clue which Sterne chiefly follows through the mazes of character, is humour; – humour of a very high and peculiar kind, perfectly original, at least in English. For that species of riotous humour arising from comic peculiarities of person; and combinations of ludicrous mischances, Sterne has little taste; though the admirably painted scene, where Obadiah on the cart horse, careering round the corner like a comet, oversets Dr. Slop in a whirlpool of mud; – and the cross bills filed by the Doctor and Susannah against each other in applying the cataplasm; show, that if he had considered this the highest walk of humour, he might have revelled in it as easily as Smollett himself. But, like Fielding, he preferred the humour which arises from bringing out by light and happy touches, and as if unconsciously, the secrets of

---

[a] System of education for Tristram. See *Tristram Shandy*, vol. 5, ch. 16.

character; only with this difference in his favour, that with Sterne the humour is steeped in sensibility. Flowing, as it does, as much from the heart as the head, it speaks also to the affections; calm smiles ripple over the countenance as we read, but tears are in the next degree. Thus, in Sterne, humour and feeling heighten and set off each other; the pathetic rises in gentle relief out of the background of the comic, and sinks gracefully and imperceptibly back into it again. It is this, for instance, which gives so irresistible a charm to the story of Le Fevre, and the Corporal's account in the kitchen of the death of Tristram's elder brother, enforced by the eloquent stroke of dropping the hat, as if a lump of clay had been kneaded into the crown of it. There is nothing sneering, nothing unkindly, nothing that revolts the better feelings in his playful irony. . . .

The two great defects of Sterne, as noticed by Sir Walter Scott, are his affectation and his indefensible indecency. For his plagiarisms from other authors, we regard as of little importance. So ingeniously are they turned to account, and so much in general does Sterne improve what he borrows, that he may fairly claim in them that right of property which the civil law allowed in articles where the labour bestowed by the borrower exceeded the intrinsic value of the material on which it was bestowed. It must be confessed, however, that few writers have carried their coolness and assurance in this respect so far as Sterne has done, who, not content with denouncing the plagiarisms of authors, has actually stolen from Burton the passage in which he exposes the iniquities of his neighbours.[27]

But the other objections less admit of defence. The affectation of Sterne is the more to be regretted, because his manner in its happiest moods is the very perfection of a lively, spirited, spoken style, idiomatic, imaginative, pliant, and varied. "Writing, when properly managed," he himself observes, "is but a different name for conversation." Unfortunately he did not always conform his practice to his precept. He is sometimes *fade*[a] in his sentimentality, and aiming after a sort of false sublime in his imagery. Some portions of the story of Maria[28] are examples of the first; the well-known personification of the recording angel in the close of Le Fevre[29] is an instance of the second. Still more unworthy of Sterne are those quackeries of the black page and the white one, the sudden transitions and affected openings of the chapters, with other harlequinades of authorship, which are carried to excess in *Tristram Shandy*.

The indecency of Sterne is more obtrusive and indefensible than that of either Fielding or Smollett; whose highly-coloured scenes

[a] Dull.

seem to be the result of an unchecked imagination, running on heedless whether its course lie through purity or filth. Sterne, on the other hand, goes coldly and deliberately in search of impurity; seeks for it in books, refines upon it, mixes it up with his reflections, and is continually insinuating some equivoque or double entendre into scenes where we can ill bear with such adulteration.

Richardson, Fielding, Smollett, and Sterne, are the four great novelists of this period (the reign of George II.) which was pre-eminently the age of novel-writing in England. For though we should indeed be sorry to undervalue the merits of Goldsmith, or the charm of his *Vicar of Wakefield*, we cannot quite rank the powers displayed in that delightful little tale, which appeared in 1763, so highly as the varied invention displayed by the writers we have named, upon the broader canvass which they selected. To use his own words, it has many faults, and a hundred things might plausibly be said to prove them beauties. Fortunately, they lie more in the minor parts, than in the essentials of the tale. In fact, the improbability of the plot is only equalled by the wonderful truth, nature and keeping of the principal character, for the "limæ labor"[a] which, in this instance, Goldsmith willingly bestowed upon his style, and on the creation and apposition of traits of character, he scrupled to waste upon the selection of his incidents. The real interest lies in the development in the character of the amiable Vicar, so rich in heavenly, so poor in earthly wisdom; – possessing little for himself, yet ready to make that little less, whenever misery appeals to his compassion; – with enough of literary vanity about him to shew that he shares the weaknesses of our nature, – ready to be imposed upon by cosmogonies and fictitious bills of exchange, and yet commanding, by the simple and serene dignity of goodness, the respect even of the profligate, and making "those who came to mock remain to pray."[30] ...

At the period when Sir Walter Scott (1814), produced the first of that long file of romances which have since obtained a more than European reputation, the public taste, in regard to novel writing, seemed to have sunk to a low ebb. ... The appearance of a great writer, who should strike out a new path through this much trodden waste, seemed at that moment in the highest degree improbable. And yet this was at once effected by the Author of Waverley, in such a manner as to raise the romance from the lowest level to the very highest position in literature. ...

The resemblance of Scott's mind to that of Shakspeare has been often remarked, and with some justice; for though even the most

---

[a] Labour with a file; i.e., minute care.

enthusiastic admirers of the romance writer, will hardly venture to claim for him an equality of powers with Shakspeare, there were strong kindred features in the character of their minds. In both we are struck with the same general and almost universal sympathies, leading to impartial and kindly views of all men and all opinions, the most remote from their own; a cheerful, healthful tone of feeling, which brightens existence about us, instead of dwelling on its evils; an avoidance of all moral casuistry, or treading on the borders of the forbidden, either in the creation of characters or of incidents; the feeling of the humourous as strongly developed as the sensibilities or the imagination; great self-possession, and a noiseless exertion of power, working out its end, not by sudden bursts, or high-wrought passages, but by a silent and steady progression, like the dawn brightening into the fulness of day.

The works of Scott produce their effect rather by the combination of many qualities than the predominance of any. . . . But his strength lies in the possession and harmonious adjustment of most of the qualities requisite to the novelist, none engrossing the whole mind, none excluding another, but all working together in kindly unison: learning arrayed in the most picturesque combinations; observation of life embodied not in abstractions, but in living forms; humour springing out of tenderness, like smiles struggling through tears; the spirit of ancient knighthood leavening the worldly wisdom of modern times; and the imagination of the poet adorning, without impairing the common sympathies and good-humoured sagacity of the man.

The department in which this combination of qualities has been most successfully displayed by Scott, was that of the historical romance – a class of fictions which he may truly be said to have created. For although fictions bearing the title of historical romances, were by no means uncommon in English literature before the time of Scott, such as the *Recess* of Miss Lee, or the *Scottish Chiefs* of Miss Porter,[31] it is apparent that they stand in a totally different class; not being, in fact, historical, except in the names of the characters. Obvious as the idea now appears, Scott was in truth, the first to show how much invention might gain by a union with reality; what additional probability, interest, and importance might be given to the fortunes of imaginary heroes, by interweaving their destinies with those of historical personages; nay, how much of romance in its finest forms lies in the characters and events of history itself invisible to the prosaic or merely philosophic observer, but obvious at once to the eye of imagination. He has carried the picturesque of history to its perfection; for without imparting to his portraits the deep and subtle traits by which Shakspeare so wonderfully individualizes the beings of his dramas, he never fails at least to present consistent and striking pictures of his historical personages in their habit as they lived, and to dispose the light and shadow about them with the most felicitous adjustment, – dress, look, gestures, manner, and the outward accompaniments of scenery, being all made important accessories, to heighten the effect of well-known peculiarities, or to hide the want of those over which Time has dropped a veil, which even Imagination can hardly raise.

In description, indeed, generally, Sir Walter Scott was unrivalled. Whatever he sees with the eye of the mind, shapes itself into words which enable us to see it too. His pictures combine in a singular way breadth and minuteness; for while he painted the details with sharpness and firmness, no one understood better the art of arrangement in masses; so that he never fails to give the spirit as well as the form of the spot, making us *feel* the solemnity and gloom of castles and druidical forests, the calm produced by the still beauty of a Highland lake, from which the morning mist is disappearing, or the healthy elevation of spirits with which we travel up some mountain height, whence we see far into the country beyond, and "feel the breath of heaven fresh blowing."

We offer no remarks upon his characters, except this, that making every allowance for repetitions, no writer of fiction since Shakespeare has enriched the portrait gallery of invention with more originals, of which we have a distinct conception; and that though his female characters have less variety and less truth than his male personages, we know no writer except Shakspeare to whom the same remark may not justly be applied.

The plots of Scott, speaking generally, are neither remarkable for excellence, nor the reverse. Examples may, in fact, be found, in the long list of his romances, both of skilful and defective plots. *Ivanhoe*, *Kenilworth*, and the *Bride of Lamermoor*, for instance, are proofs how artfully he could at times arrange his plan; the two latter having all the compactness and steady progression of the drama. Others, again, such as *The Monastery*, *St. Ronan's Well*, and *Rob Roy*, are in a high degree loose and inconsequential.

Fertile and inventive as was the genius of Scott, it cannot, we think, be denied, that during the latter half of his career as a writer of fiction, he appeared to less advantage. No wonder, indeed, when, in addition to the limits by which all invention is bounded, we consider under what depressing circumstances many of his later works were composed, that in these even the elasticity of genius itself should be somewhat outworn and deadened; that the conventional, both in character and incident, should occasionally supply the place of invention; and that mere imagery, and not always very appropriate illustration, should be substituted for the natural turns which at first enlivened the dialogue. "If there be a mental drudgery," to use his own words in his notice of Charlotte Smith, "which lowers the spirits and lacerates the nerves like the toil of the slave, it is that which is exacted by literary composition, when the heart is not in unison with the work on which the head is employed."[32] When he breaks up new ground, as in *Nigel*, *Quentin Durward*, and *The Crusaders*, his genius indeed suffers little diminution; but in *Redgauntlet*, *Anne of Gierstein*, and *The Betrothed*, the practised skill of the mechanist, recomposing old materials in new shapes, is far more visible than the freshness and spontaneity of an original inspiration. With the publication of *Kenilworth*, indeed, the sun of his fame may be said to have "touched the highest point of all its greatness;" but like that luminary during a polar summer, it seemed for a time rather to revolve than to descend, and its rays continued to look bright and beautiful, long after it was journeying towards the west.

No writer ever exercised so great an influence over the public mind, or led to so much conscious or unconscious imitation. His influence on Italy, France, and Germany we shall afterwards have occasion to notice. On the literature of Great Britain, we believe it to have exerted on the whole a most beneficial effect; not, indeed, that any professed imitation of his manner has yet appeared, which possesses great claims to genius, but that he has carried a higher spirit into novel writing; taught us how the simple feelings of peasants, and the homely pathos of humble life, and the relentings of feelings amongst the outcasts of society, might be made to blend with scenes of high imagination; that his writings are calculated to strengthen the ties of our common humanity; that they never tend to foster a bad, or to throw ridicule upon a good or generous feeling; while, speaking of them in a merely literary point of view, they taught lessons of simplicity, good taste, moderation, and skill in seizing the best points both of character and description, which have not been without their effect even on those by whom the mere manner of Scott, or his choice of subjects, have been studiously avoided....

Archibald Alison
(1792–1867)
'The Historical Romance', 1845

The son of an Anglican clergyman, also named Archibald Alison (1757–1839), best known in his day for his *Essays on the Nature and Principles of Taste* (1790), the younger Alison was trained as a lawyer and held the post of sheriff of Lanarkshire from 1835 until his death. He achieved considerable fame as a historian, especially with his *History of Europe from the Commencement of the French Revolution in M.DCC.LXXXIX to the Restoration of the Bourbons, in M.DCC.XV* (1835–42) and *History of Europe, from the Fall of Napoleon in 1815, to the Accession of Louis Napoleon in 1852* (1852–9), but he was also a prolific essayist, contributing to *Blackwood's Edinburgh Magazine* alone nearly two hundred substantial pieces in that form on a variety of topics during the quarter-century following 1831. 'The Historical Romance' was first published in *Blackwood's* in September 1845 (58: 341–56); it was subsequently reprinted in Alison's *Essays Political, Historical, and Miscellaneous*, 1850 (vol. 3, pp. 521–50).

A staunch Tory, Alison opposed parliamentary reform and free trade, believed in the necessity of slavery, and favoured the cause of the Confederacy during the American Civil War. Not surprisingly perhaps, a similar conservatism coloured his literary views. Alison revered Homer, the Greek tragedians, and Virgil, and believed that their distinctive excellence had been approached in more recent times only by Cervantes, Shakespeare, and a few seventeenth- and eighteenth-century writers. By the middle third of the nineteenth century, he held, the atmosphere in which authors worked had been polluted by a 'woful depravity of public taste' (*Essays*, vol. 3, p. 340) despite, if not because of, all the confident but shallow talk 'of the lights of the age, of the vast spread of popular information, of the march of intellect, and the superiority of this generation in intelligence and refinement over all that have gone before it' (*Essays*, vol. 2, pp. 72–3).

Among modern British novelists only Scott had managed to achieve the high goals Alison set for imaginative literature. Both the 'silver-fork' novels of fashionable life by Disraeli, Bulwer, and others (what he calls the 'Almack school') and the 'Newgate novels' – like Bulwer's *Paul Clifford* and *Eugene Aram*, Ainsworth's *Rookwood* and *Jack Sheppard*, and Dickens's *Oliver Twist* – depicting and (in the eyes of some) glorifying crime and vice that were so popular during the decade and a half preceding the appearance of 'The Historical Romance' pandered to the worst elements of the 'public taste'. As to the other work of Dickens, then the most widely admired of English novelists, it dealt too much with the unedifying rendering of middle-and lower-class life. And even the historical novelists of the 1830s and 1840s, followers of Scott though they were, generally failed to observe the 'principles' of that species of writing that mark his best fiction: the choice of 'a subject which shall be *elevated and yet interesting*'; 'the fidelity of the drawing, the spirit of the conversation, or the accuracy and brilliancy of the descriptions' taken 'from real life'; the subordination of detail to a *'sufficiently simple'* and unified story; the appeal to 'associations of general interest in the breast of the audience'); and, above all, the essentially moral purpose of awakening 'generous and elevated feelings'.

As deeply committed to the importance of 'just representations of general nature' as Samuel Johnson or Sir Joshua Reynolds (both of whom he is fond of citing), as wide-ranging (and inaccurate) in his allusions to literature as William Hazlitt, Alison shows himself to be indebted to several significant predecessors in the art of criticism, applied in 'The Historical Romance' to prose fiction rather than to painting or to the other literary genres that the novel had displaced in the public favour by mid century.

WE are constantly told that invention is worn out; that everything is exhausted; that all the intellectual treasures of modern Europe have been dug up; and that we must look to a new era of the world, and a different quarter of the globe, for new ideas or fresh views of thought. It must be confessed, that if we look to some parts of our literature, there seems too good reason for supposing that this desponding opinion is well founded. Everything, in some departments, does seem worked out. Poetry appears for the time wellnigh extinguished. We have some charming ballads from Tennyson; some touching lines from Miss Barrett; but where are the successors of Scott and Byron, of Campbell and Southey? Romance, in some branches, has evidently exhausted itself. For ten years we had novels of fashionable life, till the manners and saying of lordlings and right honourables had become familiar to all the haberdashers' apprentices and milliners' girls in London. That vein being worked out, literature has run into the opposite channel. Action and reaction is the law, not less of the intellectual than the physical world. Inventive genius has sought out, in the lower walks of life, those subjects of novel study and fresh description which could no longer be found in the higher. So far has this propensity gone, so violent has been the oscillation of the pendulum in this direction, that novelists have descended to the very lowest stages of society in the search of the new or the exciting. Not only have the manners, the selfishness, and vulgarity of the middle ranks been painted with admirable fidelity, and drawn with inimitable skill, but the habits and slang of the very lowest portrayed with prurient minuteness, and interest sought to be awakened in the votaries of fashion or the Sybarites of pleasure by the delineation of the language and ideas of the most infamous wretches who ever disgraced society by their vices, or endangered it by their crimes.

"Whatever," says Dr. Johnson, "makes the PAST or the FUTURE predominate over the present, exalts us in the scale of thinking beings."[1] The words are familiar till they have become trite; but words are often repeated when the sense is far off. It is in the general oblivion of the thought of the philosopher, while his words were in every mouth, that the cause of the want of originality in modern works of imagination is to be found. If to the "Past" and the "Future," enumerated by Johnson, we add the "DISTANT," we shall have an effectual antidote, and the only one which is effectual against the sameness of present ideas, or the limited circle of present observation. The tendency to *localize* is the propensity which degrades literature, as it is the chief bane and destroyer of individual character. It is the opposite effect of engendering a tendency to expand, which constitutes the chief value of travelling in the formation of character. If the thought and conversation of individuals are limited to the little circle in which they live, or the objects by which they are immediately surrounded, we all know what they speedily become. It is in the extension of the interest to a wider circle, in the admission of objects of general concern and lasting importance into the sphere of habitual thought, that the only preservative against this fatal tendency is to be found. It is the power of doing this which forms the chief charm of the highest society in every country, and renders it in truth everywhere the same. A man of the world will find himself equally at home, and conversation flow at once with equal ease, in the higher saloons of London or Paris, of Rome or Vienna, of Warsaw or St. Petersburg. But he will find it scarcely possible to keep up conversation for a quarter of an hour in the *bourgeois* circle of any of these capitals. It is the same with literature, and especially that wide and important branch of literature which, aiming at the exciting of interest, or delineating of manners, should in an especial manner be guarded against the degradation consequent on a narrow restriction of its subject to matters only of local concern.

The prodigious success and widespread popularity which have attended some of the most able novels of this new school of romance in late years, as well as the great ability which their composition evinces, must not blind our eyes to the degrading tendency of such compositions upon the national literature. Immediate circulation, great profit to the bookseller, a dazzling reputation to the author, are by no means to be relied on as the heralds of lasting fame. In cases innumerable, they have proved the reverse. Still less are they to be considered as proofs that the writer, be his abilities what they may, has worthily performed his mission, or elevated himself to the exalted level of which his art is susceptible. The most pernicious romances and poems that ever appeared have often been ushered into the world by the most unbounded immediate applause; witness the *Nouvelle Heloïse* of Rousseau, and *Pucelle* of Voltaire. It was just their dangerous and seductive qualities which gave them their success. Rousseau knew this well. He addressed himself with skill and perfect knowledge of the age to its passions and vices: – "J'ai vu les mœurs de mon temps, et j'ai publié ces lettres,"[a] were the first words of his *Nouvelle Heloïse*. In the school we have mentioned, there is nothing immoral or improper; but is there anything elevating or improving? The true test of real excellence is not immediate success but durable fame; it is to be found not in the popularity of circulating shops, or reading clubs, but in the shelves or the library, or the delight of the fireside. When a work suddenly attains great immediate celebrity in a particular circle or country, it is generally, though not always, an indication that it is not destined to enjoy any lasting reputation. The reason is, that it is addressed to local feelings, temporary passions, and particular desires: and it rises to eminence from interesting or gratifying them. But that is not the way permanently to attract mankind. Nothing can do so but what is addressed to the universal feeling of our nature, and has penetrated to the inmost chords, which are common to all ages and countries. The touching them alone can secure durable fame.

Where now are all the novels portraying fashionable life with which the shops of publishers teemed, and the shelves of circulating libraries groaned, not ten years ago? Buried in the vault of all the Capulets.[2] Where will the novels portraying manners in the lowest walks of life be ten years hence? He is a bold man who says they will be found in one well selected library. We do not dispute the vast ability of some of these productions. We are well aware of the fidelity with which they have painted the manners of the middle class, previously little touched on in novels; we fully admit the pathos and power of occasional passages, the wit and humour of many others, the graphic delineation of English character which they all contain. But, admitting all this, the question is – have these productions come up to the true standard of novel-writing? Are they fitted to elevate and purify the minds of their readers? Will the persons who peruse, and are amused, perhaps

---

[a] 'I have seen the manners of my time, and I have published these letters.' This is the second sentence of Rousseau's preface.

fascinated, by them, become more noble, more exalted, more spiritual beings, than they were before? Do not these novels, able and amusing as they are, bear the same relation to the lofty romances of which our literature can boast, that the Boors of Ostade, or the Village Wakes of Teniers, do to the Madonnas of Guido, or the Holy Families of Raphael?[3] These pictures were and are exceedingly popular in Flanders and Holland, where their graphic truth could be appreciated; but are they ever regarded as models of the really beautiful in painting? We leave it to the most ardent admirers of the Jack Sheppard school to answer these questions.

The doctrine now so prevalent is essentially erroneous, that the manners of the middle or lowest class are the fit object of the novelist, because they are natural. Many things are natural which yet are not fit to be exposed, and by the customs of all civilized nations as studiously concealed from the view. Voltaire's well-known answer to a similar remark when made in regard to Shakspeare, indicates, though in a coarse way, the true reply to such observations.[4] If everything that is natural, and we see around us, is the fit object of imitation, and perpetuating in literature, it can no longer be called one of the *Fine* Arts. It is degraded to a mere copying of nature in her coarsest and most disgusting, equally as her noblest and most elevating, aspects. We protest against the doctrine, that the lofty art of romance is to be lowered to the delineating the manners of cheesemongers and grocers, of crop-head charity boys, and smart haberdashers' and milliners' apprentices of doubtful reputation. If we wish to see the manners of such classes, we have only to get into a railway or steamboat; the sight of them at breakfast or dinner will probably be enough for any person accustomed to the habits of good society. Still more solemnly do we enter our protest against the slang of thieves or prostitutes, the flash words of receivers of stolen goods and criminal officers, the haunts of murderers and burglars, being the proper subject for the amusement or edification of the other classes of society. It might as well be said that the refuse of the common-sewers should be raked up and mixed with the garbage of the streets to form our daily food. That such things exist is certain; we have only to walk the streets at night, and we shall soon have ample evidence of their reality. But are they the proper object of the novel-writer's pencil? That is the question; and it is painful to think that in an age boasting its intelligence, and glorying in the extent of its information, such a question should be deemed susceptible of answer in any but one way.

These two extremes of novel-writing – the Almack and Jack Sheppard schools – deviate equally from the standard of real excellence. The one is too exclusively devoted to the description of high, the other of low life. The one portrays a style of manners as artificial and peculiar as that of the paladins and troubadours of chivalry; the other exhibits to our view the lowest and most degraded stages of society, and by the force of humour or the tenderness of pathos interests us too often in the haunts of vice or the pursuits of infamy. It is easy to see that the one school was produced by the reaction of the human mind against the other; genius, tired of the eternal flirtations of guardsmen and right honourables, sought for unsophisticated nature in the humour of low or the sorrows of humble life. But low and humble life are sophisticated[a] just as much as elevated and fashionable; and, if we are driven to a selection, we would prefer the artificial manners of the great to the natural effusions of the vulgar. We would rather, as the child said to the ogress, be eat up by the gentleman. But true novel-writing should be devoted to neither the one nor the other. It should aim at the representation of what Sir Joshua Reynolds called "general or common nature" – that is, nature by its general features, which are common to all ages and countries, not its peculiarities in a particular circle or society.[5] It is by success in delineating that, and *by it alone*, that lasting fame is to be acquired. Without doubt every age and race of men have their separate dress and costume, and the mind has its externals as well as the body, which the artist of genius will study with sedulous care, and imitate with scrupulous fidelity. But the soul is not in the dress; and so it will be found in the delineation of mind as in the representation of the figure.

All these extravagances in the noble art of romance originate in one cause. They come of not making "the past and the *distant* predominate over the present." It is like sketching every day from nature in the same scenery or country: the artist, if he has the pencil of Claude Lorraine or Salvator Rosa,[6] will, in the end, find that if the *objects* of his study are endless, their *character* has a certain family resemblance; and that, if he is not repeating the same study, he is reproducing, under different forms, the same ideas. But let him extend his observation to a wider sphere: let him study the sublimity of mountain or the sweetness of pastoral scenery; let him traverse the Alps and the Apennines, the Pyrenees or the Caucasus; let him inhale the spirit of antiquity amidst the ruins of the Capitol, or the genius of Greece on the rocks of the Acropolis; let him become imbued with modern beauty on the shores of Naples, or the combined charms of Europe and Asia amidst the intricacies of the Bosphorus – and what a world of true images, objects, and beauties is at once let into his mind! It is the same with

---

[a] Deprived of native or original simplicity.

romance. It is by generalizing ideas, by means of extended observation, that variety is to be communicated to conception, and freshness to incident; that the particular is to be taken from character, and the general impressed upon mind. But the novelist has this immense advantage over the painter – not only the present but the past lie open to his study. The boundless events of history present themselves to his choice: he can not only roam at will over the present surface of the globe, with all its variety of character, event, and incident, but penetrate backwards into the unsearchable depths of time. When will fresh subjects for description be wanting with such a field to the hand of genius? Never to the end of the word: for years as they revolve, nations as they rise and fall, events as they thicken around mankind, but add to the riches of the vast store-house from which it is to select its subjects, or cull its materials.

Look at Shakspeare – with what felicity has he selected from this inexhaustible reserve, to vary his incidents, to invigorate his ideas, to give raciness to his characters! He has not even confined himself to English story, rich as it is in moving or terrible events, and strikingly as its moving phantasmagoria come forth from his magic hand. The tragedies, the comedies, the events, the ideas, of the most distant ages of the world, of the most opposite states of society, of the most discordant characters of mankind, seem depicted with equal felicity. He is neither thoroughly chivalrous like Tasso and Ariosto, nor thoroughly Grecian like Sophocles and Euripides, nor thoroughly French like Corneille and Racine. He has neither portrayed exclusively the manners of Arthur and the Round Table, nor of the courts of the Henrys or the Plantagenets. He is as varied as the boundless variety of nature. Profoundly imbued at one time with the lofty spirit of Roman patriotism, he is not less deeply penetrated at another with the tenderness of Italian love. If Julius Cæsar contains the finest picture that ever was drawn of the ideas of the citizens of the ancient world, Juliet is the most perfect delineation of the refined passions of the modern. The bursting heart, uncontrollable grief, but yet generous spirit of the Moor – the dark ambition and blood-stained career of the Scot, come as fresh from his pencil as the dreamy contemplation of the Prince of Denmark, or the fascinating creation of the Forest of Ardennes. It is hard to say whether he is greatest in painting the racked grief of Lear, the homely sense of Falstaff, or the aërial vision of Miranda. Here is the historical drama; here is the varied picture of the human heart; and if the world is not prolific of Shakspeares, he at least has afforded decisive evidence of the vastness of the field thus opened to its genius.

The HISTORICAL ROMANCE should take its place beside the plays of Shakspeare. It does not aim at representation on the stage; it has not the powers of the actor, the deception of scenery, the magic of theatrical effect, nor the charms of music, to heighten its impression. But in exchange it has one incalculable advantage, which in the end is adequate to overbalance them all: it brings delight to the fireside. Seated in our arm-chairs, with the wintry winds howling around us, with our feet at a blazing fire, we are transported by the wand of the novelist to the most remote ages and distant countries of the earth. The lofty spirit and generous passions of chivalry; the stern resolves and heroic resolution of ancient patriotism; the graceful profligacy and studied gallantry of the court of Louis XIV.; the deep Machiavelism of Italian perfidy; the blunt simplicity of German virtue; the freeborn fearlessness of English valour; the lofty soul and poetic imagery of the North American savage; the dauntless intrepidity of his Castilian conqueror; the heart-stirring pathos of Eastern story; the savage ferocity of Scythian conquest – may be alternately presented to our view. We roam at will, not only over space but time; and if the writer is worthy of his high vocation, he can so warm the imagination by the interest of event, the delineation of character, the force of passion, or the charm of the pathetic, that the strongest impression of reality is conveyed to the reader's mind. Add to this the material appliances which are at his disposal; and which, though far inferior to mental power in rousing interest or awakening sympathy, have yet great effect in giving life to the picture, and transporting the imagination to the scenes or the ages which are intended to be portrayed. The scenery of all the different parts of the world, under every possible variety of light, colour, and circumstance; the manners, habits and customs of all nations, and all ages and all grades of society; the dresses, arms, houses, and strongholds of men in all stages of their progress, from the huntsmen of Nimrod to the Old Guard of Napoleon; the ideas of men in different classes and ranks of life in all ages – form so many additions to his pictures, which, if skilfully managed, must give them infinite variety and interest. There is no end, there never can be any end, to the combinations of genius with such materials at its disposal. If men, since this noble art has been created, ever run into repetition, it will be from want of originality in conception, not variety in subject.

The prodigious addition which the happy idea of the historical romance has made to the stories of elevated literature, and through it to the happiness and improvement of the human race, will not be properly appreciated, unless the novels most in vogue before the immortal creations of Scott appeared are considered. If we take up even the most celebrated of them, and in which the most unequivocal marks of genius are to be discerned, it seems hardly possible to conceive how their authors could have acquired the reputation which they so long enjoyed. They are distinguished by a mawkish sensibility, a perpetual sentimentality, as different from the bursts of genuine passion as their laboured descriptions of imaginary scenes are from the graphic sketches which, in later times, have at once brought reality before the mind's eye. The novels of Charlotte Smith, Mrs. Radcliffe, and Miss Burney, belong to this school;[7] they are now wellnigh unreadable. Even works of higher reputation and unquestionable genius in that age, the *Nouvelle Heloïse* of Rousseau, and *Sir Charles Grandison* of Richardson now form a heavy task even for the most ardent lover of romance. Why is it that works so popular in their day, and abounding with so many traits of real genius, should so soon have palled upon the world? Simply because they were not founded upon a broad and general view of human nature; because they were drawn, not from real life in the innumerable phases which it presents to the observer, but imaginary life as it was conceived in the mind of the composer; because they were confined to one circle and class of society, and having exhausted all the natural ideas which it could present, its authors were driven, in the search of variety, to the invention of artificial and often ridiculous ones.

Sir Walter Scott, as all the world knows, was the inventor of the historical romance. As if to demonstrate how ill founded was the opinion, that all things were worked out, and that originality no longer was accessible for the rest of time, Providence, by the means of that great mind, bestowed a new art, as it were, upon mankind – at the very time when literature to all appearance was effete, and invention, for above a century, had run in the cramped and worn-out channels of imitation. Gibbon was lamenting that the subjects of history were exhausted, and that modern story would never present the moving incidents of ancient story,[8] on the verge of the French Revolution and the European war – of the Reign of Terror and the Moscow retreat. Such was the reply of Time to the complaint that political incident was worn out. Not less decisive was the answer which the genius of the Scottish bard afforded to the opinion, that the treasures of original thought were exhausted, and that nothing now remained for the sons of men. In the midst of that delusion he wrote *Waverley*; and the effect was like the sun bursting through the clouds. After a space, shorter than is usually required for a work of original conception to make its way in society, the effect began to appear. Like the invention of gunpowder or steam, it in the end worked a change in the moral world. Envy was silenced; criticism was abashed; detraction ceased to decry – malignity to deride. The hearts of men were taken as it were by storm. A new vein of boundless extent and surpassing richness was opened as it were under our feet. Men marvelled that it had been so long of being found out. And the first discoverer worked it with such rapidity and success, that for long no one attempted to disturb him in the turning forth of its wealth.

It is curious, now that this great revolution in romance-writing has taken place, and is felt and acknowledged by all the world, to reflect on the causes, apparently accidental, by which it was brought about, and the trivial circumstances which might have turned aside, perhaps for ever, the creative mind of Scott from this its appropriate sphere of original action. The first chapters of *Waverley*, as we learn from Lockhart's Life, were written in 1808; but the work was laid aside in an unfinished form, and was almost forgotten by its author. It would probably have remained there overlooked and incomplete to the day of his death, had not the extraordinary popularity of Lord Byron's *Childe Harold* and subsequent pieces, joined to some symptoms of waning public favour in the reception of his own later pieces, particularly *Rokeby* and the *Lord of the Isles*, awakened in his mind, as he himself told us, a latent suspicion that he had better retire from the field of poetry before his youthful competitor, and betake himself to another career, in which hitherto no rival had appeared. Under the influence of this feeling of distrust in his poetical powers, the all but forgotten manuscript of *Waverley* was drawn forth from its obscurity, the novel was finished, and given to the world in July, 1814. From that moment the historical romance was born for mankind. One of the most delightful and instructive species of composition was created; which unites the learning of the historian with the fancy of the poet; which discards from human annals their years of tedium, and brings prominently forward their eras of interest; which teaches morality by example, and conveys information by giving pleasure; and which, combining the charms of imagination with the treasures of research, founds the ideal upon its only solid and durable basis – the real.

The historical romance enjoys many advantages for the creation of interest, and even the conveying of information, over history. It can combine, in a short space, the exciting incidents which are spread over numerous volumes; and, by throwing entirely into the background the uninteresting details of human events, concentrate the light of imagination on such as are really calculated to produce an impression. Immense is the facility which this gives for the creation of interest, and the addition of life, to the picture. What oppresses the historian is the prodigious number of details with which he is encumbered. As his main object is to convey a trustworthy narrative of real events, none of them can, with due regard to the credit of the narrative, be omitted. If they are so, it is ten to one that the author finds reason to repent his superficial survey before he has concluded his work; and if he is fortunate enough to escape such stings of self-reproach, he is quite certain that the blot will be marked by some kind friend, or candid critic, who will represent the thing omitted, how trifling soever, as the most important incident in the whole work, and the neglect of which is wholly fatal to its credit as a book of authority. Every traveller knows how invariably this is the case with any object which may have been accidentally omitted to be seen in any province or city; and that the only way to avoid the eternal self-reproaches consequent on having it constantly represented by others as the most interesting object to be seen, is – at all hazards of time, fatigue, or expense – to see everything. But the historical novelist is fettered by no such necessity – he is constrained to encumber his pages with no inconsiderable details. Selecting for the objects of his piece the most striking characters and moving incidents of the period he has chosen, he can throw full light upon them, and paint the details with that minuteness of finishing which is essential to conjuring up a vivid image in the reader's mind. He can give the truth of history without its monotony – the interest of romance without its unreality.

It was the power they enjoyed of abstracting in this manner from surrounding and uninteresting details, which constituted the principal charm of ancient history. The *Cyropadia* and *Anabasis* of Xenophon are nothing but historical romances. Livy's pictured page – Sallust's inimitable sketches – Tacitus's finished paintings, owe their chief fascination to the simplicity of their subjects. Ancient history, being confined to the exploits of a single hero or monarch, or the rise of a particular city, could afford to be graphic, detailed, and consequently interesting. That was comparatively an easy task when the events of one, or at most two, states on the shores of the Mediterranean alone required to be portrayed. But such a limitation of subject is impossible in modern history when the transactions of Europe, Asia, Africa, and America, require to be detailed to render the thread of events complete. Even biography is scarcely intelligible without such a narrative of the surrounding nations and incidents as makes it run into the complexity and consequent dullness of history. But the author of historical romance is entirely relieved from this necesity, and consequently he can present the principal events and characters of his work in far more brilliant colours to his readers than is possible for the historian. Certainly with some the results of his more attractive influence will be doubted; but be that as it may, it is the Henry V. or Richard III. of Shakspeare that occur to every mind when these English monarchs are thought of, not the picture of them presented, able as it is, by Hume or Turner.[9] If we hear of Richard Cœur-de-Lion, we immediately conjure up the inimitable picture of the crusading hero in *Ivanhoe* or the *Talisman*. Elizabeth of England is admirably portrayed in the pages of Hume, but the Elizabeth of *Kenilworth* is the one which is engraven on every mind; and when the romantic tale and heroic death of Mary of Scotland are thought of, it is less the masterly picture of Robertson, or the touching narrative of Tytler, that recurs to the recollection, than the imprisoned princess of the *Abbot*, or the immortal Last Sacrament of Schiller.[10]

Considered in its highest aspect, no art ever was attempted by man more elevated and ennobling than the historical romance. It may be doubted whether it is inferior even to the lofty flights of the epic, or the heart-rending pathos of the dramatic muse. Certain it is that it is more popular, and embraces a much wider circle of readers, than either the *Iliad* or the *Paradise Lost*. Homer and Tasso never, in an equal time, had nearly so many readers as Scott. The reason is, that an interesting story told in prose, can be more generally understood, and is appreciated by a much wider circle than when couched in the lofty strains and comparative obscurity of verse. It is impossible to over-estimate the influence, for good or for evil, which this fascinating art may exercise upon future ages. It literally has the moulding of the human mind in its hands; – "Give me," said Fletcher of Saltoun, "the making of ballads, and I will give you the making of laws."[11] Historical romances are the ballads of a civilized and enlightened age. More even than their rude predecessors of the mountains and the forest, they form those feelings in youth by which the character of the future man is to be determined. It is not going too far to say, that the romances of Sir Walter Scott have gone far to neutralise the dangers of the Reform Bill.[12] Certain it is that they have materially assisted in extinguishing, at least in the educated classes of society, that prejudice against the feudal manners, and those devout aspirations on[a] the blessings of democratic institutions, which were universal among the learned over Europe in the close of the eighteenth century. Like all other great and original minds, so far from being swept away by the errors of his age, he rose up in direct opposition to them. Singly he set himself to breast the flood which was overflowing the world. Thence

[a] Sighings over.

the reaction in favour of the institutions of the olden time in church and state, which became general in the next generation, and is now so strongly manifesting itself, as well in the religious contests as the lighter literature of the present day.

"Some authors," says Madame de Staël, "have lowered the romance in mingling with it the revolting pictures of vice; and while the first advantage of fiction is to assemble around man all that can serve as a lesson or a model, it has been thought that a temporary object might be gained by representing the obscure scenes of corrupted life, as if they could ever leave the heart which repels them as pure as that to which they were unknown. But a romance, such as one can conceive, such as we have some models of, is one of the noblest productions of the human mind, one of the most influential on the hearts of individuals, and which is best fitted in the end to form the moral of nations."[13] It is in this spirit that romance should be written – it is in this spirit that it has been written by some of the masters of the art who have already appeared, during the brief period which has elapsed since its creation. And if, in hands more impure, it has sometimes been applied to less elevated purposes; if the turbid waters of human corruption have mingled with the stream, and the annals of the past have been searched, not to display its magnanimity, but to portray its seductions; we must console ourselves by the reflection, that such is the inevitable lot of humanity, that genius cannot open a noble career which depravity will not enter, nor invent an engine for the exaltation of the human mind, which vice will not pervert to its degradation.

As the historical romance has been of such recent introduction in this country and the world, it is not surprising that its principles should as yet be not finally understood. It may be doubted whether its great master and his followers themselves have been fully aware of the causes to which their own success has been owing. Like travellers who have entered an unknown but varied and interesting country, they have plunged fearlessly on, threading forests, dashing through streams, traversing plains, crossing mountains, and in the breathless haste of the journey, and the animation of spirit with which it was attended, they have become, in a great degree, insensible to the causes which produced the charm which surrounded their footsteps. Yet, like every other art, the historical romance has its principles; and it is by the right comprehending and skilful application of these principles, that its highest triumphs are to be gained. They are the same as those which have long been unfolded by the great masters of composition in relation to poetry and the drama; they are to be found applied by Sir Joshua Reynolds to the sister art of painting. Yet are they not attended to by the great mass of readers, and even by authors themselves, if we may judge by the frequent failures which are exhibited, little understood or frequently neglected.

The first requisite of the historical romance is a subject which shall be *elevated and yet interesting*. It must be elevated, or the work will derogate from its noblest object, that of rousing the sympathetic passions, and awakening the generous feelings; it must be interesting, or these effects will be produced in a very limited degree. Readers of romance look for excitement; they desire to be interested, and unless they are so, the author's productions will very soon be neglected. This is universally known, and felt alike by readers and writers; but yet there is a strange misapprehension prevalent among many authors even of distinguished talent, in regard to the methods by which this interest is to be awakened. It is frequently said, that the public are insatiable for novelty; that all home subjects are worn out; and thence it is concluded, that whatever is new must possess the greatest chance of becoming popular. In the desire to discover such novelty, every part of the world has been ransacked. Stories from Persia and the East have been plentifully brought forward; the prairies and savages of North America have furnished the subjects of more than one interesting romance; Russia, Poland, Italy, Spain, as well as France, Germany, Sweden, and the United States, have been eagerly ransacked to satisfy the craving of a generation seeking after something new. The total failure of many of these novels, the dubious success of many others, though written with unquestionable talent, may convince us, that this principle of looking only for novelty may be carried too far, and that it is within certain limits only that the appetite for variety can successfully be indulged. And what these limits are, may be readily learned by attending to what experience has taught in the sister arts.

It has been said, and said truly, that "eloquence to be popular must be in advance of the audience, *and but a little in advance.*" The experience of all ages has taught, that the drama is never successful unless it appeals to feelings which find a responsive echo in the general mind, and awakens associations of general interest in the breast of the audience. It is the same with the historical romance. It may and should deviate a little from the circle of interesting association generally felt; but it should be *but a little*. The heart of the readers of novels, as well as the spectators of tragedies, is at home. The images, the emotions, the loves, the hatreds, the hopes, the fears, the names, the places familiar to our youth, are those which awaken the strongest emotions of sympathy in later years. Novelty is frequently felt as agreeable; but it is so chiefly when it recalls again in other climes, or in the events of other

71

ages, the feelings and passions of our own. We like occasionally to leave home; but when we do so, there is nothing so delightful as to be recalled to it by the touching of any of those secret chords which bind man to the place of his nativity, or the scene of his dearest associations. The novels which are to be durably popular in any country must be founded, not indeed necessarily on incidents of its own story, but on the ideas with which it is familiar, and on incidents cousin-german at least to those of its own national existence. The institutions of chivalry, the feudal system, have created, as it were, in this respect, one great family of the European nations, which renders, at least to the educated classes, the manners, emotions, and passions of the higher ranks an object of universal interest. We can sympathize as warmly with the paladins of Ariosto, or the knights of Tasso, as ever could the troubadours of Provence or the nobles of Italy. But if this lofty circle which forms the manners of chivalry is once passed, we descend to inferior grades of society. The novelist of every country will find, that what he portrays will not permanently or generally interest a wider circle than that of its own inhabitants. We can take no interest in the boyards of Russia or the boors of Poland; but little in the agas and kuzilbashes of Eastern story.[a] Novelty, as in the *Arabian Knights*, may attract in youth for a single publication; but fairy or Eastern tales will never form the intellectual bread of life. The universal admiration with which *Don Quixote* and the Waverley novels are regarded over the whole world, must not blind us to the extreme difficulty of making the manners of the middle or lower ranks, if brought forward as the main machinery of a romance, durably interesting to any but those to whom they are familiar. Even Scott and Cervantes owe great part of their success to the skill with which they have combined the noble manners and exalted ideas, engendered in the European heart by the institutions of chivalry, and as widely spread as its spirits, with the graphic picture of the manners in the different countries where the scene of their romances was laid. And it is not every man who can draw the bow of Ulysses.[14]

Ivanhoe, the *Abbot*, and *Old Mortality*, may be considered as the perfection of historical romances, so far as subject goes. They all relate to events of national history, well known to all persons possessing any information in England and Scotland, and deeply connected with the most interesting associations to those of cultivated minds. The undaunted courage and jovial manners of the Lion-hearted hero; the

[a] Boyards = members of a powerful Russian aristocratic order; agas = important military commanders and other men of distinction in the Ottoman Empire; kuzilbashes = soldiers and rulers of Turkish origin in Persia, Afghanistan, and India.

cruel oppression of Norman rule; the bold spirit of Saxon independence; the deep sorrows and ever-doubtful character of the heroic Queen of Scots; the fearful collision of Puritan zeal with Cavalier loyalty, from which issued the Great Rebellion – are engraven on every heart in the British Islands. They formed the most appropriate subjects, therefore, for the foundation or substratum of novels to be permanently interesting to the Anglo-Saxon race, with the addition of such imaginary characters or incidents as might illustrate still farther the manners and ideas of the times. Nor are such subjects of universal and national interest by any means yet exhausted. On the contrary, many of the most admirable of these have never yet been touched on. The cruel conquest of Wales by Edward I.; the heroic struggles of Wallace against the same monarch; the glorious establishment of Scottish independence by Robert Bruce; the savage ferocity and heart-rending tragedies of the wars of the Roses; the martyr-like death of Charles I.; the heart-stirring conquests of Edward III. and the Black Prince; the heartless gallantry of the age of Charles II.; the noble efforts of the Highlanders in 1715 and 1745 for their hereditary sovereign, form a few of the periods of British history, either not at all, or as yet imperfectly, illustrated by historical romance. Nor is the stock terminated; on the contrary, it is growing, and hourly on the increase. The time has already come when the heroism of La Vendée,[a] the tragedies of the Revolution, form the appropriate subject of French imaginative genius; and the period is not far distant when Wellington and the paladins of the late war, transported from this earthly scene by the changes of mortality, will take lasting and immortal place in the fields of romance.

The success of many of the novels of recent times, in the conception of which most genius has been evinced, and in the composition most labour bestowed, has been endangered, if not destroyed, by inattention to this principle in the choice of a subject. There is great talent, much learning, and vigorous conception, in the *Last Days of Pompeii* by Bulwer; and the catastrophe with which it concludes is drawn with his very highest powers; but still it is felt by every class of readers to be uninteresting. We have no acquaintance or association with Roman manners; we know little of their habits; scarce anything of their conversation in private; they stand forth to us in history in a sort of shadowy grandeur totally distinct from the interest of novelist composition. No amount of learning or talent can make the dialogues of Titus and Lucius, of Gallius and Vespasia, interesting to a modern

---

[a] Counterrevolutionary insurrection in western France between 1791 and 1796.

reader. On the other hand, the *Last of the Barons* is an admirably chosen historical subject, worked out with even more than the author's usual power and effect; and but for a defect in composition, to be hereafter noticed, it would be one of the most popular of all his productions.[15] Great talent and uncommon powers of description have been displayed in Oriental novels; but they have not attained any lasting reputation – not from any fault on the part of the writers, but the want of sympathy in the great majority of readers with the subject of their compositions. Strange to say, we feel nothing foreign in James's *Attila*.[16] So deeply were we impregnated with barbarian blood – so strongly have Scythian customs and ideas descended to our times – that the wooden palace of the chief of the Huns, surrounded with its streets of carts, and myriads of flocks and herds, in the centre of Hungary, is felt as nothing alien. On the other hand, some of Sir Walter's later productions have failed, notwithstanding great ability in the execution, from undue strangeness in the subject. *Anne of Geierstein*, and the Indian story in the *Chronicles of the Canongate*, belong to this class; and even if *Robert of Paris* had not been written during the decay of the author's mental powers, it would probably have failed, from the impossibility of communicating any of the interest of a novel to a story of the Lower Empire.[17]

In this respect there is an important distinction between the drama and the historical romance, which writers in the latter style would do well to keep in view. Tragedy being limited in general to a very short period, during which events of the most heart-rending kind are accumulated together, in order as strongly as possible to awaken the sympathy, or move the hearts of the spectators, it is comparatively of little importance where the scene is laid. Where the bones and muscles of the mind are laid bare by deep affliction, mankind in all ages and countries are the same. The love of Juliet, the jealousy of Othello, are felt with equal force in all parts of the world. We can sympathize as strongly with the protracted woes of Andromache, or the generous self-immolation of Antigone, as the Athenian audience who wept at the eloquence of Euripides or the power of Sophocles: we feel the death of Wallenstein to be as sublime as the Germans who are transported by the verses of Schiller; and they weep at the heroism of Mary Stuart, with as heartfelt emotion as the people of Scotland to whom her name is a household word. But it is otherwise with romance. It is occasionally, and at considerable intervals only, that these terrible or pathetic scenes are represented in its pages, which sweep away all peculiarities of nation, age, or race, and exhibit only the naked human heart: nineteen-twentieths of its pages are taken up with ordinary occurrences, one-half of its interest is derived from the delineation of manners, or the developing of character in dialogue, which exhibits none of the vehement passions; and the interest of the reader is kept up chiefly by the fidelity of the drawing, the spirit of the conversation, or the accuracy and brilliancy of the decriptions. If these prove uninteresting from their being too remote from ordinary observation or association, the work will fail, with whatever talent or power its principal and tragic scenes may be executed.

In proposing as the grand requisite to the historical romance, that the subject should be of an *elevating and ennobling kind*, we by no means intend to assert that the author is always to be on stilts, that he is never to descend to the description of low or even vulgar life, or that humour and characteristic description are to be excluded from his composition. We are well aware of the value of contrast in bringing out effect; we know that the mind of the reader requires repose, even from the most exalted emotions; we have felt the weariness of being satiated with beauty, in the galleries of the Vatican or the valleys of Switzerland. Brilliants require setting, and bright light can be brought out only by proportional depth or breadth of shadow. If the novelist tries to keep up exalted sentiments or pathetic scenes too often, he will fall into the mistake of the painter who throws an equal light on all parts of his picture. Probably the rule which Sir Joshua Reynolds says he found by observation had been invariably observed by Titian – viz., to have one-fourth only of his picture in very bright light, one-fourth in deep shadow, and the remaining half in middle tint,[18] may be equally applicable to the compositions of the novelist. But admitting all this – admitting further, that novels which deviate from the elevated standard may often attain a great temporary popularity, the greater, probably, owing to that very deviation – it is not the less true that the main object of the art is to awaken generous and elevated feelings; and that in no other way than by attention to this object, is durable fame to be obtained.

The celebrity arising from skill in the painting of low or vulgar manners, from power in the description of desperate or abandoned characters, how great soever it may be for a time, never fails to pass away with the lapse of time. Voltaire's romances, once so popular, are now nearly as much dead stock in the bookseller's hands; and the whole tribe of the licentious novelists of France, prior to the Revolution are now read only by the licentious youth of Paris, and a few prurient sensualists in other countries. It will be the same with Victor Hugo, Janin,[19] and George Sand, in the next generation and in other countries. All their genius, learning, and interest, will not be able to save them from the withering effect of their accumulated horrors, shocking indecencies, and demoralizing tendency.

Again, in the composition of the historical romance, the story should be *sufficiently simple*, and a certain degree of unity preserved in the interest and emotion which are to be awakened. It is not meant to be asserted by this, that the novelist is to be confined strictly to unities like the Greek drama, or that the same variety, within certain limits, is not to be presented in the pages of romance, which we see every day around us in real life. All that is meant to be advanced is, that this variety must be confined within certain limits, if the interest of the piece is to be properly kept up: and that it should be an especial object with the novelist to avoid that complication and intricacy of incidents which forms so formidable, though unavoidable, an addition to the difficulties of an historian. It is the more singular that romance writers should have fallen into this mistake, that is the very difficulty which stands most in the way of the interests of history, and which it is the peculiar advantage of their art to be able in a great measure to avoid. Yet it is the error which is most general in writers of the greatest ability in this department of literature, and which has marred or ruined the effect of some of their happiest conceptions. It has arisen, doubtless, from romance writers having observed the extreme multiplicity of incidents and events in real life, and in the complicated maze of historical narrative; and thence imagined that it was by portraying a similar combination that romance was to be assimilated to truthful annals, and the ideal founded on the solid basis of the real. They forget that it is this very complication which renders history in general so uninviting, and acceptable (compared with romance) to so limited a circle of readers; and that the annals of actual events then only approach to the interest of fiction, when their surpassing magnitude, or the importance of the characters involved in them, justifies the historian in suspending for a time the thread of inconsiderable and uninteresting incidents, and throwing a broad and bright light, similar to that of imagination, on the few which have been attended with great and lasting effects.

The great father of historical romance rarely falls into this mistake. The story, at least in most of his earlier and more popular pieces – *Waverley*, the *Antiquary*, the *Bride of Lammermoor*, *Old Mortality*, the *Abbot*, *Ivanhoe*, *Kenilworth*, *Quentin Durward*, and *Rob Roy* – is extremely simple; the incidents few and well chosen; the interest of an *homogeneous* kind, and uniformly sustained; the inferior characters and incidents kept in their due subordination to the principal ones. The subordinate characters of these admirable works, their still life, descriptions, and minor incidents, are grouped as it were around the main events of the story, and brought forward in such a way as to give variety while they do not detract from unity. It is impossible to conceive more perfect models of the historical romance, both in point of subject, conception, and execution, than *Ivanhoe* and the *Abbot*. In both, the subject is national and generally interesting – in both, the historical characters brought forward are popular, and connected with early associations – in both, the period chosen is one in which great national questions were at stake, and the conversations and characters afforded the means of bringing them prominently before the mind of the reader – in both, the incidents of the piece are few and simple; and the lesser plots or characters which they contain serve only to amuse the mind and give variety to the composition, without interfering with the unity of its general effect. How few and simple are the events in the *Bride of Lammermoor*! The tragedies of Sophocles do not exhibit a more perfect example of the preservation of the unity of emotion. Yet how interesting is the whole story – how completely does it carry along every class of readers – how well does every incident of moment prepare the mind for the dreadful catastrophe in which it terminates! How few are the incidents in the *Abbot* – how scanty the materials on which the story is built! A page riding from a castle in Dumfries-shire to Edinburgh, his introduction to the Regent Murray, and adventures during a few days in Holyrood, his attendance on the imprisoned Queen in Lochleven Castle, her escape from thence, and final overthrow at Langside – form the whole incidents out of which the web of that delightful romance has been woven. Its charm consists in a great degree in the simplicity itself, in the small number of historic incidents it records, the interest of those incidents in themselves, and the room thereby afforded for working up all the details, and the minor plot of the piece, the loves of the page and Catharine, in perfect harmony with the main event, and without disturbing their development.

It were to be wished that later writers had followed the example thus set by the father of historical romance in the selection of their subject, and the construction of their plot. But, so far from doing so, they have in general run into the opposite extreme, and overlaid their story with such a mass of historical facts and details as has not only destroyed the unity of interest, but has in many cases rendered the story itself scarcely intelligible. Take two of the most popular romances of two justly celebrated living novelists, Sir E. L. Bulwer and Mr. James – *The Last of the Barons* and *Philip Augustus*.[20] The period of history, leading characters, and subject of both, are admirably chosen;

and the greatest talent has been displayed in both, in the conception of the characters, and the portrait of the ideas and manners of the times which both present. But the grand defect of both, and which chills to a great degree the interest they otherwise would excite, is the crowding of historic incident, and complication of the story. Bulwer's novel is so crowded with rebellions, revolutions, and dethronements, that even the learned reader, who has some previous acquaintance with that involved period of English history, has great difficulty in following the story. Ample materials exist for two or three interesting historical novels in its crowded incidents. *Philip Augustus* labours equally plainly under the same defect. There is a triple plot going forward through nearly the whole piece; the story of the King and Queen, with the Papal interdict; that of Prince Arthur Plantagenet and his cruel uncle, John of England; and that of De Coucy and Isadore of the Mount. No human ability is adequate to carrying three separate stories abreast in this manner, and awakening the interest of the reader in each. The human mind is incapable of taking in, at the same time, deep emotion of more than one kind. What should we say if Shakspeare had presented us with a tragedy in which were brought forward scenes or acts about the ambition of Macbeth, the loves of Romeo and Juliet, and the jealousy of Othello? Assuredly they would have mutually strangled each other. This is just what happens in these otherwise admirable novels; the complication of the events, and the variety of interests sought to be awakened, prevent any one from taking a strong hold of the mind. Rely upon it, there is more truth in the principle of the Greek unities than we moderns are willing to admit. The prodigious overpowering effect of their tragedies is mainly owing to the unity of emotion which is kept up. It bears the same relation to the involved story of modern romance, which the single interest of the *Jerusalem Delivered* or *Iliad* does to the endless and complicated adventures of Ariosto's knights, or the sacred simplicity of the Holy Families of Raphael to the crowded canvass of Tintoretto or Bassano.

Perhaps the most perfect novel that exists in the world, with reference to the invaluable quality of unity of emotion, as well as the admirable disquisitions on subjects of taste and reflection which it contains, is Madame de Staël's *Corinne*.[21] Considered as a story, indeed, it has many and glaring defects; the journey of Lord Nevil and Corinne to Naples from Rome, is repugnant to all our ideas of female decorum; and the miserable sufferings and prostration of the heroine in the third volume, during her visit to Scotland, is carried to such a length as to leave a painful impression on every reader's mind. But abstracting these glaring errors, the conception and execution of the work are as perfect as possible. The peculiar interest meant to be excited, the particular passion sought to be portrayed, is early brought forward, and the whole story is the progress and final lamentable result of its indulgences. It is not the sudden passion of Juliet for Romeo, the peculiar growth of the Italian climate, which is portrayed, but the refined attachment of northern Europe, which is taken in more by the ear than the eye, and springs from the sympathy of minds who have many tastes and feelings in common. Nothing detracts from, nothing disturbs, this one and single emotion. The numerous disquisitions on the fine arts, the drama, antiquities, poetry, history and manners, which the novel contains – its profound reflections on the human heart, the enchanting descriptions of nature, and the monuments of Italy which it presents – not only do not interfere with the main interest, but they all conspire to promote it. They are the means by which it is seen the mutual passion was developed in the breasts of the principal characters; they furnish its natural history, by exhibiting the many points of sympathy which existed between minds of such an elevated caste, and which neither had previously found appreciated in an equal degree by any one in the other sex. It is in the skill with which this is brought out, and the numerous disquisitions on criticism, taste, and literature with which it abounds, rendered subservient to the main interest of the whole, that the principal charm of this beautiful work is to be found.

Another principle which seems to regulate the historical romance, as it does every other work which relates to man, is, that its principal interest must be sought in human passion and feeling. It appears to be the more necessary to insist on this canon, that the inferior appliances of the art – the description of manners, scenery, dresses, buildings, processions, pomps, ceremonies, and customs, has opened so wide a field for digression, that, by many writers as well as readers, they have come to be supposed to form its principal object. This mistake is in an especial manner conspicuous in the writings of Ainsworth,[22] whose talents for description, and the drawing of the horrible, have led him to make his novels often little more than pictorial phantasmagoria. It is to be seen, also, in a great degree in James; who – although capable, as many of his works, especially *Mary of Burgundy*, *Attila* and the *Smugglers*, demonstrate, of the most powerful delineation of passion, and the finest traits of the pathetic – is yet so enamoured of description, and so conscious of his powers in that respect, that he in general overlays his writings with painting to the eye, instead of using that more powerful language which speaks to the heart. It is no doubt a curious thing, and gives life to the piece, to see a faithful and graphic description of a knight on horseback, with his companion, and their respective squires, skirting a wood, mounted on powerful steeds, on a clear September morning. The painting of his helm and hauberk, his dancing plume and glancing mail, his harnessed steed and powerful lance, interests once or even twice; but it is dangerous to try the experiment of such descriptions too often. They rapidly pall by repetition, and at length become tedious or ridiculous. It is in the delineation of the human heart that the inexhaustible vein of the novelist is to be found: it is in its emotions, desires and passions, ever-varying in externals, ever the same in the interior, that scope is afforded for the endless conceptions of human genius. Descriptions of still life – pictures of scenery, manners, buildings, and dresses – are the body, as it were, of romance; they are not its soul. They are the material parts of the landscape; its rocks, mountains, and trees; they are not the divine ray of the sun which illuminates the brilliant parts of the picture, and gives its peculiar character to the whole. The skilful artist will never despise them; on the contrary, he will exert himself to the utmost in their skilful delineation, and make frequent use of them, taking care to introduce as much variety as possible in their representations. But he will regard them as an inferior part only of his art; as speaking to the eye, not to the heart; as the body of romance, not its soul; and as valuable chiefly as giving character or life to the period described, and repose to the mind in the intervals of the scenes of mental interest or pathos, on which his principal efforts are to be concentrated. Descriptions of external things often strike us as extremely brilliant, and give great pleasure in reading; but with a few exceptions, where a *moral* interest has been thrown into the picture of nature, they do not leave any profound or lasting impression on the mind. It is human grandeur or magnanimity, the throb of grief, the thrill of the pathetic, which is imprinted in indelible characters on the memory. Many of the admirable descriptions of still life in *Waverley* fade from the recollection, and strike us as new every time we read them; but no one ever forgot the last words of Fergus, when passing on the hurdle under the Scotch gate at Carlisle, "God save King *James!*" None of the splendid descriptions in the choruses of Æschylus produce the terrible impression on the mind which Sophocles has done by that inimitable trait, when, in the close of *Antigone*, he makes Eurydice, upon hearing of the suicide of her son Hæmon on the body of his betrothed, leave the stage *in silence*, to follow him by a violent death to the shades below.

The last rule which it seems material for the historical novelist to observe, is, that characteristic or national manners, especially in middle or low life, should, wherever it is possible, be drawn from real life. The manners of the highest class over all Europe are the same. If a novelist paints well-bred persons in one capital, his picture may, with a few slight variations, stand for the same sphere of society in any other. But in middle, and still more in low life, the diversity in different countries is very great, and such as never can be reached by mere reading, or study of the works of others. And yet, amidst all this diversity, so much is human nature at bottom everywhere the same, that the most inexperienced reader can distinguish, even in the delineation of manners to which he is an entire stranger, those which are drawn from life, from those which are taken from the sketches or ideas of others. Few in this country have visited the Sierra Morena,[a] and none certainly have seen it in the days of Cervantes, yet we have no difficulty in at once perceiving that Sancho Panza, and the peasants and muleteers in *Don Quixote*, are faithfully drawn from real life. Few of the inumerable readers of Sir Walter have had personal means of judging of the fidelity of his pictures of the manners and ideas of the Scotch peasants in his earlier novels; but yet there is no one in any country who does not at once see that they have been drawn from nature, and contain the most faithful picture of it. It is the fidelity of this picture which gives the Scotch novels their great charm. It is the same with Fielding: his leading characters in low life are evidently drawn from nature, and thence his long-continued popularity. When Sir Walter comes to paint the manners of the middle classes or peasants in England, from plays, farces, and the descriptions of others, as in *Kenilworth*, *Woodstock*, *Peveril of the Peak*, and the *Fortunes of Nigel*, he is infinitely inferior, and, in truth, often insupportably dull. His dialogue is a jargon mixed up of scraps and expressions from old plays or quaint tracts, such as no man on earth ever did speak, and which it is only surprising a man of his sagacity should have supposed they ever could. The same defect is more signally conspicuous in the dialogue of several of the historical romances of James.

It is the accurate and faithful picture of national character from the real life, joined to the poetical interest of his Indian warriors, and his incomparable powers of natural description, which has given Cooper his great and well-deserved reputation.[23] In many of the essential qualities of a novelist, he is singularly defective. His story is often confused, and awkwardly put together. Unity of interest is seldom thought of. He has no conception of the refined manners and chivalrous feelings of European society: though he has of late years seen much of it in many countries, he has never been able to become

---

[a] Mountain range in southern Spain.

familiar with its ideas or imbibe its spirit. His heroes, among the white men at least, are never anything above American skippers, or English subalterns or post-captains: his heroines have in general the insipidity which is, we hope unjustly, ascribed, with great personal charms, to the fair sex on the other side of the Atlantic. But in the forest or on the wave, he is superb. His *Last of the Mohicans* and *Prairie* are noble productions, to be matched with any in the world for the delineation of lofty and elevated character – the more interesting that they belong to a race, like the heroic, now well-nigh extinct. He paints the adventures, the life, the ideas, the passions, the combined pride and indolence, valour and craft, heroism and meanness of the red man, with the hand of a master. Equally admirable is his delineation of the white man on the frontier of civilisation – Hawkeye or Leather-stocking, with his various other denominations – who is the precursor, as it were, of European invasion, who plunges into the forest far ahead of his more tardy followers, and leads the roaming life of the Indian, but with the advantage of the arms, the arts, and the perseverance of the Anglo-Saxon. But he is strictly a national writer. It is in the delineation of Transatlantic character, scenes of the forest, or naval adventures, that his great powers are shown; when he comes to paint the manners, or lay the seat of his conceptions in Europe, he at once falls to mediocrity, and sometimes becomes ridiculous.

Manzoni is an author of the highest excellence, whose celebrity has been derived from the same faithful delineation from real life of national manners.[24] He has written but one novel, the *Promessi Sposi*; though various other works, some religious, some historical, have proceeded from his pen. But that one novel has given him a European reputation. It is wholly different in composition and character from any other historical romance in existence: it has no affinity either with Scott or Cooper, Bulwer or James. The scene, laid in 1628, at the foot of the mountains which shut in the Lake of Como, transports us back two centuries in point of time, and to the south of the Alps in point of scene. As might be expected, the ideas, characters, and incidents of such a romance differ widely from those of northern climes and Protestant realms. That is one of its great charms. We are transported, as it were, into a new world; and yet a world so closely connected with our own, by the manners and ideas of chivalry, our once common Catholic faith, and the associations which every person and education has with Italian scenes and images, that we feel, in traversing it, the pleasure of novelty without the *ennui* of a strange land. No translation could give an idea of the peculiar beauties and excellences of the original. As might be expected, the feudal baron and the Catholic church enter largely into the composition of the story. The lustful passions, savage violence, and unbridled license of the former, strong in his men-at-arms, castle battlements, and retainers; the disinterested benevolence, charitable institutions, and paternal beneficence of the latter, resting on the affections and experienced benefits of mankind, are admirably depicted. His descriptions of the plague, famine, and popular revolt at Milan, are masterpieces which never were excelled. The saintlike character of Cardinal Borromeo, strong in the sway of religion, justice, and charity, in the midst of the vehemence of worldly passion and violence with which he is surrounded, is peculiarly striking. It is fitted, like Guizot's *Lectures on History*,[25] to illustrate the incalculable advantage which arose, in an age of general rapine and unsettled government, from the sway, the disinterestedness, and even the superstitions, of religion.

But the greatest merit of the work is to be found in the admirable delineation of the manners, ideas, hopes and fears, joys and sorrows, of humble life with which it abounds. The hero of the piece is a silk-weaver named Renzo, near Lecco, on the Lake of Como; the heroine Lucia, his betrothed, the daughter of a poor widow in the same village; and the story is founded on the stratagems and wiles of an unbridled Baron in the vicinity, whose passions had been excited by Lucia's beauty, first to prevent her marriage, then to obtain possession of her person. In the conception of such a piece is to be seen decisive evidence of the vast change in human affairs, since the days when Tasso and Ariosto poured forth to an admiring age, in the same country, the loves of high-born damsels, the combats of knights, the manners, the pride, and the exclusiveness of chivalry. In its execution, Manzoni is singularly felicitous. He is minute without being tedious, graphic but not vulgar, characteristic and yet never offensive. His pictures of human life, though placed two centuries back, are evidently drawn from nature in these times: the peasants whom he introduces are those of the plains of Lombardy at this time; but though he paints them with the fidelity of an artist, it is yet with the feelings of a gentleman. His details are innumerable – his finishing is minute; but it is the minute finishing of Albert Durer or Leonardo da Vinci, not of Teniers or Ostade. In this respect he offers a striking contrast to the modern romance writers of France – Victor Hugo, Janin, Madame Dudevant,[26] and Sue – by whom vice and licentiousness are exhibited with vast power, but more than their native undisguised colours. – But this wide and interesting subject must be reserved for a future occasion.

Anonymous
From 'Recent Works of Fiction',
1853

In its entirety 'Recent Works of Fiction', published in the *Prospective Review* on 30 April 1853 (9: 222–47), may be read as a review of the novel *Ruth* by Elizabeth Cleghorn Gaskell. Indeed, most of the article (pp. 229–47) is given over to a minute examination of Gaskell's novel, which had appeared three months earlier; however, because this analysis is not relevant to our purposes in this volume, we are not reproducing the final two-thirds of 'Recent Works of Fiction', except for the concluding paragraph.

What gives the first third its special interest is the fact that the reviewer here develops a coherent theory of the novel, its nature, and its function in the mid nineteenth century, on which he then proceeds to base his detailed consideration of *Ruth*. Far more significant than mere entertainment, he argues, the novel has become 'the chosen medium for the discussion of the vexed and difficult questions, moral, religious, social and political, which agitate the minds of men'. It cannot serve this high purpose if it confines itself to photographic realism ('redundancy of commonplace'), if it concentrates on 'the repulsive', or if it trivializes vital ethical questions. Rather, the novel must appeal to the imagination and the moral sense by a carefully crafted rendering of fundamental issues of human conduct in a world that is inexorably governed by the laws of God.

Ruth was particularly well suited to illustrate a theory of this kind, for it addressed some deeply troubling concerns. Not only does the protagonist bear and raise an illegitimate son, but her protector, the Dissenting clergyman Thurstan Benson, and his sister Faith persuade themselves that Ruth should be 'passed off as a widow' – a well-meant piece of deception, but a lie all the same, 'on which the fate of years moved' (ch. 11). There are a number of other characters in *Ruth* whose positions are at best morally ambiguous: Ruth's first employer; her seducer; his mother; the man in whose family Ruth serves as governess until her past comes to light. Gaskell herself clearly had a didactic purpose in mind in writing the novel, and it is not surprising that most of the early reviewers seized on its moral rather than its aesthetic aspects. For our critic, however, these aspects of *Ruth* are mutually supportive, and finally indistinguishable from each other.

The *Prospective Review*, in which this essay appeared, was a quarterly with strong Unitarian leanings that ran from 1845 to 1855, during most of which time it was published by John Chapman. George Eliot, Eliot's friends the Hennells and the Brays, and Arthur Hugh Clough were regular readers. It is known that James Martineau, Francis William Newman, Charles Wicksteed, Richard Holt Hutton, Richard Monckton Milnes, Walter Bagehot, and William Caldwell Roscoe were among those who wrote for the *Prospective*, but the identity of most contributors is unknown: articles were unsigned; no reliable marked file has come to light; there are no relevant financial records, because contributors were not paid for their work. It has not been possible, therefore, to establish the authorship of 'Recent Works of Fiction'.

THE novel has been styled the modern Epos, but if in ancient times, Calliope[a] was represented as holding in her hand the three great Epics of antiquity, her modern representative ought rather to be typified as a female Briareus,[b] furnished with fifty heads, and a hundred hands, and might even then not unreasonably complain of the fatigue to which she is subjected in the service of her numerous votaries. The avidity with which works of fiction are perused, aspiring, as they do, to delineate emotions and experiences in which all human beings are equally interested, cannot excite surprise. "Man is dear to Man," and the desire for sympathy is one of the deepest instincts of his nature; yet his inner mind is shrouded in a veil of mystery; his emotions, whether of joy or of sorrow, lurk often unsuspected in the recesses of his heart, and his most cherished thoughts shrink from exposure, except when conveyed in an imaginative form. All genuine fiction, however, is the idealized transcript of actual experience; and as the architects of old built their souls into the stately minsters, whose storied aisles embody the aspirations of a by-gone age, so the heart of humanity has enshrined itself in the glowing pages of romance, where stand revealed those hidden passages of experience, which in actual life are witnessed only by the eye of Him who seeth in secret; and as we listen to the wail of sorrow or the tones of joy, uttered, it may be, in a foreign language, and coming to us from a distant time, our heart responds to the sympathetic touch, and we recognise the deep truth of the poet's words, "that we have all of us one human heart."

It is not merely as the record of past emotion, as the silent witness through each succeeding generation to the great doctrine of Human Brotherhood, that we value fiction; we regard it as fulfilling a high and a holy mission in the present; it conjures up an ideal world in the midst of our prosaic realities, and men, absorbed in selfish interests, are awakened to more generous sympathies,[1] and their hearts, severed in the turmoil of the world, find a bond of fellowship and reunion in the affections and antipathies inspired by the creations of the poet: –

[a] Muse of epic poetry.
[b] Fifty-headed, hundred-handed giant who sided with Zeus in the Olympians' war against Briareus's fellow-Titans.

for books, we know,
Are a substantial world, both pure and good;
Round these, with tendrils strong as flesh and blood,
Our pastime and our happiness will grow.[2]

Fiction has yet another claim to our regard as a vehicle for the transmission of opinion; the results of speculative inquiry, when presented in an abstract form, wear, to the ordinary mind, an aspect so severe and uninviting, that we joyfully hail the imaginative faculty which invests dead principles in the living hues of experience, and thus brings them home to the conscience and apprehension of humanity. We accordingly find that as society awakens to a consideration of its vital interests, the province of fiction expands; it becomes the chosen medium for the discussion of the vexed and difficult questions, moral, religious, social and political, which agitate the minds of men; and the various theories adopted for their solution endeavour to obtain a hearing, by assuming an imaginative expression, and embodying themselves in a concrete form.

The vast influence thus acquired by works of fiction, and the prominence which they assume as an element of modern civilization, renders it important to determine the laws of taste by which they should be regulated; – a consideration the more worthy of regard when we reflect how closely interwoven are the various lines of thought, and that by the law of reciprocation, a wrong bias impressed upon any one of its manifestations has a tendency to spread beyond its immediate sphere; and hence literature, while it reflects the character of the age in which it is produced, becomes, in its turn, one of the most powerful agencies by which that character is modified.

The highest function of the critic is to act as the interpreter of genius, which, working under the impulse of its creative instincts, may be, and we believe frequently is, unconscious of the deep truths embodied in its own productions; the critic's eye, "made quiet by the power of harmony,"[3] sees into the life of a work of art, penetrates its hidden meaning, and detects the subtle beauties which escape the notice of the superficial observer.

His subordinate function is to determine the laws of taste in harmony with which genius itself must consent to work, if it would remain within the sphere of beauty, and send forth its creations, "unmixt with baser matter,"[4] to charm and elevate the minds of contemporaries, and to live for ever in the thought of humanity.

It would be impossible within the compass of an article to dwell individually upon the numerous works of fiction, with which our imaginative literature has recently been enriched, and from the perusal of which we have derived both instruction and pleasure. From the ample field outspread before us, we shall therefore select "Ruth," not only from its high merit as a work of art, but from the deep interest attached to the moral questions which it involves. Before proceeding to our pleasant task of hearty appreciation, we shall take this opportunity of pointing out what appear to us some false tendencies, manifested in the imaginative literature of the day; "Ruth" being reserved for after consideration, is not included in the following strictures, which are offered in no irreverent or depreciating spirit, but rather from an earnest desire that an agency so replete with power and blessing as fiction, should be wielded with full efficiency, and enlisted heartily in the sacred cause of truth and goodness.

Novels may be divided into two classes, the epic, and the dramatic; the former, proposing as their aim a comprehensive survey of life, are necessarily slow in their development; we cannot accelerate the march of Providence, nor with impatient hand gather prematurely its slowly-ripening fruits; ample scope is thus allowed for digression and disquisition; and the readers, like travellers through a pleasant country, instead of hurrying to the goal, are contented to linger by the way, and to enjoy the rich prospects which open round them as they advance. Other novels on the contrary, by the rapidity of their action, the small number of characters introduced, and the limitation of the field of view, bear more affinity to the drama, which exhibits the concentrated essence of life, rather than life itself. Now it would seem reasonable that the extent of canvas should bear some proportion to the dimensions of the picture: fashion, however, having prescribed a certain framework, as characteristic of the legitimate novel, the author is under the necessity of contracting or dilating his matter in accordance with the prescribed limits; a process by which his movements are greatly embarrassed. It is unquestionably a difficult problem to expand into three volumes thought which would naturally embody itself in a much smaller compass; and to this vicious practice may, we think, in some degree be attributed the diffuseness of style which characterizes a large portion of our modern literature.

For the full enjoyment of fiction, too, the imagination must be in a productive mood; the figures then start into life, and the various aspects of nature flit through the mind, forming a background to the living scene; a redundancy of commonplace, however, effectually paralyses the imagination, and shuts the portals of the ideal world; there is nothing by which the effect of a work of art is more impaired, than by the too frequent intermingling of insignificant details, and we feel assured that if from many works of fiction the superfluous matter were eliminated, they would gain in power what they would lose in bulk. Occasionally recourse is had to still more desperate measures; one work of fiction, which obtained a high and deserved reputation, was returned to the author by the publisher, with the request that a hundred pages might be added; the consequence was the introduction of an episode, by which the symmetry and significance of the whole were greatly impaired; the absurdity of such a proceeding in reference to the plastic arts would be obvious at once, and reminds us of Addison's witty description of certain Greek poems, which were to be cramped or extended to the dimension of the frame prepared for them; they were obliged, he says, to undergo the fate of those persons whom the tyrant, Procrustes, used to lodge in his iron bed; if they were too short he stretched them on a rack; and if they were too long he chopped off a part of their legs, till they fitted the couch prepared for them.[5] The publisher's apology would doubtless be that a more saleable article was thus produced. Alas for art, when it thus becomes the slave of Mammon! It is another manifestation of the tendency only too characteristic of the age, "to degrade the cow of Isis into the milch cow, and to count what the butter will fetch in the market."[6]

Another false tendency to which we would advert, manifests itself, we think, in the kind of characters selected as the subjects of fiction. From certain instinctive tendencies in the human mind, there is a degree of pleasure derived from any faithful imitation of Nature; but that from her exhaustless treasure-house of beauty, artists, relying upon this principle, should voluntarily select the repulsive for the exercise of their art, seems an unaccountable perversity. Literature, it is true, must be based upon reality; there is, however, a high and generous, as well as a low and grovelling, reality; and the true artist, in embodying the spirit of the age instead of introducing us to a region of sordid and vulgar fact, depicted with revolting minuteness, gives greater prominence to its ennobling elements, and though not ignoring the existence of evil, yet veils it in a poetic form. It is not the function of art simply to reproduce the noise and turbulent present, but to impart rhythmical beauty to its manifold aspects, and by introducing us into a region of calmer and loftier thought to win us to a nobler life.

As in painting no executive skill, no richness of colour, can redeem a trivial conception and faulty design, so in literature no grace of style or harmony of diction can impart interest to ignoble views of life, and types of character essentially mean.

True fiction hath in it a higher end
Than fact; –
    *   *   *   *   *
'Tis not enough to draw forms fair and lively,
Their conduct likewise must be beautiful;
A hearty holiness must crown the work,
As a gold cross the minster dome, and show
Like that instonement of divinity,
That the whole building doth belong to God.[7]

Our final stricture has reference to a practice against which we beg to enter our most earnest protest; we refer to the levity with which vice is not unfrequently alluded to. The effect of custom in deadening our impressions is well known, and it is a trite, but not the less important, observation, that familiarity with vice tends to diminish the horror with which it is at first instinctively regarded. Let not the novelist plead in excuse "that it is not his province to play the moralist." The artist might with equal truth justify the introduction of a distorted limb, on the plea that anatomy is no concern of his. Life is profoundly moral, and it is only our superficial glance which fails to recognise God's holy law, underlying its complicated phenomena; could we penetrate the recesses of the human heart, and see the tide of emotion coloured to remotest time by a momentary impulse; or could we disentangle the web of life, and trace the outward consequences of actions, weaving their dark or golden threads through the many-coloured texture, we should see God's holiness abundantly vindicated, and perceive that His moral government is regulated by laws as inflexible as those which govern the material universe. The fact of the highest artistic genius having manifested itself in a polytheistic age, and among a people whose moral views were essentially degraded, has, we think, fostered the erroneous notion, that the sphere of art has no connection with that of morality. The Greeks, with penetrative insight, detected the essential characteristics of man's organism as a vehicle of superior intelligence, while their intense sympathy with physical beauty made them alive to its most subtle manifestations, and reproducing their impressions through the medium of art, they have given birth to models of the human form, which reveal its highest possibilities, and the excellence of which depends upon their being individual expressions of ideal truth. Thus, too, in their descriptions of Nature, instead of multiplying insignificant details, they seized instinctively upon the characteristic features of her varying aspects, and not unfrequently embodied a finished picture in one comprehensive and harmonious word. In association with their marvellous genius, however, we find a cruelty, a treachery, and a license, which would be revolting if it were not for the historical interest which attaches to every genuine record of a by-gone age. Their low moral standard cannot excite surprise when we consider the debasing tendency of their worship, the objects of their adoration being nothing more than their own degraded passions invested with some of the attributes of deity. Now, among the modifications of thought introduced by Christianity, there is perhaps none more pregnant with important results than the harmony which it has established between religion and morality. The great law of right and wrong has acquired a sacred character when viewed as an expression of the divine will; it takes its rank among the eternal verities, and to ignore it in our delineations of life, or to represent sin otherwise than as treason against the supreme ruler, is to retain in modern civilization one of the degrading elements of heathenism. Conscience is as great a fact of our inner life as the sense of beauty, and the harmonious action of both these instinctive principles is essential to the highest enjoyment of art, for any internal dissonance disturbs the repose of the mind, and thereby shatters the image mirrored in its depths.

We are far from maintaining that the novelist should usurp the function of the preacher; his mission is to delineate life, in all its richness and harmony, and we are well aware that in actual experience the indirect teachings of example come home to the heart with far greater power than those delivered in the tone of direct exhortation; we may remark, incidentally, that highly as we appreciate Bulwer's last effort, "My Novel,"[8] rich as it is in lessons of wisdom, and abounding in passages of rare beauty, we cannot but think that its artistic value is marred by the prominence given to the didactic element. The characters thereby lose their spontaneity, and want the breath of life; they seem not so much to have sprung into being from the fervent depths of a creative imagination, like the goddess of beauty emerging from the wave,[a] as to have been called into existence for the purpose of embodying certain moral ideas. The moral tone should be felt through a work of fiction, like the pulse of health through a living organism, never obtruding itself into notice, but imparting grace and elasticity to every movement; the love of what is pure and honourable should be brought home to our hearts, heightened by the rich glow of the imagination, and while our charity is fostered by being made to feel how much that is excellent may possibly co-exist with moral evil, we must never be seduced by levity or sophistry, into a forgetfulness of its deadly character.

[a] Aphrodite, who sprang from the foam of the sea; Greek *aphros* = foam.

The unobtrusiveness of the moral elements in 'Ruth' constitutes, we think, one of its greatest charms, and enhances its merit as a work of art. A passage from the volume of life, one of the saddest contained in that mysterious record, is transcribed for our perusal, and is left, without comment, to suggest its appropriate lesson. But as life itself, with its myriads of living agents, "encircled by the mystery of existence," may justly be regarded as an allegory, the significance of which depends upon the right reading of the truths underlying its outward manifestations; so every episode in life partakes of an allegorical character, and invites to a deciphering of its hidden meaning, and an unfolding of its teachings. It is in this spirit that we turn to the narrative before us, which seizes upon the mind with the strong grasp of reality, and through its graceful diction, graphic delineation of nature, and skilful portraiture, fully maintains the high reputation which the author has already achieved as a writer of fiction. In the pages of her recent work she exhibits one phase of a vast social evil, which claims the earnest consideration of the wisest and noblest minds, and which, in its manifold bearings, involving the deepest questions in ethical science, is manifestly beyond the scope of a single work of fiction; we shall endeavour to point out a few of the truths which she has conveyed through the medium of her touching tale, and in order to render our remarks intelligible, we shall preface them by a brief outline of its more prominent features....

In conclusion, we thank our author for directing public attention to a subject fraught with such painful interest, and one, the consideration of which is encompassed with so many difficulties, as that which she has embodied in her touching narrative. The one-sidedness of her view may, we fear, have a tendency, in some quarters, to lessen her influence as a moral teacher; from the reticence, however, necessarily induced by artistic considerations, we are by no means entitled to infer the absence of that full knowledge, and mature consideration of the subject, in its manifold bearings, which would be essential to invest her opinions with authority. We are aware also that many earnest thinkers would consign this subject to the sphere of silence, and regard it as altogether beyond the region of art; we respect their scruples though we cannot sympathize with them; so long as evils are ignored, and any allusion to them held to be inconsistent with good taste, no earnest conviction can be generated in the public mind; to the remedial power of truth, embodied in earnest words, moral maladies the most inveterate must eventually yield. And let not those who are labouring in the great cause of social amelioration, be appalled at the magnitude of the evils with which they are called upon to grapple, or feel tempted to despise the day of small things; as in the material universe, the tiny seed lodges in the hollow of the rock, and by its expansive force gradually undermines the superincumbent mass; so in the subtler regions of the mind, the germs of truth strike root, and spread forth their delicate fibres; and mountains of error and wickedness are loosened from their foundations, and the cheerful daylight shines in, where once reigned darkness and the shadow of death.

James Fitzjames Stephen
(1829–1894)
From 'The Relation of
Novels to Life', 1855

In 'The Relation of Novels to Life' (*Cambridge Essays Contributed by Members of the University*, 1855, p. 161), James Fitzjames Stephen refers to two of Thackeray's characters as 'literary barristers'. The same term could be applied to Stephen himself, though without the condescension that his use of it for Arthur Pendennis and George Warrington in this essay suggests. Stephen's record of achievement in the law as well as in letters was a formidable one.

The son and grandson of distinguished men both named James Stephen and a graduate of Cambridge, Stephen became a barrister in 1854. He was appointed a Queen's Counsel in 1868, a member of the governor-general's legislative council in India in 1869, and a judge of the Queen's Bench Division of the High Court of Justice in 1879. Following his resignation from the latter post because of ill health, Stephen was created a baronet in 1891. His publications include a number of substantial books on criminal law and the law of evidence.

Having been introduced to the editor of the *Saturday Review* by Henry Sumner Maine, Regius Professor of Civil Law at Cambridge, Stephen began writing for that new periodical with its second number in November 1855. During the next dozen years or so, he produced more than 150 reviews and almost as many 'middles': Merle M. Bevington, the historian of the periodical who attributes this large body of work to him, agrees with the judgement of Stephen's friend T. H. S. Escott that Stephen '*was* the *Saturday Review*' during this period. A good many of his contributions to the *Saturday Review* were reprinted in *Essays by a Barrister* (1862) and three series of *Horae Sabbaticae* (1892). Stephen also wrote – on legal, literary, and a variety of other subjects – for the *Edinburgh Review*, the *Fortnightly Review*, *Fraser's Magazine*, the *Contemporary Review*, the *Cornhill Magazine*, the *National Review*, the *Nineteenth Century*, and *Macmillan's Magazine* (the *Wellesley Index to Victorian Periodicals* ascribes nearly a hundred pieces in these magazines to him); and he was a mainstay of the *Pall Mall Gazette*, an evening newspaper of high quality, from its beginning in February 1865 until his departure for India nearly five years later.

Owing to the mass and scope of Stephen's criticism, his ideas about literature, and fiction in particular, are difficult to describe succinctly. Possibly because of his Evangelical background and his legal training, he took a hardheaded approach to belles-lettres, scoffing at the pretension and the sentimentality of many nineteenth-century authors. Though he believed that novel-reading could affect, most often adversely, morals and behaviour, he had no sympathy with the novel of social purpose. Indeed, one wonders how seriously he took English fiction. In his review of *Madame Bovary*, for example, he raised grave objections to the tone of the work and what he regarded as Flaubert's purpose in writing it, but did not think its example would be harmful in his own country. 'There is no fear that our novelists will outrage public decency. Their weaknesses forbid such dangerous eccentricity quite as much as their virtues.'

Another difficulty with classifying Stephen's ideas arises from his dogged independence and refusal to subscribe wholeheartedly to any system. For instance, his assertion in 'The Relation of Novels to Life' that 'The first requisite of a novel is, that it should be a biography' can be traced back to Thomas Carlyle's question about 'Fictional Narratives': 'What are all these but so many mimic Biographies?' ('Biography', 1832), and he certainly agreed with much in Carlyle's political thought, especially his belief in the necessity of strong government; but Stephen's published estimates of Carlyle's work were at best mixed. A similar inconsistency is seen in what is today Stephen's best-known book, *Liberty, Equality, Fraternity* (1873): though Stephen considered himself a utilitarian, this is a sustained attack on John Stuart Mill's *On Liberty*.

Our selection from 'The Relation of Novels to Life' omits some of Stephen's examples and illustrative quotations as well as a lengthy discussion of *Robinson Crusoe* (pp. 187–92), which leads into his concluding judgement that Defoe's novel, admirably, is as close to a literal transcript of real life as it is possible for a work of fiction to be.

WE have discarded many of the amusements of our forefathers. Out-of-door games are almost inaccessible to the inhabitants of cities; and if they were not, people are too much tired, both in nerve and muscle, to care for them. Theatres and spectacles are less frequented than they used to be; while the habit of reading has become universal. These causes increase the popularity and the influence of novels, and, measured by these standards, their importance must be considered very great.

The majority of those who read for amusement, read novels. The number of young people who take from them nearly all their notions of life is very considerable. They are widely used for the diffusion of opinions. In one shape or another, they enter into the education of us all. They constitute very nearly the whole of the book-education of the unenergetic and listless.

Familiar as the word 'novel' may be, it is almost the last word in the language to suggest any formal definition; but it is impossible to estimate the influence of this species of literature, or to understand how its character is determined, unless we have some clear notion as to what is, and what is not, included in the word.

The first requisite of a novel is, that it should be a biography, – an account of the life, or part of the life, of a person. When this principle is neglected or violated, the novel becomes tiresome; after a certain point it ceases to be novel at all, and becomes a mere string of descriptions.

The *Arabian Nights*, perhaps, contain as slight a biographical substratum as is consistent with anything like romance. The extravagance of the incidents and scenery is their principal charm, and the different characters might be interchanged amongst the different stories, almost without notice. Who would relish the *Diamond Valley* and the *Roc's Egg* the less, if they were introduced in the *History of the three Calendars*, or in the *Adventures of Prince Caramalzaman*? and who would notice the change if either of those personages were to be substituted for *Sinbad the Sailor*? Who, on the other hand, could interchange the incidents, or the personages, of the *Memoirs of a Cavalier*,[1] and *Robinson Crusoe*?

Perhaps the essentially biographical character of novels will be more fully displayed by comparing less extreme cases. In what does the superiority of Fielding over Mr. Dickens consist? Is it not in the fact that *Tom Jones* and *Joseph Andrews* are *bonâ fide* histories of those persons; whilst *Nicholas Nickleby* and *Oliver Twist* are a series of sketches, of all sorts of things and people, united by various grotesque incidents, and interspersed with projects for setting the world to rights?

There is a class of books which wants only a biographical substratum to become novels. In so far as it is an account of Sir Roger de Coverley, and the Club, the *Spectator*[2] is one of the best novels in the language; and if the original conception had been more fully carried out, that fact would have been universally recognised. It employs fictitious personages to describe manners and characters, and it sustains the interest which they excite by fictitious incidents. Yet no one would call those parts of the *Spectator* which are not biographical a novel.

Novels must also be expressly and intentionally fictitious. No amount of carelessness or dishonesty would convert into a novel what was meant for a real history. It would, for example, be an unjustifiable stretch of charity to consider the *Histoire des Girondins*, or the *Histoire de la Restauration*,[3] as romances. On the other hand, a very small amount of intentional fiction, artistically introduced, will make a history into a novel. All the events related may be substantially true, and the fictitious characters may play a very subordinate part, and yet the result may be a novel, in the fullest sense of the word. In the *Memoirs of a Cavalier*, Gustavus Adolphus, Charles, and Fairfax occupy the most prominent places. The scenes in which they take part are generally represented with great historical fidelity. The cavalier himself, and his adventures, are only introduced as a medium for the display of the events through which he passes; but they are introduced so naturally as incidents in his life, and the gaps between them are filled with such probable and appropriate domestic occurrences, that the result is the most perfect of all historical novels.

We understand, then, by the word *novel*, a fictitious biography. Books written primarily for purposes of instruction, or for the sake of illustrating a theory, do not fall within this definition, because they are not, properly speaking, biographies. If we suppose the hero to have been a real person, and then consider whether the object of the book was to deduce some moral, or to illustrate some theory, by his life, or to describe the man as he was, we shall be able to say whether the book is, or is not, a novel.

Thus, we should not call Plato's *Dialogues* novels, though they resemble them more nearly than any other ancient books. Nor should we call the 'Vision,' in Tucker's *Light of Nature*,[4] a novel, although it would fall expressly within the terms of our definitions, if it were not written merely to illustrate a theory. The miraculous separation of Search's body from his vehicle – the inconvenience which he sustained from the rays of light – his conversation with Locke – his interview with his wife – his absorption into the mundane soul – and his re-introduction into his body, form an imaginary posthumous biography, with a beginning, middle, and end; but it cannot be called a novel, inasmuch as Search and his adventures are introduced solely in order to give life to a philosophical speculation, which is never for an instant lost sight of.

Pilgrim's Progress and the *Holy War* come nearer to the character of novels. The artistic bias of Bunyan's mind was so strong, that we should be inclined to think that he sacrificed the allegory to the story more frequently than the story to the allegory. The death of Faithful, for example, is an incident which, if the book is a novel, is as well conceived as executed; but it is inconsistent with the allegory, which would have required that Faithful should go to Heaven in the sense of travelling along the actual highroad till he got there. So, too, the Siege of Mansoul is much more like the Siege of Leicester than the temptations of the Devil.

There is another class of books which would be excluded from our definition by the word 'fictitious.' As fiction is sometimes used as a mere vehicle for opinions, so it is sometimes a mere embellishment of facts. There is a class of books in which the life of a real person is made to illustrate some particular time or country, and in which just so many fictitious circumstances are introduced as may be necessary to give a certain unity to the scenes described. The most perfect instances of this form of writing with which we are acquainted is M. Bungener's *Trois Sermons sous Louis XV.*,[5] which is partly a history of French Protestants in the eighteenth century, partly a fictitious biography of the real man Rabaut.[6] It has the inconvenience of constantly suggesting to the reader the impression that the author considers him incapable of taking an interest in the subject unless it is baited with a certain amount of fiction.

It is commonly said that novels supply the place of comedies; and it would perhaps be hard to put into words the distinction between them, otherwise than by the definition which we have suggested. A drama is the representation of an incident – a novel is the history of a life. Thus, the plays which composed an Æschylean trilogy consisted of the representation of separate incidents in the life of some person or the fortunes of some royal house; but if they had been permitted to run into each other, such an interference would have been a violation of the rules of dramatic art, and would have made them into a novel.

It is not always easy to say what is incident and what is biography. Shakspeare's historical plays do not fall very appropriately under either division. Some, for example, of Crabbe's tales, are miniature novels, others undramatized plays. It cannot, however, be doubted that in cases upon which no one hesitates our distinction holds good. Thus, *Waverley* is undeniably a novel, and *Romeo and Juliet* is undeniably a play. We should have been displeased if Shakspeare had introduced into his play anything not bearing upon the single subject of the love of the principal persons in it. It is, on the other hand, one of the beauties of *Waverley* that it incidentally illustrates a great number of subjects in which the hero of the novel had not personally much interest.

Novels, in the proper sense of the word, are used for a greater number of purposes than any other species of literature. Their influences on their readers may, however, be reduced within a very narrow compass. In early boyhood and in mature life they are read merely for amusement; and indulgence in them will be beneficial, or otherwise, according to the ordinary rules upon that subject. But at that time of life which intervenes between these two periods they exercise a far greater influence. They are then read as commentaries upon the life which is just opening before the reader, and as food for passions which are lately awakened but have not yet settled down to definite objects.

It may be questioned how far the habit of reading novels contributes to knowledge of the world. The undue prominence given to particular passions – such as love, the colouring used for artistic purposes, and a variety of other circumstances, are so much calculated to convey false impressions, that it may be plausibly doubted whether the impressions formed are, in fact, better than none at all.

Such a judgment appears to us too severe. If a young man were, according to Mr. Carlyle's suggestion, to be shut up in a glass case from eighteen to twenty-five, and were, during that period, to be supplied with an unlimited number of novels, he would no doubt issue from his confinement with extremely false notions of the world to which he was returning; but if, during such an imprisonment, he had made it a point of conscience never to open a novel, he would, in the absence of extraordinary powers of observation and generalization, be strangely puzzled on re-entering life.

What we call knowledge of the world is acquired by the same means as other kinds of knowledge, and consists not in mere acquaintance with maxims about life, but in applying appropriate ideas to clear facts. This application can only be made by a proper arrangement and selection of the material parts of the facts observed; and this arrangement is effected, to a very great degree, by guesses and hypotheses. No one will be able to make any use of his experience of life, or to classify it in such a manner as to add to his real knowledge, unless he is provided in the first instance with some schemes or principles of classification, which he starts with, and which he enlarges, narrows, or otherwise modifies as he sees cause....

... Novels, perhaps, offer a greater number of such hypotheses than are to be derived from any other source; and though they give them in a very confused, indefinite manner, they gain in liveliness and variety what they want in precision.

It is, however, by the materials which it affords for self-examination that novel reading enlarges our experience most efficiently. It was, if we are not mistaken, Lord Chesterfield's advice to his son, that if he wished to understand mankind he ought to be always saying to himself, 'If I were to act towards that man as he acts towards me, he would feel towards me as I feel towards him.'[7] The thought that they often do act like characters represented in novels, and that people do in consequence feel towards them as they themselves regard such characters, must occur, we should think pretty frequently, to novel readers. It would be a great effort of self-denial to many of us to read *Murad the Unlucky*, or *To-morrow*;[8] and we should think that few men could become acquainted with *George Osborne* or *Arthur Pendennis*[9] without acquiring a consciousness of a multitude of small vanities and hypocrisies which would otherwise have escaped their attention. To produce or to stimulate self-consciousness by such means, may not be altogether a healthy process, but it is unquestionably one which has powerful effects.

In a large class of readers, novels operate most strongly by producing emotion. Strange as it seems, many people sympathize more intensely with fictitious than with historical characters. Persons who would read Carlyle's *History of the French Revolution* unmoved, would not be proof against such books as *Uncle Tom's Cabin*, or the *Heir of Redcliffe*;[10] and we suspect that Mr. Dickens has caused a great deal more emotion by some of his luscious death-bed scenes, than by what we have always considered one of the most fearful stories, both in matter and manner, which we ever read, the papers entitled *Transported for Life*, in *Household Words*.[11] Habitual emotion, whatever may be the exciting cause, produces some moral effects. A man who had really seen a negro flogged to death, or had attended a young man on his wedding tour, in a fatal illness, would probably be in some respects altered for a longer or shorter time afterwards. Whatever would be the effect of habitually witnessing such scenes, the same effect would follow in a much slighter degree from habitually reading descriptions of them; but in order to make the parallel complete we must suppose the witnessing of the scenes to be as much a matter of choice as the reading of the novels; a person who went to see a man die because he liked it would receive very different impressions from one who saw such a sight because he could not help it.

It is sometimes broadly stated that emotion produced by fiction is an evil, and tends to harden the heart. This statement goes further than its authors suppose. The parables are fictions, but we do not think any one was ever hurt by emotion produced by reading the parable of the Prodigal Son, or that of Dives and Lazarus. Emotion, also, is of many kinds. Laughter implies emotion. Is it wrong to laugh at Falstaff or Mrs Quickly? Admiration is an emotion. Even amusement, in so far as it involves interest, and is not a mere suspension of thought, implies emotion. So, too, wonder is an emotion. No one thinks it wrong to produce these emotions by fiction. In fact, the emotions of tenderness or terror are the only ones which are objected to; and since the objection will not lie against producing emotion by fiction, but only against producing those particular emotions, it must be contended that the emotions are bad in themselves, and ought only to be submitted to when unavoidably forced upon the mind. Few people would maintain this proposition when nakedly set before them.

It may however, be remarked, that it is not easy to say what is and what is not fiction for these purposes. Is the story of *Lucretia*[12] fiction, within the meaning of this objection? Or has it only become so since the publication of Niebuhr's *History*,[13] and as to so many people as have read it? Or would it cease to be fiction if its substantial truth were to be established by new evidence?

Would *Mansfield Park* cease to be fiction for the purposes of the objection, if it were to appear that Miss Austen had drawn from the life, and that the grouping and connexion alone of the circumstances were invented by her? Or, if the intention of the author be considered as the test of fiction, it would be necessary to contend that a description of incidents which in all essential particulars occurred as described, ought not to produce emotion, merely because the person describing them was not aware of the degree in which his description coincided with the facts.

The moral effects of novel reading being the enlargement of the reader's knowledge of the world, and the excitement of his feelings, in what respects do such effects differ from those which similar objects might excite in real life? In other words, what adjustments and allowances must we make before the suggestions of novels can be accepted as additions to our experience?

If novels were perfectly-executed pictures of life, they would increase the reader's knowledge of life, just as paintings add to his knowledge of scenery and of incident; but no information, or only very false information, is to be derived from the pictures either of novelists or of painters, unless proper allowance is made, not only for the limitations imposed on them by the rules of their art, but also for the faults of conception and of execution most common amongst them.

One of the most obvious causes which makes novels unlike real life is the necessity under which they lie of being interesting, an object which can only be obtained by a great deal of *suppressio veri*,[a] whence arises that *suggestio falsi*[b] of which it is our object to point out the principal varieties.

Who would infer from one of the trial scenes which occur in almost

[a] Suppression of the true.
[b] Suggestion of the false.

every one of the *Waverley Novels*, what a real criminal trial was like? The mere *coup d'œil*[a] presented by the judges, the barristers, the prisoner, the witnesses, and the crowd of spectators, might be pretty accurately represented to any sufficiently imaginative reader by the account of the trial of Fergus McIvor and Evan Dhu Maccombich.[14] The *State Trials*[15] would give a juster notion of the interminable length of the indictments, the apparently irrelevant and unmeaning examinations and cross-examinations of witnesses, the skirmishing of the counsel on points of law, and the petitions of the prisoners, often painfully reasonably, for some relaxation of the rules of evidence, or procedure; but to any one who seeks mere amusement, such reading is intolerably tedious, and even when accomplished, it gives a very faint representation of the actual scene as it appeared to those who sat or stood, day after day, in all the heat, and dust, and foul air of the court-house at Carlisle or Southwark, half understanding, and – as the main points at issue got gradually drowned in their own details – half attending to the proceedings on which the lives and deaths of their friends depended. A man really present on such an occasion, and personally interested, would probably bring away impressions which a life-time would not destroy. In a novel, such a scene is at once more and less interesting than it is in fact. There are more points of interest, more dramatic situations; the circumstances are more clearly defined, and more sharply brought out than they ever would be in real life; but at the same time, that from which such circumstances derive their interest is wanting; the necessity of thought and attention, the consciousness that what is passing is most real and serious business, which it is not open to the spectators to hurry over, or to lay down and take up again at pleasure. In one word, the reality. It is in order to supply the absence of this source of interest that recourse is had to the other.

If we imagine a novel written for a reader seeking, not amusement, but information, it would be not only insupportably dull, but would be more laborious reading that any other kind of literature. Suppose that in addition to the present novel of *Waverley*, we had the muster-roll of Captain Waverley's troop, with extracts from the *Army List* of that time as to Gardiner's[16] dragoons; – suppose we had full statements of the route of the Pretender's[17] army, short-hand writers' notes of the proceedings of all his councils of war; – suppose the MSS. of the Jacobite divinity of Waverley's tutor, or at any rate, the plan of the work, with copious extracts, were actually printed, and all the proceedings against Fergus McIvor, and respecting the pardon of

[a] Spectacle.

Waverley and the Baron[18] incorporated in the book; – and suppose on the part of the reader sufficient interest and patience to go through all this mass of matter, no one can doubt that he would know much more about Waverley and his fortunes than ordinary readers do know. If, however, *Waverley* had been composed upon this principle, the conversations and descriptions, which give it all its charm, would have been greatly curtailed. A person who had toiled, notebook and atlas in hand, through all sorts of authorities, geographical, historical, antiquarian, and legal, about the Highland line, black-mail, and the heritable jurisdictions, would have little taste for the conversations between Waverley, Rose Bradwardine, Evan Dhu, and the Baron, upon the same subjects. They contemplate a frame of mind altogether different.

The *suppressio veri* which occurs in novels may therefore be considered as an essential feature of that kind of literature, but it involves a *suggestio falsi* which is not so obvious, and has more tendency to mislead readers.

It requires but very little experience of life to be aware that the circumstances stated in a novel form a very small part of what must have actually occurred to the persons represented; but it requires more experience to see in what respects the fact that all dull matter is suppressed, falsifies the representation of what is actually described.

The most remarkable of all the modifications with which novels represent real life consists in the way in which such suppressions distort their representations of character.

These representations differ from the thing represented much as a portrait differs from a real face. A child would probably prefer the portrait to the face, because its colours are more definite, smoother, and less altered by the various disturbing causes which act upon the living body. This difference is a consequence of yielding to the temptation, under which novelists continually labour, of taking an entirely different view of character from those who seek not to represent, but to understand it.

The easiest way of representing character is to represent it as a set of qualities which belong to different men, as colour, weight, and form belong to different substances; to represent brave actions as resulting from a quality of courage in one man, or wise actions from a quality of wisdom in another, just as knives cut because they are sharp, or lead sinks because it is heavy. No one who takes his views of character from life would accept this as a fair representation of it. Whatever ultimate differences not resolvable by any analysis there may be between one man and another, no one can seriously doubt that far the most important differences between men are differences of habit. What we call character is little else than a collection of habits, whether their formation is to be traced to original organic differences or to any other causes.

Almost everybody likes and dislikes the same things. Everybody likes praise, everybody likes knowledge, everybody likes distinction, everybody likes action; but everybody likes rest, and ease, and safety, and dislikes trouble, risk, and defeat. The difference between different people is that in some, for whatever reason, the passions which involve immediate self-denial conquer those which involve immediate self-indulgence, whilst in others the opposite happens, and thus some habits are acquired with great ease and completeness, others at the expense of a good deal of effort and self-restraint, and therefore much less completely. A man may be a very brave man, and yet do very cowardly things, as he may be very prudent, and yet do very foolish things.

Probably no one can look back upon his own history without recalling innumerable inconsistencies in his own conduct and in the conduct of those about him, with the principles which it has been their most earnest desire to recognise, and the habits which they have been forming for years. But though life is full of shortcomings and inconsistencies arising from this cause, novels are not. The difficulty of conceiving or representing differences which vary in every case would of course be very great, and the flow of the story would be interrupted by them. Character, in novels, therefore, is represented as far more homogeneous and consistent than it ever really is. Men are made cowards or brave, foolish or wise, affectionate or morose, just as they are represented as being tall or short, red-haired or black-haired, handsome or ugly.

It is to this origin that we are indebted for the mass of melodramatic or merely conventional characters, which form the staple of some novel writers, and which appear in greater or less numbers even in the most distinguished.

The heroes of the Waverley novels, one and all, belong to this class. They have certain characters assigned to them, and act accordingly throughout the whole story, never rising above or falling below a certain ill-defined, but well-understood, level of thought and conduct which is appropriated to such persons. There is no effort, no incompleteness, about these characters. Any one of them could be described by a certain number of adjectives. All of them possess muscular and amatory qualifications for their office of hero, all of them are brave, most of them generous, some determined, and some irresolute, but none of them display the variety, the incompleteness, the inconsistency, which almost all men show in real life.

If we look either at history or at the very highest class of fiction, we shall find it impossible to exhaust a man's character by adjectives. Who could describe Cromwell, or William III., or Voltaire, or Falstaff, or Hamlet in this manner? It is only by reflection and comparison that we can tell what kind of persons Shakspeare's characters were intended to represent, just as it is only by studying and reflecting upon the different actions of their lives that we can become acquainted with any real personage whatever, historical or contemporary. The great mass of characters in novels may be weighed and measured, and their qualities may be enumerated, with as much ease and precision as we could count the squares in a chess-board and describe their colours.

A novelist always has some kind of scheme in his mind, according to which he draws his picture; and this scheme becomes sufficiently obvious to the reader long before he has finished the novel. In real life, on the contrary, we are obliged to take people as they come, and to form our opinions of their characters as time and opportunity happen to display them to us.

Men whose opinion is worth anything upon such matters are very cautious indeed in describing characters by a few broad phrases; for no lesson is sooner learnt than that such general language requires to be modified in innumerable ways before it can, with any kind of correctness, be applied to any individual case. In life character is inferred from actions, in most novels actions are ascribed to particular people in order to illustrate the author's conceptions respecting their character. Language, therefore, is as inadequate, when applied to real persons, as it is adequate and exhaustive when applied to the common run of fictitious ones.

Even the most prominent figures in a novel are represented in a very imperfect manner. The object of a fictitious biography is to enlist the curiosity, which a real biography presupposes. It therefore seeks to lay before the reader rather a vivid picture than an historical account of a character. To exhibit a great man as he really is the novelist would have to be himself a greater man than the person represented, and the few cases in which this has really been done are universally recognised as the very highest efforts of genius. Hamlet, King Lear, and Henry V., Satan in *Paradise Lost*, and to some extent perhaps Prometheus, not only act as people capable of great things might act, but they absolutely do the great things themselves before us. It is, however, only in the very highest class of fiction that this is possible. In ordinary novels the labour necessary to effect such an object would be improvidently invested. If any one of the numerous biographies of popular clergymen which are so common in the present day were from beginning to end an entire fiction, it would be no doubt the most extraordinary feat of imagination ever performed. But few people, and those members of a very limited class, would care to read it. Novelists, therefore, are generally in the habit of representing people rather by their behaviour in the less than in the more important affairs of life. They say, A. B., being otherwise a remarkable man, acted thus or thus in relation to his marriage. We assume, for the purposes of the novel, that he was a remarkable man *aliunde*,[a] and we consider the representation successful or not according as it corresponds or otherwise with this assumption.

There is always, however, a certain amount of risk that the reader will suppose that the author means to describe a man as he is, instead of giving a mere sketch, more or less perfect, of certain features in his manners. Hence they might come to draw a wider inference from the book than it was calculated to support, and to suppose that, because in this or that particular case, certain qualities were displayed by particular symptoms, there is, therefore, a necessary and universal connexion between the characters and the symptoms. Thus Byron suggests to many persons an association between misery and gloom on the one hand, and genius on the other, though, if we look at the books themselves, we have only Lord Byron's own word for the power or capacity of any kind, of Lara, and the Giaour, and the rest. No doubt he only exercised an author's prerogative in making such statements respecting them as matter of fact; but all that he shows of their characters is not in any way inconsistent with their having been as weak as they were bad. Byron's is an extreme case, but almost every writer who has obtained any considerable popularity has, more or less, misled his readers in this manner. To be able to do so is a proof, which few people can give, of the power of interesting and enlisting sympathy....

The hero-worship of authors is a love passing the love of women. The hero of a novel is the child of the author's experience, of his love, of his passions, of his vanity, of his philosophy; yet he is not a picture of himself in such a sense as to establish between them that unlimited liability for each others' shortcomings which is the essence of partnership. A hero is an embodied day-dream, with paper and ink for flesh and blood; and all of us know how large a part we ourselves play in our own day-dreams. The hero of a novel may not be like the author. He may be ludicrously unlike; but it is hardly possible that the furniture of

[a] In other respects.

his mind should not have been supplied by the author from his own mental stores, although its arrangement in the two men may differ. The reason is, that we know our own feelings, but we only know other men's actions, and infer from them that they feel as we should feel if we were to act in the same manner. Therefore, when we are to describe feelings as they present themselves to us upon introspection, and not as we view them in, or infer them from, other people's acts, we must necessarily draw from ourselves, as we have no other models. I know that when A. was angry he spoke harshly, that B. imputed ungenerous motives, that C. misrepresented, and so on; but I can only infer the feelings of A., B., and C., when they so acted, from my own experience of my own feelings when I acted in the same way. But though a writer cannot but invest his characters with many of his own feelings, he by no means necessarily identifies himself with all or any of them. Conscious that he is likely to be charged with drawing from himself, he probably avoids doing so explicitly and consciously, whilst he allows the favourite points of his own character to look out upon him, more or less, from his canvas. An author, under such circumstances, has some resemblance to an artist colouring a photograph. The main lines are drawn for him, and recal his own features, but he is at liberty to add what he pleases. Sometimes, probably, he paints his hero as he would wish to be, sometimes as he would wish not to be; but, unless such characters as he represents at full length, with all their feelings and mental peculiarities, have some relation to him, it is hard to say to what they are related.

Whatever may be the origin of the fact, we take the fact to be quite certain, that there is a large class of novels in which all the incidents are arranged so as to give prominence to one particular view of life, and to present it, as it might be supposed to present itself to the eyes of some one person, who, (with some modifications) acts as hero in a whole series of novels.

Perhaps there is no one thing which so entirely distorts facts as this habit. It is like looking at the world through coloured spectacles; and it engenders a wretched class of imitators, who, as we seriously believe, do harm in society.

The vexed question, as to the morality of representing bad characters in a novel, is possibly to be solved upon this principle. If it is universally true that the representation of wicked characters is objectionable, it would be hard to deny that all representation of human character is objectionable; inasmuch as there is no character which does not contain some admixture of wickedness. On the other hand, it is impossible to deny that there are some vices which can hardly be represented without mischief both to the writer and the reader. It would appear that the morality or immorality of such representations by no means depends upon the heinousness of the characters described. It would be difficult to imagine a more wicked character than Iago, or a less immoral play than *Othello*. The Bible is full of descriptions of most atrocious crimes of all sorts, and it would be natural to suppose that the fact that they are related historically would make them more, and not less, injurious than they would be if related as fictions, because the interest is greater.

The moral effect of men upon each other depends upon their intimacy. No one is made wicked by knowing that bad people exist. Most people would become wicked if all their intimate friends were so. Characters in novels may be considered as being more or less intimate acquaintances, and as they are represented upon two different principles, they may be divided into two classes.

The characters of one class are represented from without – those of the other class from within. The classification is neither exact nor complete, because almost all characters are depicted partly from one point of view, partly from the other; but these are the limits towards which such representations approximate in a greater or less degree. We should say that the latter class exercise very little moral influence over any one. They are merely more or less honest and accurate representations of facts. The other class of characters exercises the same *kind* of influence over readers as actual acquaintance with the living persons. In order to ascertain the *degree* of influence, we must not only suppose the acquaintanceship to have been limited to the time consumed in reading or thinking over the novel, and to the circumstances mentioned in it, but as existing subject to those deductions which we have indicated above as implied in the existence of novels. How far such acquaintanceship is injurious or otherwise, is a question for individuals.

It is to be observed, however, that the immoral writing which gives the greatest and most reasonable offence, is immoral specifically, and consists of detailed descriptions of subjects on which the mind cannot be suffered to rest without injury. This class of offences is mostly of a sufficiently obvious kind. It is nearly allied to what, in our own time and country, is a far more probable evil – a conscious delicacy, which suggests improper thoughts by carefully avoiding all mention of vices which must be referred to if life is to be depicted at all, and which would excite no improper feelings if referred to without unnecessary detail. . . .

The incompleteness, and consequent incorrectness of the information conveyed by novels, distorts facts even more than characters. The most familiar of all illustrations of the defect is to be found in novels of adventure. Captain Marryat, Cooper, and other writers of that class, not only suppress a great many facts for the sake of interest, but, by the very fact of such suppression, they entirely falsify the characters of those which are represented....

The circumstances which, when combined and arranged, form a novel, would, in reality, lie widely scattered over the surface of life, the attention of the actors in them being diverted to other affairs, quite unfit for the purposes of a novelist. Thus, when any of these events occurred, it would not strike those who were concerned in it, or who were witnesses of it, as being in any degree a romantic incident. Its connexion with the other circumstances which impart to it its romantic character, would be so overlaid by the other affairs of life, that their relation to each other would escape observation....

... It is of the essence of a novel to assume not only the infallibility of the narrator as to the matters of fact which he relates, but also as to the bearing of the facts related upon each other; and it would lead to constant mistakes to suppose that the circumstances which in a novel prove the guilt, or the love, or the wisdom, which the novelist attributes to his hero, would prove the same things in real life. A still more curious illustration of this is the alterations of facts which occur in historical novels. As novels cannot be taken to be histories without a good deal of management and allowance, so history cannot be readily woven into novels without corresponding distortions....

Somewhat similar in its effects is the habit of supposing that the importance of events in real life is commensurate with their importance in novels. The well-known dogma of Aristotle, that the object of a tragedy is to excite terror and pity, might be paraphrased by saying that it is the object of a novel to describe love ending in marriage. Marriage in novels occupies almost always the position which death occupies in real life; it is the art of transition into a new state, with which novelists (with some very rare exceptions) have little or nothing to do. No doubt, a happy marriage is to a woman what success in any of the careers is to a man. It is almost the only profession which society, as at present constituted, opens to her. The mistake of novelists lies not so much in overrating the importance of marriage, as in the assumed universality of the passion of love, in their sense of the word. The notion which so many novels suggest – that if two people who have a violent passion for each other marry, they have necessarily acted wisely, – is as unfounded as the converse, that if two people marry without such a passion, they act unwisely.

It would be impossible for any one to dispute altogether the existence of some such passion as is the foundation of most novels; but it may safely be affirmed that it is very uncommon, that it is a very doubtful good when it exists, and that the love which the Prayer Book seems to consider as a condition subsequent to marriage, is something much more common and very different.[a] In novels it is considered as the cause, in the Prayer Book as what ought to be the effect of marriage; and we suspect that the divines have been shrewder observers of human nature than the men of the world. In the morality of almost all novelists, the promise ought to be, not 'I will love,' but 'I declare that I do love.' The wisdom or otherwise of a step upon which so much of the happiness of life must turn, is made to depend, not on the mutual forbearance and kindly exertions of the two persons principally interested, but upon their feeling an exceptional and transitory passion at a particular moment.

To attempt to give an accurate definition, or even description of love, would be presumptuous, if not pedantic; but it may safely be affirmed that one of its most important constituent parts, if not its essence, is to be found in a willingness to discharge the duties implied in the relation of the persons loving, in order to please or benefit each other. Love between the sexes is not the only kind of love in the world. Its specific peculiarities arise, like the specific peculiarities of all other kinds of love, from the peculiar relations and duties implied in the relation of husband and wife, which, however, operate principally by giving colour to the common sentiments of friendship and confidence, and, above all, to those which spring from the habits of society. To use the language of a very great man (employed in maintaining a proposition which to some may seem questionable) –

> It must be carefully remembered, that the general happiness of married life is secured by its indissolubility. When people understand that they must live together, except for a very few reasons known to the law, they learn to soften, by mutual accommodation, that yoke which they know they cannot shake off, and become good husbands and good wives from the necessity of remaining husbands and wives. For necessity is a powerful master in teaching the duties. If it were once understood that, upon mutual disgust, married persons might be legally separated, many a couple who now pass through the world with mutual comfort, with attention to their common offspring, and to the moral order of civil society, might have been at this moment living in a state of mutual unkindness, in a state of estrangement from their common offspring, in a state of the most licentious morality.[19]

The habit of finishing a novel with the marriage of the hero and heroine, is quite in accordance with the view of love which we have

[a] The priest's questions to the couple being married are in the future tense: e.g., 'Wilt thou love...?'

been reprobating. It would seem ludicrous to conclude the history of a man's professional career with the act of his entering upon his profession; but it is an all but universal practice to conclude a representation of him, as a social and feeling being, with his marriage. Why? Because a person is supposed to enter on a profession in order to do something in it, and to marry only to gratify his passions.

The necessity of interesting the reader by what is represented, and the necessity of suppressing all that is dull, taken together, are the reasons why novelists fall into the habit of distorting facts in order to produce an unnatural excitement of feeling.

In real life, the announcement of a person's death, or marriage, produces a certain effect, varying with our attachment to the person concerned. The same announcement about a fictitious character would produce no effect at all by its own weight; therefore, in order to make it affecting, novelists are obliged to have recourse to what we now call sentimentality. 'Affectation,' if the word were used in a more restricted sense than it generally bears, would be a more correct, though perhaps less expressive, name for the habit of mind which we wish to describe.

Etymologically, 'sentimental' ought to mean, capable of sentiment; and, inasmuch as sentiment is nothing else than feeling, every man, and indeed every animal, might be described as being in that sense 'sentimental;' but the meaning which we popularly attach to the word has become considerably extended in some respects, and much narrowed in others. It denotes, not a capability of any sort of feeling, but the habitual indulgence of one particular class of feelings; that is to say, tenderness, and principally tenderness by way of association, and it is seldom used without implying disapprobation. There are certain secondary pleasures attendant upon almost all kinds of sorrow. Sorrow calls out many good qualities, the recollection of which is in itself pleasant. The sorrow of others furnishes an occasion for the feelings of pity and generosity, as well as for that less amiable gratification implied in the '*Suave mari magno.*'a There is a certain interest and sympathy of which people in unfortunate circumstances are the object, both at their own hands and at the hands of others, such as Charles Lamb has very agreeably described in his essay on the *Pleasures of Sickness.*[20] Now, when a man describes sorrow in writing, painting, or speaking, not substantively, but with an eye to these alleviations and associations, we call such a description sentimental. Thus, the description of Lefevre's death, in *Tristram Shandy*, is

---

a Opening words of Lucretius's *De Rerum Natura* II, the first two lines of which make the point that we enjoy watching the suffering of others.

sentimental, because it is impossible to read it without feeling that it is introduced in order to set off Uncle Toby's generosity and Lefevre's affection for his son; but no one would call Burns' address to *Mary in Heaven*[21] sentimental, because there the grief is in the substantive part of the poem, and the description of scenery merely an accessory.

For our present purposes, therefore, 'sentimentality' may be described as being that way of writing which makes use of emotions of tenderness or the like, as accessories for the purpose of heightening an artistic effect, whether that effect is to be produced by the description of other feelings, or merely by the skilful handling of details. The state of human affairs is probably such that no one could conceive a consistent story without being naturally and unavoidably led to describe many painful things, and no one can be blamed for describing such subjects in a spirited manner, if he describes them gravely, and because they lie straight in his path; but we do not know of a habit more likely to injure the interests, both of art and of morals, than that of describing death and kindred subjects as accessories to matters of inferior importance, or for the sake of displaying skill in handling details.

There is one writer in our own day who entirely exemplifies our meaning: this is Mr. Dickens. . . .

Another consequence of the suppression of so large a proportion of the facts which in real life carry on the business of the world is to be found in the invention of masses of what the critics in the last century used to call 'machinery,' and what is perhaps better known in the present day under its theatrical slang name of 'business.' . . .

Mr. Dickens seems to us the greatest master of this kind of artifice, but his method is most peculiar. It consists in giving an entirely factitious prominence to minute peculiarities. He constantly gives expression, almost personality, to inanimate objects. He invests the most ordinary affairs of life with a certain charm and poetry. It is abundantly clear that this is what none but a man of genius could do. Nor is it an illusion which would be likely to deceive any one. Nobody ever lived in the world without finding plenty of dulness in it, and no quantity of verbal artifice would make him forget it; but though artifices like these may not deceive, they are still deviations from reality, and are to be allowed for before a novel can be considered as a picture of life.

There are dwarfs in real life, and the circumstance of bodily deformity no doubt exercises a powerful influence over character, but a little imp, with some slight resemblance to a man and a vast preponderance of the devil, like Quilp, or a 'recluse,' like the Black Dwarf,[22] are what Addison calls 'machines'[23] peculiar to novelists, and without representatives in real life.

III

Descriptions of scenery, especially in modern novels, often act as machines. We are tolerant of improbability and of gaps in a story, such as 'five years elapsed,' &c. &c., when they are covered by pictures of still life, such as the charming descriptions of South America, which fill up about half a volume and three very uneventful years in the wanderings of Sir Amyas Leigh, knight.[24] Such, too, are some of Mr. Dickens's descriptions of nature, which contain extremely picturesque sentences, but generally offend our taste by their obvious effort and elaboration; such, for example, is the account of the great storm at Yarmouth or of the Swiss valley, in *David Copperfield*. They would furnish very good drop-scenes to a theatre; but in the history of a man's life we can dispense with drop-scenes. The descriptions of nature in *Gil Blas*,[25] in Defoe, occasionally in Fielding, and continually in Smollett, are never obtrusive or over elaborate. They are the simple vivid impression left by striking scenery upon men who had no inclination to go about the world in the spirit of landscape painters, but who could appreciate a fine view when it came in their way. Gil Blas' journey through the Asturias, the Cavaliers' wanderings in Yorkshire, the hill on which Tom Jones and Partridge lost their way, and the infinite variety of pictures hinted at rather than drawn, in Roderick Random's journey to London, are instances of our meaning.

It is a great beauty in a novel, when the story, as it were, tells itself, without the introduction of machines to help it out.

Perhaps the most remarkable result of the arbitrary power which novel writers exercise in the selection of facts to be represented and facts to be suppressed, is to be found in the morality which they teach.

Nothing is more common than for novel writers to set out with the assumption of the truth of certain maxims of morality, and to arrange the facts of their story upon the hypothesis that every violation of those maxims entails all sorts of calamity; instead of looking at the world, and seeing for themselves whether, in point of fact, experience confirms them in the notions which they have formed as to the sanctions provided for the enforcement of such maxims. Those who act thus do not see that the honour which they intend to pay to morality is mere lip-service, and conceals a real doubt as to whether there is such a thing as a natural sanction of morality at all. If they believe that human nature and society are so constituted that the laws of morality are self-executing, they ought to recollect that the sanctions are adjusted by some fixed rule, and if so, the question, what those sanctions are, can be learnt only from experience. . . .

A novel with a moral bears the same relation to other novels as a panegyric to a biography. Instead of illustrating the particular virtues of his subject simply and naturally, the novelist is always on the watch for opportunities of bringing them in at any cost, and, if we may trust our own experience, seldom fails to make the reader utterly rebel against the maxim, or hero, as the case may be. . . .

In this, as in almost every department of novel literature, Mr. Thackeray appears to us to have conferred immense benefits on novel readers. He is the only writer that we know who does not shrink from allowing all kinds of villany to go unpunished, except by its own badness, and who makes his readers feel without preaching or effort how complete a punishment that is. The reason of this may perhaps be, that few authors feel so strongly as Mr. Thackeray that mere wealth and success in life are not all that we ought to live or to wish for; and that it is a beggarly reward, after all, for goodness, to make it heir to a large estate and a fine house. We think that Mr. Morgan[26] 'living to be one of the most respectable men in the parish of St. James's,' and Becky Sharpe keeping one of the most well-conducted stalls in Vanity Fair, are really far more edifying representations than any number of saints, pampered, very strangely to all readers of the New Testament, with all sorts of luxury, and any number of sinners consigned to a fate to which they certainly were not accustomed, when they were not plagued like other men, nor afflicted like other men, – when they had children at their desire, and left the rest of their substance to their babes.

We would recommend to all who think it necessary to warp facts in order to justify morality, the words of one of the greatest of English wits and poets: –

> Think we, like some weak prince, th' Eternal Cause
> Prone for his favourites to reverse his laws?
> .   .   .   .   .
> 'If' sometimes virtue wants while vice is fed,
> What then? is the reward of virtue bread?
> That vice may merit, 'tis the price of toil,
> The knave deserves it when he tills the soil;
> The knave deserves it when he tempts the main,
> Where folly fights for kings, or dives for gain.
> .   .   .   .   .
> What nothing earthly gives, or can destroy –
> The soul's calm sunshine, and the heart-felt joy, –
> Is virtue's prize: a better would you fix?
> Then give humility a coach-and-six,
> Justice a conqueror's sword, or Truth a gown,
> Or public spirit its great cure – a crown.[27]

In conclusion, we will indicate – it would require a book to do more – a few of the principal causes of the imperfect representations of life by novelists.

The most remarkable of these are traditional plots, the requisitions of which can hardly be complied with without a considerable warping of facts. The great majority of these plots are composed of two elements, – the adventurous, and the amatory . . . .

It has always seemed to us that the confusion of the two classes of plots of which we have spoken, spoils all novels in which it exists. The wonderful superiority of Swift and Defoe over all succeeding novelists, is owing, to a great extent, to their almost absolute freedom from this fault. Grant Gulliver his postulates, and his book is as sober, dignified, and probable as Arthur Young's *Travels in France*.[28] Smollett and Fielding have but very little of the dramatic element in their plots. *The Vicar of Wakefield* has a sort of sentimental, operatic atmosphere cast over it by Burcham's incognito, and Squire Thornhill's marriage. If Olivia's character had never been reinstated at all, the story would have been far more life-like.

Next to those of Swift and Defoe, we should most unquestionably place the plots of Fielding. They are marvellous in their simplicity and nature; and the various adventures by which they are illustrated form, as they would in real life, not the ground-work of the story told, but mere ornaments and episodes.

The whole story, for example, of *Joseph Andrews* may be told in a sentence: Joseph Andrews being dismissed from his place in London, goes into the country and marries Fanny Williams. The adventures related are merely incidental, and might all be struck out of the book without disarranging the continuity of the story. Most novels are, as it were, articulated by means of various more or less well-known dramatic contrivances.

Another curious case of an extrinsic disturbing force acting upon novels is to be found in the habit, which of late years has become so common, of using novels to ventilate opinions.

It is a common, but not, we think, a very fair objection to such books, to complain that the author does not give his critics a fair shot – that he shelters himself behind his hero, and expresses, not his own, but his puppets' opinions.

To those who consider authors as a sort of waste, over which they are entitled to common of abuse, some comfort may be given by the reflection, that by abusing the hero instead of the author, and by abusing him for those qualities which he shares with the author, they may still inflict a reasonable amount of pain; but those who are willing to consider that the object of such novels is rather to display the manner in which opinions act upon those who hold them, than to inculcate the opinions on their own grounds, will probably be content with considering how far the representation is honest.

Opinions and states of mind may, no doubt, be as legitimately made the subjects of representation as adventures, but the dangers of partiality, of dishonesty, of false morality on the part of authors, and of hasty misconception on the part of readers, is obviously at a maximum in this class of books. *Pendennis* is, perhaps, the most notable and trustworthy specimen of the class which could be mentioned. The irresolute, half-ashamed, sceptical hero, conscious of his own weakness, conscious of his own ignorance, conscious, too, of his capacity for both power and knowledge, – half envious of the vigorous delusions with which he sees one part of mankind possessed, half sympathizing with the vigorous pleasure-hunting of another class, – governed by tastes and circumstances instead of principles, but clinging, firm to old habits, to traditional lessons of truth and honour, – jotting down, sketch-book in hand, all the quaint irregularities or picturesque variations of the banks as he drifts, half-pleased, half-melancholy, down the river of life, not very bad, nor very good, nor very anything – looking, half-respectfully, half-derisively, at what the world venerates, – despising, more or less, though on other grounds, what it hates, – is one of the saddest, as it is one of the most masterly memorials of the times in which he lived which any writer ever drew for posterity.

Our most remarkable writer of this kind, after Mr. Thackeray, appears to us to be, beyond all comparisons, Mr. Kingsley. That he is a poet and a man of genius, that he has almost unrivalled power of description, and that he reproduces, with a fidelity almost marvellous, the feelings of that particular generation and class in which his lot is cast, no one, we think, who belongs to the same class and generation can doubt. The perplexities of Lancelot Smith,[29] the certainties of Amyas Leigh – who is a Lancelot Smith without perplexities, – the opinions, or rather sentiments of Alton Locke[30] and his friend – who may be like tailors, but are most unquestionably like gentlemen accidentally reduced to that occupation, – are most undeniable likenesses of the genus Englishman, species Cantabrigian tempore[a] 184-. Mr. Kingsley knows much more about Alexandria in the days of Cyril,[31] and about England in the days of Elizabeth, than we do; therefore we shall only say that it is very curious that their inhabitants should have so exactly, so curiously, and intimately resembled that particular class to which we have referred, as, from Mr. Kingsley's novels, we find they did.

[a] At the time.

Novels are also made use of at the present day, as social or political *argumenta ad misericordiam*,[a] – when they fall within the remarks which we have made upon novels written with a moral. Such, for example, are Mrs. Gaskell's novel of *Mary Barton*, written in order to bring forward certain observations of the author, and apparently to advocate a particular set of feelings respecting the condition of the poor in Manchester; and her novel of *Ruth*, written, apparently, to show that the regulations of society, with respect to female virtue, sometimes produce hardship. We have already expressed our opinion upon the general question of the introduction of morality into novels; historically considered, all these novels will have to be read with large allowances, on the score of their having been, to a great extent, party pamphlets. It is curious to observe how the artistic bias of the writer's mind gets the better of her theories. *Mary Barton* remains an excellent novel after its utter uselessness, politically speaking, is fully recognised. That poor people out of work in Manchester were very discontented and very miserable, and that being so, they behaved much as the authoress of *Mary Barton* describes their behaviour, will continue to be a fact worth representing, however notorious it may always have been, long after everybody has recognised the truth, that that fact has little or nothing to do with either the cause or the remedy of their wretchedness.

Ruth has much in it that is beautiful, even in the eyes of those who cannot see that if it were literally true it would prove anything at all. All that it shows is, that it is possible to put a case of a person who, for violating the letter, and not the spirit of the law, gets more severely punished than she would have been if the law had been made to provide for her individual case. This must be the case with all human laws. What has to be proved is that the punishments of the social law, on the subject to which *Ruth* refers, are too severe, when not only the letter, but the spirit also, of the law is violated. You do not prove that imprisonment is too severe a punishment for theft by putting the case of a child being so punished, though it had hardly realised the notion of property: you must show that it is unjust to imprison a common-place London pickpocket.

A person who reads either *Ruth* or *Mary Barton* without notice of the various social and political discussions which suggested these novels, will hardly be able to derive much experience from them. It is like reading *Caleb Williams* without knowing that Godwin was the author of *Political Justice*.

The personal character of the authors is the last disturbing force which is to be taken into account.

---

[a] Arguments designed to arouse compassion.

Life puts on very special colours when it is looked at through the medium of the feelings of a man like Swift, who seems to have been, in sober earnest, very much the kind of person that Byron wished himself to be thought. The *sæva indignatio*[a] which prompted him constantly to write what, if not inscribed with, is continually suggestive of lamentations, and mourning, and woe – showed him all things in a sort of glare, which, like the light of some distant conflagration, forms a background to all the playfulness and irony of *Gulliver's Travels*, and becomes, at last, their one great characteristic; so that after being amused at Lilliput, interested in Brobdignag, and astonished at Laputa, we feel the same kind of relief on finishing the account of the Houyhnhms as we experience on passing into the open air and cheerful streets from the ulcers and abortions of a medical museum.

Goldsmith, on the other hand, saw everything *couleur de rose*.[b] If young Primrose[32] has to travel through Europe, he makes rather a pleasant business of it. He enjoys himself more, as he tells us, with his crown piece over a bowl of punch, than the old crimp[c] to whom he has just paid its last companion with his fifty thousand pounds. When he lands on the continent he finds ways and means to see the world, not unpleasantly; he gets his board and lodging from 'those who are poor enough to be very merry,' and disputes his way cheerfully through university towns as yet unknown to tourists.

Now if anyone were to draw from Swift's book the moral that life was utterly foul and monstrous, or from Goldsmith the conclusion that even to a penniless vagabond it was a pleasant amusement, – he would be transferring to the picture the colour of the glass through which he looks at it. It would be a curious thing to construct a scale of the allowances necessary to be made in the books of different authors on this ground, like the rates of going which are ascertained for chronometers at the Greenwich Observatory.

We do not know a better corrective for timidity and despondence than the tone of 'unabashed' Defoe. Most men would have described Robinson Crusoe's career as something between life in a mad-house and life in gaol. So, too, Lockhart's *Life of Scott* is a not uninstructive commentary on the *Waverley Novels*. There is another side to that prosperous, easy-going enjoyment of life, and fine scenery, and middle-age costume, which is to be taken into account before we can let the stalwart heroes – who are constantly 'accompanying their thanks with a kiss,' and plausibly settling all the difficulties of the world, – walk out of the canvas into real life. All those volumes of

[a] Fierce indignation.   [b] Through rose-coloured glasses.
[c] One who induces men by fraud or force to enter naval or military service or – as in the case of Mr Crispe in *The Vicar of Wakefield* – to go to the American colonies as indentured servants.

correspondence about plate, linen, and furniture – all the adding house to house, and field to field – the final bankruptcy – the tragical and fruitless efforts which followed it – and the gradual breaking up of a great genius and an iron frame, are melancholy proofs that the world has more in it after all than is to be solved by the sort of boisterous, noisy, straightforward sense – sense in more ways than one – which the *Waverley Novels* seem to suggest as that sum of the whole matter which the Wise Man expressed somewhat differently.

In conclusion, we will take as an illustration of the manner in which the disturbing forces of which we have spoken may be minimized, an instance of a novel which appears to us to be, in these particulars, almost faultless; and which adds to the information and excites the feelings of its readers in a manner almost as natural and complete as if it were a real history of real facts. We allude to *Robinson Crusoe*. . . .

Taken as a whole, there is probably no book in the range of novel literature which would form an addition to the experience of its readers so nearly equivalent to that which it would have formed if it had been literally true. In so far as a novel is a poem, or a satire, or a play, or a depository for beauties, *Robinson Crusoe* has been surpassed again and again; but if a novel is properly and primarily a fictitious biography, and if we have fairly stated its general objects and effects, it is not only unsurpassed, but we may almost say unsurpassable.

It may perhaps be regretted that novels should form so large a part of the reading of young men, though it is doubtful whether in any case they are an unmixed evil. Those who idle over novels would, in their absence, idle over something else; those who are unnaturally excited by them would find a vent for that habit of mind elsewhere. But be they good or bad, useless or necessary, they circulate over the land in every possible form, and enter more or less into the education of almost every one who can read. They hold in solution a great deal of experience. It would therefore surely be a most useful thing to provide rules by which the experience might be precipitated, and to ascertain the processes by means of which the precipitate might be made fit for use. We are not so vain as to suppose that we have done much towards the accomplishment of such a task. We have done our best to point out the limits and directions of the instructions which are wanted.

William Caldwell Roscoe
(1823–1859)
From 'W. M. Thackeray,
Artist and Moralist', 1856

William Caldwell Roscoe graduated from the University of London in 1843. Called to the bar in 1850 after a period of study at the Middle Temple, he practised for only two years before delicate health (he suffered from asthma) and a probably exaggerated sense of his intellectual unfitness for the law caused him to abandon it. Following his marriage in 1855, he lived mostly in North Wales, where he was a partner in a granite quarry, until he succumbed to typhoid fever in his thirty-sixth year.

Throughout the 1850s Roscoe was active as a man of letters. He wrote two tragedies, *Eliduke, Count of Yveloc*, and *Violenzia*, and a good deal of poetry; he was one of the editors of the *Prospective Review* from July 1852 until it ceased publication in February 1855; and he contributed essays to several periodicals. Most of his critical prose apeared in the *National Review*, edited by his sister's husband, Richard Holt Hutton; indeed, every number of that quarterly from the first in July 1855 until Roscoe's death four years later contains substantial work from his pen.

In the 'Memoir of the Author' that introduces his two-volume edition of *Poems and Essays by the Late William Caldwell Roscoe* (1860), Hutton – himself one of the most accomplished of Victorian critics – bestows high praise on Roscoe's critical writings, calling them 'quite worthy to rank beside the critical essays of Hazlitt and Coleridge' (vol. 1, p. cvi). Whether or not this is an exaggeration possibly growing out of long friendship, deep affection, and family piety, it is clear that Roscoe's criticism retains much of its interest and that 'W. M. Thackeray, Artist and Moralist' is a representative specimen. It first appeared in the *National Review* for January 1856 (2: 177–213) and is reprinted in *Poems and Essays* (vol. 2, pp. 264–308). Our text of the essay is complete except for eight of Roscoe's longer quotations from Thackeray and, in all but one of these cases, the sentences that introduce them.

Roscoe always insisted that the faithful depiction of external human reality – what he calls in the essay on Thackeray the 'painting of manners' – was an inescapable part of the novelist's task. In his view, the fiction of Charlotte Brontë lacked 'permanent interest' because, without adequate opportunity to observe 'the forms of social intercourse, and the ordinary modes of expression', she was able to depict only a 'school of manners ... drawn out of her own head' (*Poems and Essays*, vol. 2, p. 342). Roscoe did commend her for her 'strong imagination' (vol. 2, p. 338), but – as the novels of Bulwer demonstrate more strikingly than those of Charlotte Brontë – a writer's art may be irreparably flawed by its 'severance from the truths of nature': 'it must rest on reality; there must be some sense in which imagination, even in its wildest flights, keeps harmony with the universe in which we live, or we recoil from its births as distorted and monstrous' (vol. 2, p. 392). Even though it may soar out of control, however, imagination is essential to the writer of fiction provided that it is properly disciplined and properly used. Thackeray is by no means the only major novelist whom Roscoe found deficient in imagination: for example, though Defoe's ability to render details is admirable according to Roscoe, his work is ultimately unsatisfactory because he 'abides in the concrete; he has no analytical perception whatever.... He has an enormous reconstructive and a very narrow creative imagination' (vol. 2, p. 235).

As the title, the content, and the structure of his essay on Thackeray will suggest, Roscoe laid great stress on the morality of fiction. But he was no narrow-minded fanatic on this subject. It was quite plain to Roscoe that a novel addresses the moral nature of the reading audience and that the conscientious modern novelist is obliged to consider what kind of moral response such a work will arouse as he or she selects and arranges the materials that go into it. *Wuthering Heights*, for instance, he judged to be 'revolting'. 'Unsparing vindictiveness and savage brutality are depicted in all their native deformity. Art throws aside her prerogative to dwell on beautiful and hint at hideous things, and lays bare to day the base actualities of coarse natures and degraded lives' (*Poems and Essays*, vol. 2, pp. 317–18). But he acknowledged that mature readers are able to distinguish between unsavoury subject matter and the ethical truths it may teach, especially when the novelist's world is remote from theirs. Defoe's novels 'deal frankly with matters about which our better modern taste is silent, and use language which shocks modern refinement'; nevertheless, despite their candor and grossness, 'they contain a deeper moral, not the less important because the writer was unconscious of its existence' (vol. 2, pp. 262–3). Even immature readers, children, are more discriminating than zealous guardians of their supposedly vulnerable virtue believe, Roscoe held. In his review of *George Cruikshank's Fairy Library* (1854), Roscoe dismissed as 'sacrilegious' such well-intentioned but clumsy attempts to purge fairy tales of morally questionable elements and convert them into edifying tracts. In such stories we find ourselves 'in the land of romance, far away from the realities of life; and the child's instincts appreciate this, and he is in no danger of adopting the guile of Puss in Boots, or the marauding disposition of Jack of the Bean-stalk. They bring him neither good nor evil in a moral point of view; but they supply food for his imagination and his sense of humour' (vol. 2, p. 518). In the world of Thackeray's writings, by contrast, the reader is very close to home; and Thackeray's moral responsibility, therefore, is quite clear.

WE are not among those who believe that the "goad of contemporary criticism" has much influence either in "abating the pride" or stimulating the imagination of authors.[1] The human system assimilates praise, and rejects censure, the latter sometimes very spasmodically. A writer or labourer of any sort rarely profits by criticism on his productions; here and there a very candid man may gather a hint; but for the most part criticism is only used by an author as a test of the good taste of his judge. It is a fiction, in fact, long religiously maintained in the forms of our reviews, that we write for the benefit of the reviewee. In most cases, and at any rate in that of a mature and established author, this didactic figment would be as well put aside. A new work, a body of writings, by a man who has attained a wide audience and produced a considerable impression on his times, constitutes a subject for investigation; we examine it as we do other matters of interest, we analyse, we dissect, we compare notes about it; we estimate its influences; and as man is the most interesting of all studies, we examine what light it throws on the producing mind, and endeavour to penetrate from the work to some insight into the special genius of the writer; – and all this for our own pleasure and profit, not because we think our remarks will prove beneficial to him who is the subject of them. Mr. Thackeray has outgrown even the big birch-rod of quarterly criticism. A long and industrious apprenticeship to the art of letters has been rewarded by a high place in his profession. He is reaping a deserved harvest of profit and fame; he can afford to smile at censure; and praise comes to him as a tribute rather than an offering. We propose, then, simply to say what we have found in the books we have read, and what light they appear to us to throw upon the genius of the author, more particularly in the two capacities we have indicated in the heading of this article.

As an Artist, he is probably the greatest painter of manners that ever lived. He has an unapproachable quickness, fineness, and width of observation on social habits and characteristics, a memory the most delicate, and a perfectly amazing power of vividly reproducing his experience. It is customary to compare him with Addison and Fielding. He has perhaps not quite such a fine stroke as the former; but the *Spectator* is thin and meagre compared with *Vanity Fair*. Fielding has breadth and vigour incomparably greater; but two of his main excellencies, richness of accessory life and variety of character, fly to the beam when weighed against the same qualities in Thackeray. Fielding takes pride to himself because, retaining the general professional identity, he can draw a distinction between two landladies. Thackeray could make a score stand out – distinct impersonations. It is startling to look at one of his novels, and see with how many people you have been brought into connection. Examine *Pendennis*. It would take a couple of pages merely to catalogue the *dramatis personæ*; every novel brings us into contact with from fifty to a hundred new and perfectly distinct individuals.

When we speak of manners, we of course include men. Manners may be described without men; but it is lifeless, colourless work, unless they are illustrated by individual examples. Still, in painting of manners, as distinguished from painting of character, the men must always be more or less subsidiary to their clothing. Mr. Thackeray tells us of a room hung with "richly carved gilt frames (with pictures in them)." Such are the works of the social satirist and caricaturist. He puts in his figures as a nucleus for his framework. A man is used to elucidate and illustrate his social environment. This is less the case with Mr. Thackeray than with most artists of the same order. He might almost be said to be characterised among them by the greater use he makes of individual portraiture, as he certainly is by the fertility of his invention. Still, at bottom he is a painter of manners, not of individual men.

The social human heart, man in relation to his kind – that is his subject. His actors are distinct and individual, – truthfully, vigorously, felicitously drawn; masterpieces in their way; but the personal character of each is not the supreme object of interest with the author. It is only a contribution to a larger and more abstract subject of contemplation. Man is his study; but man the social animal, man considered with reference to the experiences, the aims, the affections, that find their field in his intercourse with his fellow-men: never man the individual soul. He never penetrates into the interior, secret, *real* life that every man leads in isolation from his fellows, that chamber of being open only upwards to heaven and downwards to hell. He is wise to abstain; he does well to hold the ground where his pre-eminence is unapproached, – to be true to his own genius. But this genius is of a lower order than the other. The faculty that deals with and represents the individual soul in its complete relations is higher than that which we have ascribed to Mr. Thackeray. There is a common confusion on this subject. We hear it advanced on the one side, that to penetrate to the hidden centre of character, and draw from thence, – which of course can only be done by imagination, – is higher than to work from the external details which can be gathered by experience and observation; and on the other hand, that it is much easier to have recourse to the imagination than to accumulate stores from a knowledge of actual life, – to draw on the fancy than to reproduce the living scene around us. The answer is not difficult. It is easier, no doubt, to produce faint vague images of character from the imagination than to sketch from the real external manifestations of life before our eyes; and easier to make such shadows pass current, just because they are shadows, and have not, like the others, the realities ready to confront them. But take a higher degree of power, and the scale turns. It is easier to be Ben Jonson, or even Goethe, than Shakespeare. In general we may say, that the less elementary the materials of his art-structure, the less imagination does the artist require, and of the less creative kind; – the architect less than the sculptor, the historian less than the poet, the novelist less than the dramatist. Reproducers of social life have generally rather a marshalling than a creative power. And in the plot and conduct of his story Mr. Thackeray does not exhibit more than a very high power of grouping his figures and arranging his incidents; but his best characters are certainly creations, living breathing beings, characteristic not only by certain traits, but by that atmosphere of individuality which only genius can impart. Their distinctive feature and their defect, as we have before stated, is this, that not one of them is complete; each is only so much of an individual as is embraced in a certain abstract whole. We never know any one of them completely, in the way we know ourselves, in the way we imagine others. We know just so much of them as we can gather by an intercourse in society. Mr. Thackeray does not penetrate further; he does not profess to show more. He says openly this is all he knows of them. He relates their behaviour, displays as much of the feelings and the character as the outward demeanour, the actions, the voice, can bear witness to, and no more. It is exactly as if you had met the people in actual life, mixed constantly with them, known them as we know our most intimate friends. Of course this is all we can *know* of a man; but not all we can imagine, not all the artist can, if he chooses, convey to us. We don't know our nearest friends; we are always dependent on our imagination. From the imperfect materials that observation and sympathy can furnish we construct a whole of our own, more or less comformable to the reality according to our opportunities of knowledge, and with more or less completeness and distinctness according to our imaginative faculty; and every man, of course, is something really different from that which every man around him conceives him to be. But without this imaginative conception we should not know one another at all, we should only have disconnected hints of contemporary existence.

It is perhaps the highest distinguishing prerogative of poetry or fiction, or whatever we choose as the most comprehensive name for that art which has language for its medium, that it gives the artist the power of delineating the actual interior life and individual character of a living soul. It is the only art that does so. The dramatist and the novelist have the power of imagining a complete character, and of presenting before you their conception of it; and the more complete this is, and the more unmistakably they can impress you with the idea of it in its fulness and in its most secret depths, the nearer they attain to the perfection of their art. Thackeray leaves the reader to his own imagination. He gives no clues to his character, as such; he is not leading to an image of his own. He probably has a very distinct, but no complete conception of them himself; he knows no more of them than he tells us. He is interested more in the external exhibitions of character and the feelings than in character itself; his aim is not to reproduce any single nature, but the image that the whole phenomenon of social life has left impressed on his mind. . . .

Individual character, however, is the deeper and more interesting study; and the writings prompted by genius which delights more in the habits and qualities and casual self-delineations of man than in man himself, always disappoint us by our half-acquaintance with the personages of the story. As for the subsidiary middle-distance people, this matters little. We know as much as we wish to do of Sir Pitt Crawley, of Lord Steyne, of the Major, of Jack Belsize, of Mrs. Hobson Newcome, of Mrs. Mackenzie; but how glad should we be to see more into the real heart of Major Dobbin, of Becky, even of Osborne of Warrington, of Laura; even of shallow and worldly Pendennis, how partial and limited, how merely external, is our conception! What do we know really of the Colonel,[2] beyond that atmosphere of kindliness and honesty which surrounds one of the most delightful creations poet ever drew? But why complain? Distinctness and completeness of conception are two qualities divided among artists; to one this, to the other that; rarely, perhaps never, has any single man been gifted with a large measure of both. If Mr. Thackeray's genius is not of the very highest order, it is the very highest of its kind. The vividness, the accuracy of his delineation goes far to compensate for a certain want of deeper insight. Let us be grateful for what he gives us, rather than grumble because it is not more. Let us take him as that which he is – a daguerreotypist of the world about us. He is great in costume, in minutiæ too great; he leans too much on them; his figures are to Shakespeare's what Madame Tussaud's waxworks are to the Elgin Marbles – they are exact figures from modern life, and the resemblance is effected somewhat too much by the aid of externals; but there is a matchless sharpness, an elaborateness and finish of detail and circumstantiality about his creations. He has an art peculiarly his own of reproducing every-day language with just enough additional sparkle or humour or pathos of his own to make it piquant and entertaining without losing vraisemblance. His handling of his subject, his execution, are so skilful and masterly, that they for ever hold the attention alive. He takes a commonplace and makes a novelty of it, as a potter makes a jug out of a lump of clay by turning it round in his hands; he tells you page after page of ordinary incident with the freshness of a perennial spring. He is master of the dramatic method which has of late preponderated so much over the narrative. Perhaps the greatest attraction of his writings consists in the wonderful appropriateness of the language and sentiments he puts into the mouths of his various characters; and he not only makes them express themselves, but he manages, without any loss of dramatic propriety, to heighten the tone so as to give some charm or other to what every one says; and not only this, but with an ease which veils consummate dexterity, he makes these dramatic speeches carry on the action and even convey the author's private inuendo. . . .

If the power of producing the impression of reality were the test of the highest creative power, Thackeray would perhaps rank higher than any one who has ever lived, – higher than Defoe.[3] But Thackeray's mode of creating an impression of reality is more complicated than Defoe's. It is not that simple act of force by which the latter identifies himself with his hero. It arises in great measure from his way of knitting his narrative on at every point to some link of our every-day experience. His fiction is like a net, every mesh of which has a connecting knot with actual life. Many novelists have a world of their own they inhabit. Thackeray thrusts his characters in among the moving everyday world in which we live. We don't say they are life-like characters; they are mere people. We feel them to be near us, and that we may meet them any day. Dickens creates a race of beings united to us by common sympathies and affections, endeared to us by certain qualities, and infinitely amusing in their eccentricities. Still, we all know perfectly well they are not really human beings; though they are enough so for his purpose and ours. No one supposes that Carker every really rode on that bay horse of his to the city with those shining teeth; that Traddle's hair really had power to force open a pocket-book. We know that the trial of Bardell v. Pickwick is an imaginary contribution to our judicial records, and that Edith Dombey exists only in highflown language and the exigencies of melodrama.[4] But the Major frequents Bond Street, Mrs. Hobson Newcome's virtue is a thing of this life and of London, and it is but one step from questioning the existence of Becky's finished little house in Curzon Street to admitting the philosophy of Berkeley.[5] All artists have an ultimate aim which shapes their working. Miss Bronte wishes to depict marked character; Dickens bends himself to elicit the humorous element in things; Bulwer supposes that he has a philosophy to develop; Disraeli sets himself to be himself admired. Thackeray only desires to be a mirror, to give a true but a brilliant reflection; his vision is warped, no doubt, by peculiarities of his own; but his aim is to reproduce the world as he sees it.

His conception of a story is, like his conception of a character, incomplete. There is no reason why he should begin where he does, no reason why he should end at all. He cuts a square out of life, just as much as he wants, and sends it to Bradbury and Evans.[6] In *Vanity Fair* and *Pendennis* the characters are at large, and might at any moment be gathered in to a conclusion. The *Newcomes* begins with the history of Clive's grandfather, and the reasons are independent of art which cause it to conclude before the death of his grandchildren. This, however, is little more than a technical shortcoming, and certainly does not much affect the reader, to whom skill in the conduct of the story is infinitely more important. And in the conduct of his story, in the management of his narrative, in the interlinking of incident, the way in which one character is made to elucidate another, in which every speech and every entrance carries on the action, in the ease, the grace, the hidden skill with which the intricate complication of interests and events are handled and developed, Mr. Thackeray justly claims our highest admiration. In all that belongs to execution he shows a mastery that almost makes us think he has some secret peculiar power, so effortless is his brilliancy, so easy his touch. His tale is like a landscape growing under the instinctive rather than conscious hand of a master.

The novelist who draws the external life of men is subject to this disadvantage: he is more dependent on his experience than the one who makes individual character his end. It is true, we apprehend, that a poet can, by the force of imagination, and the excitement of particular parts of his nature so as to produce temporary identification, create a character which he has never seen. Goethe bears witness to the fact in his own case. He tells us he drew in his youth characters of which he had no experience, and the truthfulness of which was justified by his mature observation.[7] His evidence is peculiarly valuable, both because no man estimated observation higher, and because his great skill in it would enable him to apply an adequate test to the accuracy of the delineations which he speaks of as springing ready-formed from the resources of his own nature. Of course, even granting that a man could be entirely independent of observation in his conception of a character, he would still require it in order to find a field for the display of that conception; and the more knowledge he commands, the better can he develop his idea. Less, however, will suffice for such an artist than for one who works like Thackeray or Fielding. These are absolutely bounded by the limits of their observation, and consequently in constant danger of self-repetition. Mr. Thackeray is remarkable rather for his exhaustless ingenuity in making the most of the knowledge he possesses than for any very wide range. His fertility becomes the more remarkable when we survey the resources on which he draws. His field is not an extensive one. He stands on the debatable land between the aristocracy and the middle classes – that is his favourite position – and he has evidently observed this form of life mainly from dining-rooms and drawing-rooms. He surveys mankind from the club-room and from country-houses; he has seen soldiers chiefly at mess-dinners; is not familiar with lawyers, though he is with the Temple; has seen a good deal of a painter's life, and must of course have had a considerable knowledge of the professional world of letters, though he is shy of profiting by this experience. He is not at home in provincial life in England, especially town-life, nor has he any extensive acquaintance with the feelings and habits of the lower classes. His knowledge of men about town is profound, exhaustive; his acquaintance among footmen vast. He may have more materials in store; but he begins to indicate a check in the extent of his resources. We know the *carte-du-pays*[a] pretty well now, and have a notion where the boundary-fence runs. The extraordinary thing is the immense variety of the surface within it.

There is one direction, however, in which Mr. Thackeray's resources have always been remarkably limited. It is curious how independent he is of thought; how he manages to exist so entirely on the surface of things. Perhaps he is the better observer of manners because he never cares to penetrate below them. He never refers to a principle, or elucidates a rule of action. But this latter is a characteristic which belongs rather to his character as a moralist than an artist. What we are now concerned with is the absence from his books of what we are accustomed to call ideas. In this respect Thackeray is as inferior to Fielding, as in some others we cannot help thinking him superior. Fielding, you cannot help seeing as you read, was a reflecting man; you feel that his writings are backed by a body of thought, though it is far from an intrusive element in them. Defoe always leaves the impression of an active, vigorous intellect. The force of Thackeray's writings is derived from the strength of his feelings; great genius he

[a] Map of the country.

has, and general vigour of mind, but not the *intellectus cogitabundus*.[a]
Read his charming and eloquent Lectures on the Humorists. You
would suppose that thought would ooze out there if any where; but
there is no trace of it. He simply states his impressions about the men;
and when he speaks of their personal characters, every deference is to
be paid to the conception of one who has so sensitive an apprehension
of the distinguishing traits of various natures. We are far from wishing
for a change in the method of the book; we believe the sort of quiet
meditative way in which Mr. Thackeray touches and feels about and
probes these men is more valuable and instructive than any elaborate
reasonings on them would be, and infinitely better calculated to
convey just impressions of what they really were like. But the omission
of thought is not the less a characteristic feature; and on one of the
pages, where a note of Coleridge is appended to Thackeray's estimate
of Sterne, it is curious to see two such utterly opposite modes of
approaching a subject brought into juxtaposition.[8] Thackeray never
reasons, he never gains one step by deduction; he relies on his
instincts, he appeals to the witness within us; he makes his statement,
and leaves it to find its own way to the conviction of his readers; either
it approves itself to you, and you accept it, or it does not, and you leave
it. The highest moral truths have been thus enunciated, perhaps can
only be thus enunciated; but Mr. Thackeray does not enunciate great
truths. The most he does is to generalise on his social observation. He
is not absolutely destitute of some of those distilled results of a wide
knowledge of men which properly come under the head of wisdom;
but they are very disproportioned to the extent and penetration of his
perception. He occupies a good deal of space in half-meditative,
half-emotional harangues on the phenomena of life. Where these do
not immediately deal with the affections, they owe their novelty and
value to their form alone; and it would not be difficult to enumerate
his chief ideas, and count how often they occur. He impresses on us
very constantly that 'the Peerage'[9] is the Upas-book[b] of English
society; that our servants sit in judgment on us below stairs; that good
wages make a better nurse than love; that bankers marry earls'
daughters, and *vice versâ*; that the pangs of disappointed passion stop
short of death; that no man making a schedule of his debts ever
included them all. We need not go through the list; and trite as such
sayings seem when stripped bare for enumeration, the author for ever
invests them with some fresh charm of expression or illustration,
which goes far to preserve them from becoming wearisome. It is with

[a] Thoughtful comprehension.
[b] Poisonous or evil book.

the feelings and the affections that Mr. Thackeray is at home. They supply with him the place of reasoning-power. Hence he penetrates deeper into the characters of women than of men. He has never drawn, nor can he ever draw, a man of strong convictions or thoughtful mind; and even in women he deals almost exclusively with the instinctive and emotional side of their nature. This feature gives a certain thinness and superficiality to Mr. Thackeray's works. He nowhere leaves the mark of a thinker. Even his insight is keen and delicate rather than profound. But his deep and tender feeling makes him sensitive to those suggestions which occupy the boundary-land between the affections and the intellect, the country of vain regrets and tender memories, of chastened hopes and softened sadness, the harvest-field in every human soul of love and death. The voice of Mr. Thackeray's tenderness is at once sweet and manly; and when he will allow us to feel sure he is not sneering at himself, its tone is not unworthy to speak to the most sacred recesses of the heart. . . .

Is there in the range of fiction any thing more touching than the conception which took the shattered heart of the old Colonel to rest among the pensioners of Grey Friars?

Mr. Thackeray's pathos is good; but his humour is better, more original, more searching. He never rests in the simply ludicrous or absurd. Irony is the essence of his wit. His books are one strain of it. He plays with his own characters. In the simplest things they say the author himself gets a quiet backstroke at them. It is not enough for him to depict a man ridiculous, he makes him himself expose his own absurdities, and gathers a zest from the unconsciousness with which he does so. He treats his *dramatis personae* as if he were playing off real men. His wit is not a plaything, but a weapon, and must cut something whenever it falls; it may be a goodnatured blow, but it must touch some one. He never fences against the wall. His satire is most bitter when he is most cool. He is skilful in the management of sneer and inuendo, and can strike a heavy blow with a light weapon. For his broadest absurdities he chooses the form of burlesque, and then he likes to have a definite something to parody. He is one who does not laugh at his own story. It is not often he makes his reader laugh; but he can do it if he will. Foker is the best of his more laughable creations.[10] In general he is grave, composed, even sad, but he is never uninterested in the personal adventures he is engaged in narrating; his sympathies are always keenly alive, though often he prefers to conceal how they are enlisted. At bottom he has a warm, almost a passionate interest in his own creations. They are realities to him as to the rest of the world.

His peculiar powers must tempt him to personality, but in any open form of it he does not now indulge. The early days of Blackwood and Fraser are gone by.[11] There was a time, however, when he gave 'Sawedwadgeorgeearllittnbulwig' a very severe, though not ungenerous shaking; and when himself attacked by the *Times* he turned and bit fiercely and sharply.[12] He is apt to wear the forms of his wit to tatters. Jeames, with his peculiar dialect, in the *Yellowplush Papers* and elsewhere, was entertaining and instructive, but has been allowed to grow wearisome. Orthographical absurdity is an exhaustible subject of merriment, and Mr. Thackeray's wit is somewhat too much dependent on his nice appreciation of distinctions of pronounciation, and the slavish subserviency he compels from the art of spelling. He can mimic in print as well or better than Dickens. His sense of humour differs from that of the latter, however, in being almost exclusively called forth by the peculiarities of persons themselves, or personal relations. He very rarely is struck with the ludicrous in things alone, as Dickens often is; his description of Costigan's hairbrush, as "a wonderful and ancient piece,"[13] stands almost by itself; he rarely even makes fun out of a man's personal appearance, except so far as his dress or air indicate some mental trait or characteristic. The mode of his caricaturing, too, is quite different. Dickens collects all the absurdities and laughter-moving elements in a thing, and heaps them together in a new image of his own. Thackeray pictures the thing as it is, only bringing out its ludicrous or contemptible features into sharp relief.

His genius does not lead him to the poetic form; he has just that command of verse which one would expect from a man of his great ability; he can make an able use of it, and his power of language gives him great command of rhyme and sufficient facility. His verses are generally reproductions; free renderings from another language with new point and application, parodies or humorous narratives of actual incident. Among these the "Chronicle of the Drum" is the best. It is thoroughly French, dramatic, and spirit-stirring. "Jacob Homnium's Hoss" far surpasses all his other humorous efforts in verse. . . .[14]

His sense of beauty is warm and lively. If he had as much of the negative sense of good taste which discards the ugly and jarring elements as he has of the positive sense which detects and appreciates the beautiful, his works would be far pleasanter reading. He sees beauty every where; his love of it mingles with the affectionateness of his nature, and throws a softening grace over his pages, relieving a bitterness which without it would sometimes be scarcely sufferable. Though his genius leads him to deal with men, external nature has no light charms for him. He does not often paint landscape, but he can do so in brief exquisite touches. Most of us are familiar with some such a German scene as this:

Pleasant Rhine gardens! Fair scenes of peace and sunshine; noble purple mountains, whose crests are reflected in the magnificent stream; who has ever seen you that has not a grateful memory of those scenes of friendly repose and beauty? To lay down the pen, and even to think of that beautiful Rhineland, makes one happy. At this time of summer-evening the cows are trooping down from the hills, lowing, and with their bells tinkling, to the old town, with its old moats, and gates, and spires, and chestnut-trees, with long blue shadows stretching over the grass; the sky and the river below flame in crimson and gold; and the moon is already out, looking pale towards the sunset. The sun sinks behind the great castle-crested mountains; the night falls suddenly; the river grows darker and darker; lights quiver in it from the windows in the old ramparts, and twinkle peacefully in the villages under the hills on the opposite shore.[15]

Of his bad taste his works furnish only too abundant evidence. It was a happy idea to look at society from the footman's point of view; but a very little of that sort of fun suffices. And Mr. Thackeray does not scruple to surfeit us. We have rough Warrington's excellent authority for the assertion, that "Mrs. Flanagan the laundress, and Betty the housemaid, are not the company a gentleman should choose for permanent association;"[16] and we are not surprised at that "most igstrorinary" burst of indignation with which Jeames's career draws to its close in the *Yellowplush Papers*.[17]

The advantage of using such a mouthpiece, if it be an advantage, is this, that it gives an opportunity of saying things more vulgar, biting, and personal, than a man's self-respect or shame would allow him to say out of his own mouth. It is a *quasi* shifting of the responsibility. But if we give Sheridan credit for his wit, we must give Thackeray credit for his vulgarity. This feature greatly disfigures his works, and shows itself not only in the gusto and ease with which he enters into the soul of a footman, but in a love of searching out and bringing into prominent view the more petty and ignoble sides of all things. We don't quarrel with a humorist for exposing the vulgar element in a vulgar man, and in taking all the fun he can out of it. Self-delineative dramatic vulgarity, used in moderation, is one of the fairest and readiest sources of laughter. What we quarrel with is vulgarity in the tone of the work; a charge for which it is not very easy to cite chapter and verse, as it is a thing which is felt by the instinct rather than detected by observation; but we will adduce one instance of the sort of thing we allude to. In the first volume of *The Newcomes* we are told how Warrington and Pendennis gave a little entertainment at the Temple, including among their guests little Rosey and her mother. It is a very pleasant charming picture, and the narrator speaks of the

"merry songs and kind faces," the "happy old dingy chambers illumi-
nated by youthful sunshine." What unhappy prompting, then, makes
him drop this blot on his description: "I may say, without false
modesty, that our little entertainment was most successful. The
champagne was iced to a nicety. The ladies did not perceive *that our
laundress, Mrs Flanagan, was intoxicated very early in the afternoon.*"
And before the end of the description we are not spared another
allusion to "Mrs. Flanagan in a state of excitement."[18] It is vulgar,
surely, to mar the pure and pleasant impression of the scene with this
image of the drunken laundress not only introduced, but insisted on.

Not from false taste, but from something deeper, – a warp in the
very substance of his genius, – arises another unwelcome characteristic. *Vanity Fair* is the name, not of one, but of all Mr. Thackeray's
books. The disappointment that waits upon human desires, whether
in their fulfilment or their destruction, the emptiness of worldly
things, the frailty of the affections, the sternness of fate, the hopeless-
ness of endeavour, *vanitas vanitatum*, – these are his themes. The
impression left by his books is that of weariness; the stimulants
uphold you while you read; and then comes just such a reaction as if
you had really mingled closely in the great world with no hopes or
ambitions outside it; you feel the dust in your throat, the din and the
babbling echo in your ears. Art may touch the deepest sources of
passion: awe and grief and almost terror are as much within her
province as laughter and calm; she may shake the heart, and leave it
quivering with emotions whose intensity partakes of pain; but to
make it unsatisfied, restless, anxious, – this is not her province. To
steep it in the turmoil, the harass, the perpetual shortcomings of actual
life, may possibly be sometimes permissible. But this must only be for
a brief period – it is a very exceptional source of excitement; and to
drop the curtain and leave the mind jaded with small discontents,
perplexed with unsolved difficulties, and saddened with the shortcomings of fruition, – this is to be false to the high and soothing
influences of art, and to misuse the power she gives. Those old
story-books show a deeper sense of her true province who marry a
couple and tell us they lived happily till they died, than Mr. Thackeray,
who cannot forbear from turning over one more page to show us the
long-beloved and hardly-won Amelia scarcely sufficing to her
husband, and who brings back the noble-hearted Laura to teach us
that she cannot escape the consequences to her own demeanour and
character of having married a man so far inferior to herself.

As a Moralist, his philosophy might be called a religious stoicism
rooted in fatalism. The stoicism is patient and manly; kindly though

melancholy. It is not a hardened endurance of adverse fate, so much as an unexamining inactive submission to the divine will. . . .

His fatalism is connected with a strong sense of the powerlessness of the human will. He is a profound sceptic. Not a sceptic in religious conviction, or one who ignores devotional feeling, – far from it; but a sceptic of principles, of human will, of the power in man to ascertain his duties or direct his aims. He believes in God *out of the world*. He loves to represent man as tossing on the wild sea, driven to and fro by wind and waves, landing now on some shining fortunate isle, where the affections find happy rest, and now driven forth again into the night and storm; consoled and strengthened now and then by the bright gleams above him; dexterous with his helm to avoid or conquer the adverse elements; but destitute of all knowledge of navigation, and with no port to steer for and no compass to guide his course. Pleasure, he tells you, may and perhaps should be plucked while you are young; but he warns you the zest will fail; he warns you that gratified ambition will taste like ashes in the mouth, that fame is a delusion, that the affections, the sole good of life, are often helpless under the foot of adverse fortune, and neither so powerful nor so permanent as we dream; and he can only recommend you to enjoy honestly, to suffer bravely, and to wear a patient face. He speaks to you as one fellow-subject to another of the Prince of this world. He has no call to set things right, no prompting to examine into the remedy. His vocation is to show the time as it is, and especially where it is out of joint. His philosophy is to accept men and things as they are.

He is a very remarkable instance of the mode in which the force of the intellect affects the moral nature and convictions. We apprehend he never asked "why?" in his life, except perhaps to prove to another that he had no because. With a very strong sense of the obligation of moral truthfulness, and the profoundest respect for, and sympathy with, simplicity and straightforwardness of character, he has no interest in intellectual conclusions. He would never have felt sufficient interest to ask with Pilate, "What is truth?"[19] Always occupied with moral symptoms, intently observing men, and deeply interested in their various modes of meeting the perplexities of life, he never attempts to decide a moral question. He rarely discusses one at all; and when he does so, he is studiously careful to avoid throwing his weight into either scale. Elsewhere ready enough to show in his proper person, he here shrinks anxiously out of sight. Sometimes he warns you expressly he will not be responsible for what he is putting into the mouth of one of his characters; or more often he treats the subject like a shuttlecock, raps it to and fro between two dramatic disputants, and lets it fall in the middle for those to pick up who list.

From this form of mind springs, in great measure, that scepticism to which we have alluded. A writer can scarcely help being sceptical who sees all sides of a question, but has gathered no principles to help him to choose among them; who has no guiding rules to which to refer, and whose instincts alone prevent the field of his conscience from being an absolute chaos. Only by these instincts he tests the character of men and the propriety of actions; and wherever they alone can serve as guides, they do so faithfully, for in him they are honest and noble. . . .

. . . *Pendennis* is throughout the least agreeable of Mr. Thackeray's fictions. A work more purposeless, or one in which all grounds of action and elements of judgment are more distorted and confused, it is scarcely possible to imagine. Arthur Pendennis is represented as a young man of warm impetuous feelings, a lively intellect, much self-conceit, and a natural selfishness of disposition fostered by early indulgence. The highest and sole attractive points in his character are a sense of honour and a capacity for love. In early youth he is carried away by an impetuous passion for an uneducated woman, whose beauty is her sole attraction. Forcibly weaned from his first devotion, he goes to college, where his sole ambition is for social display, and where he falls a victim to his vanity and weakness. Returning home, he idles away some time, entangling himself more or less with a clever wicked little flirt in the neighbourhood. He goes to London, takes to review-writing as a means of support, strives to write honestly; has written a novel, dresses it up for the public, publishes it, and gains a reputation by it; moves meanwhile, by the interest of his uncle – a thorough man of the world and of the clubs – among high circles of fashionable life, and loves to study them and all other forms of life; lives in every way – in earning his maintenance, in intellect, in emotion – from hand to mouth; has no ambition, no convictions, and is utterly destitute of any object in life and of any incitement to action beyond the temporary requisitions or the chance stimulants of the day. . . .

Pendennis was decidedly becoming worldly, and was very far from being what every man ought to be, and what most men, let us hope, are in at least some higher degree than he was. But Mr. Thackeray must not argue as if we were in danger of charging him with worldliness because he went down into the battle of life and accepted his place among those conditions which the divine wisdom has appointed for the activity of man. It is not this that makes him worldly, but because he has no life and no interests above this struggle to ennoble and give a meaning to it. Because he floats down the stream aimless, and with no thought beyond the momentary excitements of the rapid course. Because he is utterly immersed in worldly interests and worldly enjoyments; because his ends, as far as he can be said to have any, as well as his activity, are worldly. This is why we condemn Pendennis. Following this life, he comes accidentally across a charming little porter's daughter, who falls violently in love with him, and for whom he conceives a sudden passion. Not the man to marry thus, he rises superior to trifling with a temptation, and shows resolution and, what he is never indicated as wanting, generous and honourable impulse. Subsequently he consents to marry his old flirting little friend, for whom he has no love (as he honestly tells her), because she brings him wealth and a seat in Parliament. He finds that so dishonourable a condition is annexed to the acceptance of these advantages that he is bound to refuse them; but in doing so he will not break the engagement of honour which binds him to Blanche Amory, although he has discovered that the true leaning of his heart is towards Laura, his mother's ward, who has loved him from old times. The faithlessness of his *fiancée* rescues him, and allows him to marry her whom he really prefers. He does so, and the spirit of his life remains that which was before indicated. He continues a kind-hearted, conceited, clever, self-centered, sceptical man of this world purely. The history concludes with a few sentences, in which the author briefly vindicates it as being a picture in conformity with the actual arrangements of divine providence; and invites us, "knowing how mean the best of us is," to "give a hand of charity to Arthur Pendennis, with all his faults and shortcomings, who does not claim to be a hero, but only a man and a brother."[20] We must be allowed to observe in passing, that though we dare not refuse the hand of charity to Mr. Pendennis, it costs a struggle to give it; and that any thing further, such as affection or respect, we are quite unable to feel. We have no wish to be intimate with him. We find him intensely disagreeable, ill-bred, and ostentatiously offensive. But this is purely a personal matter, and may be referred partly to envy of his superior talents, partly to disgust at his inordinate self-conceit. What we have to do with is the moral view taken by the author. It is characteristic that, while professing to lay bare the weaknesses and shortcomings of Pendennis's worldly life, he does not once touch the root of the matter, or indicate the true want of this wasted spirit. To a mind like Arthur's, which measures the emptiness of all worldly subjects of ambition, it is more than to any other essential that it should have some gleam of insight and some practical interest in the higher diviner life which embraces this. And Arthur, orthodox, church-going Christian as he no doubt is, is a practical atheist. With a pure and awful reverence for the manifestations of holiness in others, gazing on a woman praying as with the reverted eyes of one justly banished from Paradise, and himself not without pious impulses, he lives without God in the world. And if we were to lay our hand on the most deep-seated failing of Mr. Thackeray's works, we should find it, not in his sneers or in his contemptuous estimate of human nature, but in the low level on which the whole body of his creation stands, and in the narrow boundaries within which the whole is enclosed. We should have no quarrel with an artist who should paint the world as it is, ay, and in far truer colours than Mr. Thackeray dares to use; but then he must embrace the true scope of life, he must not ignore those higher connections from which alone it acquires a purpose, and reduce it to a medley fit only to move the laughter of fools and the tears and scorn of the wise. It is not enough to gaze on the varied conditions of man, and say, We accept them, they are manifestations of the divine will. One can almost imagine that the faith of an animal rises to this uninformed acceptance of the conditions of existence. To man it is granted to touch here and there the general clue of the divine purpose, and to hold ever by that thread which belongs to his individual soul; to him is given a modifying will, a power of choice, and an active energy; of him that highest of all things has been said, that he may be a fellow-worker with God. Even in the minutiæ of his daily life he may follow that service which is perfect freedom, and only not be a servant because he has the higher tenderer invitation to be a child. Is it answered, that these themes are too serious for the novelist, the entertainer of lighter hours, the comic-tale writer? Then we say, that as long as a writer confines himself to fragmentary sketches of life, to its superficial humours or sentiments, the answer is good; and that we have no objection whatever to take the entertainment at its full worth, and laugh gaily with Grimaldi in the pantomime or Mathews in the farce.[21] But Mr. Thackeray never cultivated this sort of literature in spirit, though he may for a time have availed himself of its ordinary forms. His genius is too large, too penetrating, too grave to move in this sphere. He professes to paint human life; and he who does so, and who does not base his conception on that religious substructure which alone makes it other than shreds of flying dreams, is an incomplete artist and a false moralist. And Mr. Thackeray cannot be sheltered behind the assertion that a fitting reverence precludes the intermingling of religious ideas with light literature, – first, because what we ask for does not demand a constant presence of the religious element on the surface, or indeed that it should appear there at all, –

only that the spirit of the work and the picture of life should recognise it as at the foundation, or even only not utterly lose sight of it as a fundamental element in the conception of this world; and secondly, because he does not scruple (and fitly, we think) reverently to introduce the topic of religion, and to picture a humble spirit looking upwards for consolation and support; – because, while he includes the *sentiment*, he excludes the *realities* of religion, and has no place for those aspirations of the higher life, only to form the field for which, was this world he deals with created. And this further quarrel we have with Mr. Thackeray's picture – that he gives a worldly view of the world; that through sarcasm and satire there shines every where a real undue appreciation of worldly things – most, of those things he is most bitter against – money and rank; and above all, a debasing sensitiveness to the opinion of those around us, apart from any regard for them and independently of any respect for their judgment. He reads as if he had a consciousness in himself of too great an appreci-ation of these things, against which his moral indignation is always in arms, and to which his honesty compels him to give expression; as if the bitterness of his jests were founded on that temper the poet speaks of –

> Out of that mood was born
> Self-scorn, and then laughter at that self-scorn.[22]

Otherwise, by what strange distortion can a man of Mr. Thackeray's mind and heart have allowed himself to become absorbed in the contemplation of meanness and false shame and the world's low worship of mere worldly advantages? How can he have permitted so unpleasant a subject to grow on him till it has become the atmosphere of his thoughts? As Swift rakes in dirt, so Thackeray in meanness. He loves to anatomise its every form, to waylay and detect it at every corner, to turn it inside out, to descant on it, to conjugate it. He sees English society worshipping a golden and titled calf, and he angrily dashes down the image; but that is not enough; he grinds it to powder, and mingles it in every draught he gives us. We know there are these things in the world; but the question is, whether an author is well employed in constantly forcing them on our attention. All will agree that the less a man can be affected by them the better; we know these meannesses and basenesses are in our own natures; but the true way to deal with them is, looking upwards, to tread them under foot, not to go scraping about with our noses to the ground and taking credit for our humility and honesty when we lay them bare. They grow thick enough in our own soil and in our neighbours', if we choose to devote ourselves to the search. Any man will succeed in distorting and confusing his moral judgment, if he will but search long enough among his mixed motives to lay hold of the mean or selfish element, and do but give it attention enough when he has found it. Grant, if you will, that an element of self-interest mingles in all we do; are we likely to lose it by always looking for it? Is there any thing less edifying than Mr. Thackeray's way of showing up the meannesses and mixed motives of our neighbours, and then turning sharply on his readers, crying, "You're as bad, I'm as bad, we are none of us better than our neighbours; allow me to continue to excoriate them"? The remedy for these failings is not in exposing and railing at them. It is in raising men out of the atmosphere of them. The highest and the surest escape is the same we spoke of before, as transmuting life by a divine alchemy from barrenness, emptiness, and vanity into a harvest-field of rich opportunities and a battle-field for high ambition. Just in the degree in which a man's secret soul is occupied by a life at once within and outside this life will the small vexations of life and the pettinesses of others and even of himself fail to trouble him; the more he can absorb himself in a loftier pursuit, the more heedlessly will he brush through the nettles which Mr. Thackeray will have us sit down in to examine.

But apart from these considerations, any vivid interests powerful enough thoroughly to occupy a man suffice to set him free from this morbid and one-sided scrutiny of himself and his neighbours. But Mr. Thackeray not only narrows the field of life – he ignores the main avenues which, within the boundaries of the world he describes, are available as an escape both from an unhealthy sensitiveness to the meanness around us and within us, and from that burdening ever-presence of self under which almost all his characters labour.

Wide as is his knowledge of men, he seems to have little acquaintance with affairs. He paints men almost entirely in their moments of relaxation. He never describes a man carried out of himself by strong practical aims and interests. He is unwilling to recognise, seems scarcely to believe, that men ever have disinterested motives, or can be deeply occupied by other things than the demands of the feelings or the exigencies of gaining a livelihood. He laughs to scorn the idea that a man in writing, for instance, can have any higher object than to gain a money reward. He will have it that writing is a trade, and that all the writer can aspire to in the way of lofty aims is to write honestly, and without false exaggeration of sentiment or wilful distortion of fact. And on this latter point he speaks strongly and well, and with a vivid consciousness of some of an author's most immediate sources of temptation. It is true, perhaps, that the art of letters has become unduly subservient to money gains, that even men of genius are apt to consider too closely not what their own conception of what is best and highest prompts them to, but what will tell best in securing a popular acceptance; and that they too often wait timidly and obsequiously on the public taste of the day. Yet this spirit is not so universal as Mr. Thackeray would have us think. Letters still leave a man free to be true to himself and his art, as well as to the ordinary exigencies of honesty. Even if they did not, there are plenty of other careers in which a man may forget himself in devotion to something beyond him. And in the case of the painter, indeed, Mr. Thackeray can see that while the artist labours for bread, his very choice of his profession as a means of making bread shows his love for it, and that as he who preaches the Gospel may justly live by it, the fact that he lives by his art is by no means inconsistent with a conscious devotion to its own high ends, or with his finding in a pure love for it the truest and most powerful source of his activity. . . .

As a rule, however, the author of *Vanity Fair* never represents a man as taken out of himself, except in some instances by the passions or the affections which approach nearest to instincts. He produces his characters on the stage generally only in their hours of idleness or amusement; and though he may indicate external occupation, he never (save, perhaps, in the sketch of J. J.[23]) indicates an absorbing external interest. All his characters are self-engrossed, most of them self-seeking. Of Pendennis he tells us openly, "ours, as the reader has possibly already discovered, is a selfish story, and almost every person, according to his nature more or less generous than George, and according to the way of the world, as it seems to us, is occupied about Number One."[24] The occasion which calls out this expression of conviction indicates the source from which it springs. No man can set too high a value on the affections, but too exclusive a one he easily may; and this, as we have before indicated, is Mr. Thackeray's danger. He sees that the purest passion, the strongest personal friendship, and still more, the holy instinct of maternal love, – which he so admires and reverences that he seems to approach the subject on bended knee, – have mingled in their very essence a tincture of self; and finding it here, it seems easy to him to assume that no province of human life can possibly be free from it. Whereas, in fact, the affections are the strongholds of self-occupancy. Warm feelings, devoted instincts of attachment, are but a blessed gift from heaven, a part of the granted *nature*, and in their action simply the indulgence of a delightful emotion. Through the intellect and the will is a man's escape from self;

thought and action are the conditions of self-forgetfulness; and love only loses its element of self in active service for the beloved object. Brooding over an attachment is the gratification of the highest pleasurable instinct granted to man; it is not conscious self-seeking, it is self-gratification; to labour for the sake of love is at once to escape from self, and the reverse of self-seeking. And as the highest virtues have the deepest temptations by their side, perhaps the most devout soul is the most in danger of a subtle spirit of self-occupancy, and most needs a field of active service; and on the other hand, the conditions of life offer the easiest escape from self-occupation in proportion as they lie farther from the domain of sentiment – science more than art, and active life more than science; and that pursuit offers the least tempta-tion to selfishness which affords a man the widest and most absorbing sphere of exertion in the interest of others. Government is the employment which gives a man the least excuse for being self-occupied, though no doubt it may present him with formidable temptations to gratify what selfishness he has. In his want of interest in the active concerns of life, and in his emotional and artistic nature, are probably to be found the grounds of Mr. Thackeray's belief in the universality of self-occupation, which by want of intellectual discrimi-nation he confounds with self-seeking or selfishness.

Some of Mr. Thackeray's lesser works are infused throughout with a genial kindly spirit; such are the *History of Mr Samuel Titmarsh and the Great Hoggarty Diamond* (which it is pleasant to hear is a favourite with the author), and the *Kickleburys on the Rhine, Dr Birch's School,* &c. In these, foibles are pleasantly touched with cheerful happy raillery, and a light, gay, yet searching tone of ridicule, and a tender pleasing pathos, pervade the story: "the air nimbly and sweely recom-mends itself:"[25] the wit plays freshly and brightly, like the sun glittering through the green leaves on the wood-paths. But in the mass of his works the tendencies we have before spoken of give a dark and unpleasing ground to the whole picture; and on it he draws in strong black and white. His general view of English society is a very low and unrelieved one. It is a true but a strictly one-sided represen-tation, selected partly for its amusing elements, partly from an unhappy idiosyncrasy of the author. An opposite picture might be drawn as flattering as this is satirical; and neither, of course, would be complete. On this stage move many figures fair and dark. The author's skill by no means forsakes him when he chooses to draw upon our love and admiration: Dobbin and Amelia, Warrington and Laura, and Helen; Lady Esmond, Colonel Newcome, and the sweet, placid, tear-worn, but somewhat shadowy image of Madame de Florac, rise up at once before the mind.[26] But he puts such characters apart; they shine like glowworms, brightly, but with no influence in the surrounding darkness. They are in his world, but scarcely of it; they are never allowed to leaven his general conception of society. A lump of sugar here and there cannot soften the bitterness of the whole cake. It would be unjust, perhaps, to say that his genius is more at home in his darker portraitures; but they certainly gain an undue significance, if only from this, that they are always represented in their proper sphere of activity, where their whole cleverness and energy is brought into light, whereas his fairer characters are invariably those whose excellence consists in the goodness of their instincts and emotions, and, with the single exception of Colonel Esmond, no external field of any interest is found for them to occupy. It is unfortunate, too, that Mr. Thackeray finds the main sources of wit and amusement in the most close connection with some form of vice or wickedness. How often is his laughter spun out of baseness, and crime, and misery! Degrading selfishness, heathen worldliness, abandoned honour, broken oaths, dice, drunkenness, every form of viciousness but one are made the subjects of sparkling satire, witty jests, the universal charity of mockery, and scorn tempered by scepticism. The company of bad men and women in the world is not elevating. How can they be elevating made amusing in books? The 'terrible death-chant of the contrite chimney-sweep,' in which Sam Hall conveys the lesson of his example,[27] enforced by maledictions, has a grim humour about it true enough, – might almost be said to be a work of genius; but we don't take our daughters to hear it sung. Wickedness has its funny side; but it grates on our ears to hear English ladies talking as they do sometimes of "that charming little Becky." We don't say that a vicious or even a degraded nature is not a fit subject for the artist, – no doubt it is; we do not say it is an unfit subject even for comedy; but we do say it ought not to be comically treated. We do maintain that there is a sin against good taste and right moral influence in mingling too intimately real vice and the ridiculous; they may be alternated, but not mixed, still less almost chemically combined, after Mr. Thackeray's fashion. You sap the force of moral resentment when, by smiling raillery or farcical laughter, you make tolerable the stern realities of sin. We know no book with so repulsive a contrast between the broad farce, almost buffoonery, of its form, and the hideous and utterly unrelieved baseness and wickedness of its subject-matter, as is exhibited in the history of "Mr. Deuceace," told in the characteristic orthography of "Jeames."[28] Mr. Thackeray has in his heart an eager hatred of baseness and hypocrisy. It bursts out unmistakably sometimes. It is hidden, no doubt, under all his air of persiflage; but it is part of his art to preserve a mask of neutrality; and an occasional protest has no weight against the tone of universal toleration, and the bantering mood which shakes these glittering sparks of wit out of the devil's devices. Sin is fire; and Mr. Thackeray makes fireworks of it.

And not only the witty emblazonment is bad, the elaborate detail is bad; and this applies not alone to the descriptions of the more serious vices, but to the lesser meannesses which we have before mentioned as occupying so undue a space of Mr. Thackeray's attention. It can be good for none of us to mingle so pleasantly and so closely with old Sir Pitt Crawley, with Becky, with old Osborne, with Major Pendennis, or even his nephew, with Costigan, with Altamont, with Blanche, with Lord Steyne, with many of those snobs. It is bad for us to be constantly rubbed against vice or sin of any kind; and we do not know whether the constant minutiæ of selfishness, of weakness, of false ambition, of cringing meanness and vulgarity, are not more harmful than the details of murder and other violent crime. Ainsworth and Thackeray differ in this respect only in the greater refinement and reconditeness of the latter. Why do we condemn the French school of novels? Because of the danger and debasement which lie in familiarising the ideas they contain. If we rightly think Richardson's *Pamela* unfit reading on account of its prurient minute details of a seduction, may we not protest against some portions of Mr. Thackeray's works which bring us so unintermittingly in contact with other degrading weaknesses of our nature, accompanied by something of a similar zest in the author, which has great power to infect the reader? On Richardson's subject, we should not, in the present day, tolerate such minuteness for an instant; on that matter we have an almost absurd apprehension of the dangers of infection. We not only avoid details, we shun the subject altogether: an author who means to be read must not come within a mile of it, – he must cripple his creations of character and his pictures of life in order to avoid it. Mr. Thackeray is fully aware of this; mere commercial self-preservation makes it necessary to hold aloof. But if the instinct which avoids familiarity with one particular form of vice and sinfulness be true, as we believe it to be, though overstrained, ought not the same instinct to apply in due proportion to other forms of vice and sinfulness?

It is no vindication of the dark tints of Mr. Thackeray's painting to say that base natures and low motives throng life itself, that it is not a Jenny and Jessamy world,[a] and that we must all mix in it. The fact is, that a vast number of Mr. Thackeray's readers learn more of the soiled

[a] A romanticized world of affectation and make-believe.

aspects of the world from his pages than from any experience of their own. And if it be said that these considerations would too go far in curtailing the range of art, we reply, that the author limits its range by the same considerations, but so as to incur a double evil; for while he cuts himself off from almost a whole side of human life in order to accommodate himself to modern taste and female readers, he certainly retains much which any but the world's standard of taste would willingly see excluded. Conventionally he is thoroughly unexceptionable. Practically his writings are too cramped for the indurated apprehensions of men who know the world; too tarnished for those who are unsophisticated, whether men, women, or children. A broad and lifelike picture of wickedness, even baseness, is not objected to. Iago and Blifil leave no stain on the mind; but incessant pottering over small meannesses bears the same relation to Shakespeare's and Fielding's treatment of this subject as, in another subject, Paul de Kock's novels[29] do to *Tom Jones*. The most condensed illustration of this morbid tendency is republished from the *Comic Almanac* in the first volume of Mr Thackeray's *Miscellanies*, – the "Fatal Boots." It is the cleverest piece of irony since *Jonathan Wild*, and perhaps the most subtle and complete delineation of an utterly base and selfish nature ever written. It is more painful and humiliating reading than *Jonathan Wild*; because the greater crimes of the latter remove him further from us, and because he is distinguished by some power of intellect and force of character utterly denied to the abject Stubbs, whose autobiography reads like the smell of bad cabbages.

It is the evil of all satire, that it depends for its force upon a minute and vivid delineation of faults and vices which it never is advantageous to drag into light. Its only useful sphere is personality. It is not often that personal satire is defensible; but in that, or the near approaches to it, is the only practical and possibly advantageous exercise of the art. You can make one man feel the lash, and direct a storm of indignation against him which may punish him or terrify him into a new course. And so it is possible to attack effectively a small class, or an opinion or course of action, which admits of practical change or abandonment. You may satirise General Simpson[30] or the *Times*, and possibly produce an effect, though it is not probable; you may satirise the Palace Court, the peace-party, or the conduct of the war, and it may be with a result: but you cannot scourge abstract vices; you cannot hope to be practically employed when you satirise hypocrisy, or mammon-worship, or false adulation of rank, or the worldly estimate of temporal advantages which results in wretched marriages or selfish singleness. For one who learns from Mr. Thackeray to amend a folly of his own, how many will gain a sharper insight into those of their friends! And to none of our tendencies does Mr. Thackeray minister so effectively as to this. His social satire is fair and honest, "strikes no foul blow," as he himself says of it; but it is so searching, so minute, deals with such real incident of every-day occurrence, that it forms a sort of public gossip. It is a treasury of general observation, out of which to make particular applications. It gives us an insight we never had before into the weaknesses of our neighbours, makes us rich in new sources of contempt, and indicates clearly the channels of false shame. We can test our friends' daily life by it, and cry, "Isn't that like Mrs. Kewsy?" and "The very way the Portmans go on."[31]

As a set-off against these unpleasing elements in Mr. Thackeray's writings, there is one whole side of his genius which casts a pure and pleasant sunshine over his pages. He has a heart as deep and kind as ever wrote itself in fiction. His feelings are warm and impetuous, his nature honest, truthful, honourable. Against cruelty, against baseness, against treachery, his indignation flames out quick and sudden, like a scorching fire. With what is manly, frank, and noble, he has a native inborn sympathy. If his sense of the ludicrous, and his wit, are too often nourished upon wickedness and depravity, he is familiar with another and truer connection, and has an exquisite felicity and moving power in the mingling of humour and pathos. If his works as a whole want purpose and depth, and clearness of moral conviction, if they accept sin simply as part of what is, instead of as a departure from what should be, yet they preach throughout lessons of example more telling than precept, and enclose many and many a passage well fitted to stir the spirit and to move the heart. If his wicked and mean creations are too predominant and too detailed, he has some at least whose great goodness and white purity relieve by fair gleams the dark and clouded landscape. They are emotional characters: but are not these the very ones which practically take the strongest hold on our affections; and the errors of impulse those which, however long the preacher may preach, we shall always the most readily excuse? Who ever painted a manly generous boy with so free and loving a pencil as the author of *Dr. Birch's School*, of Champion Major,[32] and of young Clive Newcome? Who else has that fine touch that can picture us so delicately and so clearly the fresh innocence of girlhood, the tender passion of a loving woman, or the absorbing devotion of a mother? Who can trace in firmer strokes fidelity and courage and temperate endurance in a man? In every page, alternating with bitterness, and sometimes an unsparing cruelty of sarcasm, there shines out a kindly affectionate nature, soft compassion, and humble reverence. It is as if

his nature, like his writings, were full of strongly-contrasted elements,
lying closely side by side. Whatever his defects, – and they are great, –
he must always take his stand as one of the masters of English fiction;
inferior to Fielding, because he wants his breadth and range, the
freeness of his air, and the soundness of his moral healthfulness; but
his rival in accuracy of insight and vigour of imagination; and
perhaps, as we have before said, more than his rival in fertility. And
since Fielding's time, though characters have been drawn more
complete than any one of Mr. Thackeray's, no fiction has been written
in the school to which his imagination belongs which can bear a
moment's comparison with *Vanity Fair*. This is hitherto his masterpiece, and will probably always remain so. There is a *vis*[a] in it greater
than in any of his other works – the lines are more sharply, deeply cut,
the whole more marked with the signs of special and peculiar genius.
Our pleasure in it alternates vividly with dislike – almost repulsion;
but our admiration is compelled by all parts of it, and our eagerest
sympathy by some. Dobbin and Amelia will always remain living
inmates of the English mind. They have both of them, Amelia
especially, had much injustice done them by their author; but as their
images lie longer in our breasts, and we mediate upon them, the sneers
and inuendoes fade away, and we see them undefaced, and recognise
that Dobbin's devotion was not selfishness, and Amelia's characteristic tenderness not weakness. Just as with living people small obscur-
ations and accidents fall away, and we estimate the whole character
better in absence, so it is with these: we know them better, and love
them more trustfully in memory than on the actual page. Thackeray's
genius is in many respects not unlike that of Goethe; and such another
woman as Amelia has not been drawn since Margaret in *Faust*.

Of his other great works, *Pendennis* is the richest in character and
incident, and the least pleasing; the *Newcomes* the most humane, but
less vigorous and concentrated than any of the others; *Esmond* – the
later parts at least – by far the best and noblest. We have no temptation
to discuss the merits of its imitative style and scenery, observing only
that though a modern mind shines through the external coat, yet
probably no other man could have gathered so many minute and
characteristic indicia of the times of which he writes, and so artfully
have blended them together. It is as a tale we look at it; and though to
most men such a subject, so treated, would have afforded more than
ordinary temptations to an overloading of character with costume and
external detail, with Mr. Thackeray the reverse is the case. He is freed
from his devotion to the petty satire of modern conventions, and has

[a] Strength.

fewer calls for the exercise of small contempts. The main characters, Esmond, his mistress, and Beatrix, are the ablest he has drawn; they are not less vivid than his others, and more complete. Esmond is strong, vigorous, noble, finely executed as well as conceived, and his weakness springs from the strength of a generous and impulsive nature. He is no exception to the observation that Mr. Thackeray never endows a hero with principles of action. Esmond is true to persons, not to ideas of right or duty. His virtue is fidelity, not conscientiousness. Beatrix is perhaps the finest picture of splendid, lustrous, physical beauty ever given to the world. It shines down every woman that poet or painter ever drew. Helen of Greece,

> Fairer than the evening air
> Clad in the beauty of a thousand stars,[33]

is the only one who approaches her. And both her character and that of her mother are master-pieces of poetical insight; the latter blemished, however, here and there with the author's unconquerable hankering to lay his finger on a blot. He must search it out, and give it at least its due blackness. He will not leave you to gather that it must be there, – he parades it to the day, and presses it to your reluctant eyes. It comes partly from the truthfulness of his nature, which cannot bear that a weakness should be concealed, and partly probably from a mistaken apprehension of the truth that the artist must be true to nature. There was a time when a good deal of parade was made and some very diluted philosophy spun out of the distinction between "the true" and "the real." But this simple fact there is, that a man may be true to nature and yet depart from all her manifested forms; and that it is a higher striving to be faithful to such an inborn conception than to mutilate and distort it for the sake of finding room in it for certain observed facts. Mr. Thackeray sometimes does this, oftener he does what is quite as unpleasing. When in a character, especially a woman's, he comes upon a defect, he does not allow it to speak itself, or show itself naturally, and sink with its own proper significance into the reader's mind. He rushes in as author, seizes on it, and holds it up with sadness or triumph: "See," he says, "this is what you find in the best women." Thus he gives it an undue importance and vividness, and troubles and distorts the true impression of the whole character.

In the same spirit he lays hold of the petty dishonesties and shams of social life. Almost all these have their origin in vanity, and in its hasty and habitual gratification the meanness of the devices is overlooked, at any rate not often wilfully adopted with a consciousness of its presence. Such contrivances are follies of a bad kind; but to stigmatise them as deliberate hypocrisies is to give a very false significance to the worst ingredient in them.

In the *Newcomes* "the elements are kindlier mixed" than in any of the other fictions; there is a great softening of tone, a larger predominance is given to feeling over sarcasm. As before, the book is a transcript from life; but the life is more pleasantly selected, and the baser ingredients not scattered with so lavish a hand. If the execution be somewhat inferior, as perhaps it is, the characters of Clive and Ethel less clearly and vividly defined than we have by long use to high excellence begun to think we have a right to expect they should be, and the former unattractive in his feebleness, if the journey through the story be rather *langweilig*,[a] sometimes from over-detail, sometimes from long and superficial moralisings over the sins of society, – yet there is much to reconcile us to these shortcomings in exchange, in some greater respite from the accustomed sneer. We have said before that the genius of Thackeray has many analogies to that of Goethe. He is like him, not only in his mode of depicting characters as they live, instead of reproducing their depths and entirety from the conception of a penetrative imagination, but also in his patient and tolerant acceptance of all existing phenomena, and his shrinking not merely from moral judgment but from moral estimate. The avoidance of the former, springs in Thackeray from kindly feeling, from the just and humble sense we all should have that our own demerits make it unseemly for us to ascend the judgment-chair, and from a wide appreciation of the variety and obscurity of men's real motives of action; the latter, a very different thing, springs from this same wide insight, which makes the task more than ordinarily difficult, especially to an intellect not framed to take pleasure in general conclusions, and from his imagination being one which does not naturally conceive in separate wholes, and most of all from an insufficient sense of the duty incumbent on us all to form determinate estimates of the characters and moral incidents around us, if only to form the landmarks and bearings for our own conduct in life. These features remain in the *Newcomes*. There is the same want of ballasting thought, the same see-saw between cynicism and sentiment, the same suspension of moral judgment. The indignant impulse prompts the lash, and the hand at once delivers it; while the mind hangs back, doubts its justice, and sums up after execution with an appeal to our charity on the score of the undecipherable motives of human action, the heart's universal power of self-deception, and the urgency of fate and circumstance.

[a] Tedious.

David Masson
(1822–1907)
From 'British Novelists Since Scott': Lecture IV of 'British Novelists and Their Styles', 1859

Though best remembered today for his seven-volume *Life of John Milton* (1859–94), David Masson also produced an impressive body of other books and essays during a career as journalist, critic, historian, editor, and university teacher that spanned more than half a century. His *British Novelists and Their Styles* is notable as the first book-length treatment of the theory and history of the novel in English.

Born in Aberdeen, Masson was educated at the Grammar School and Marischal College in that city before going on to study divinity at the University of Edinburgh. Having abandoned his intention of becoming a minister in the Church of Scotland, he assumed the editorship of an Aberdeen weekly in 1842 and two years later turned to writing as a profession, first for the Edinburgh publishing house W. and R. Chalmers and then as a freelance, contributing to such periodicals as *Fraser's Magazine*, the *Quarterly Review*, the *Westminster Review*, the *Leader*, and the *North British Review*, as well as to the *Encyclopaedia Britannica*.

In 1847 Masson moved to London, where he made many literary acquaintances, and by 1853 his own reputation as a man of letters was such that he was appointed Professor of English Literature at University College London. Later he also agreed to edit two important new periodicals as they began publication in an increasingly crowded and competitive market: the monthly *Macmillan's Magazine*, which first appeared in November 1859; and the weekly *Reader*, whose four-year life began on 3 January 1863. In 1865 Masson became Professor of Rhetoric and English Literature at the University of Edinburgh, a position in which he enjoyed great success and which he held until his retirement three decades later.

In its original form, which was slightly revised for publication, *British Novelists and Their Styles* consisted of a series of four lectures delivered before the Philosophical Institution of Edinburgh in March and April 1858. In the first, Masson defines the novel, linking it to and contrasting it with narrative poetry, and traces the early development of the genre, through the end of the seventeenth century. The second lecture is devoted to the eighteenth-century novel and the third – obviously 'prepared for an Edinburgh audience', as

Masson reminds the reader in a 'Prefatory Note' to the volume – to 'Scott and His Influence'. Lecture IV (pp. 208–308 in the 1859 Macmillan edition), from which the following substantial excerpt is taken, brings Masson's account up to the present (i.e., the late 1850s) and ends with his 'hopes as to the Novel of the future'.

In his first portion of the lecture, not reproduced here (pp. 208–32), Masson cites statistics to show that, at least in quantitative terms, the novel has become a 'formidable' presence in Victorian life: the rate of publication accelerated dramatically between the appearance of Scott's first novel, *Waverley*, in 1814 and his death in 1832, when it reached one hundred titles a year – a level it maintained during the intervening quarter-century. He also classifies the nineteenth-century British novel into thirteen categories, giving examples and assessing the strengths and weaknesses of each: (1) the novel of Scottish life and manners; (2) the novel of Irish life and manners; (3) the novel of English life and manners; (4) the fashionable novel; (5) the illustrious criminal novel; (6) the traveller's novel; (7) the novel of American manners and society; (8) the Oriental novel, or novel of Eastern manners and society; (9) the military novel; (10) the naval novel; (11) the novel of supernatural phantasy; (12) the art and cultural novel (now commonly referred to by the German term *Bildungsroman*); and (13) the historical novel.

Masson's extended discussion of Dickens and Thackeray, the two foremost novelists of the decade and indeed the age, notes resemblances but stresses differences between them. Though both began as novelists of English life and manners, placing special emphasis on London, each has also produced examples of the traveller's novel and the historical novel. But Dickens's style is 'more diffuse and luxuriant' than that of Thackeray, who writes with 'an Horatian strictness and strength' (p. 240); Dickens's range of subject matter is wider than Thackeray's; in 'general philosophy', Dickens is 'the more genial, kindly, cheerful, and sentimental', Thackeray 'the more harsh, caustic, cynical, and satiric writer' (pp. 243–4).

More significantly, his treatment of Dickens and Thackeray enables Masson to contrast 'the Real school' of novel writing, represented by Thackeray, with 'the Ideal, or Romantic school', represented by Dickens, an opposition that Masson had already established eight years earlier in his joint review of Thackeray's *Pendennis* and Dickens's *David Copperfield* in the *North British Review* for May 1851 (15: 57–89). (Even then it was common to play off the two novelists against each other; Masson began his 1851 review by observing that 'the two names now almost necessarily go together'.) Rather than placing one school above the other, however, Masson argues that both have distinctive virtues and that 'each writer is to be tried within his own school by the kind of success he has attained within it'. He welcomes the developments that have occurred in each school as the awareness of realistic and romantic novelists alike has expanded following the revolutionary year 1848; and as he contemplates the future of the novel, which he believes will be a bright one, he looks forward to a further broadening and deepening of the outlook of writers in both schools as well as the establishment of a more solid intellectual foundation for the work of those turning out widely read didactic 'Roman Catholic novels, Anglo-Catholic novels, Evangelical novels, Broad-Church novels, Christian Socialist novels, Temperance novels, Woman's Rights novels, etc.' (p. 264).

The following selections from 'British Novelists Since Scott' are taken from pp. 248–53, 292–305, and 308 of the 1859 Macmillan edition of *British Novelists and their Styles*.

... Thackeray is a novelist of what is called the Real school; Dickens is a novelist of the Ideal, or Romantic school. (The terms Real and Ideal have been so run upon of late, that their repetition begins to nauseate; but they must be kept, for all that, till better equivalents are provided.) It is Thackeray's aim to represent life as it is actually and historically – men and women, as they are, in those situations in which they are usually placed, with that mixture of good and evil and of strength and foible which is to be found in their characters, and liable only to those incidents which are of ordinary occurrence. He will have no faultless characters, no demigods – nothing but men and brethren. And from this it results that, when once he has conceived a character, he works downwards and inwards in his treatment of it, making it firm and clear at all points in its relations to hard fact, and cutting down, where necessary, to the very foundations. Dickens, on the other hand, with all his keenness of observation, is more light and poetic in his method. Having once caught a hint from actual fact, he generalizes it, runs away with this generalization into a corner, and develops it there into a character to match; which character he then transports, along with others similarly suggested, into a world of semi-fantastic conditions, where the laws need not be those of ordinary probability. He has characters of ideal perfection and beauty, as well as of ideal ugliness and brutality – characters of a human kind verging on the supernatural, as well as characters actually belonging to the supernatural. Even his situations and scenery often lie in a region beyond the margin of everyday life. Now, both kinds of art are legitimate; and each writer is to be tried within his own kind by the success he has attained in it. Mr Thackeray, I believe, is as perfect a master in his kind of art as is to be found in the whole series of British prose writers; a man in whom strength of understanding, acquired knowledge of men, subtlety of perception, deep philosophic humor, and exquisiteness of literary taste, are combined in a degree and after a manner not seen in any known precedent. But the kinds of art are different; and I believe some injustice has been done to Mr. Dickens of late, by forgetting this when comparing him with his rival. It is as if we were to insist that all painters should be of the school of Hogarth. The Ideal or Romantic artist must be true to nature, as well as the Real artist; but he may be true in a different fashion. He may take hints from Nature in her extremest moods, and make these hints the germs of creations fitted for a world projected imaginatively beyond the real one, or inserted into the midst of the real one, and yet imaginatively moated round from it. Homer, Shakspeare, and Cervantes, are said to be true to nature; and yet there is not one of their most pronounced characters exactly such as ever was to be found, or ever will be found in nature – not one of them which is not the result of some suggestion snatched from nature, in one or other of her uttermost moments, and then carried away and developed in the void. The question with the Real artist, with respect to what he conceives, is, "How would this actually be in nature; in what exact setting of surrounding particulars would it appear?" and, with a view to satisfy himself on this question, he dissects, observes, and recollects all that is in historical relation to his conception. The question with the Ideal artist is, "What can be made out of this; with what human conclusions, ends, and aspirations can it be imaginatively interwoven, so that the whole, though attached to nature by its origin, shall transcend or overlie nature on the side of the possibly existent – the might, could, or should be, or the might, could, or should have been?" All honor to Thackeray and the prose fiction of social reality; but much honor, too, to Dickens, for maintaining among us, even in the realm of the light and the amusing, some representation in prose of that art of ideal phantasy, the total absence of which in the literature of any age would be a sign nothing short of hideous. The true objection to Dickens is, that his idealism tends too much to extravagance and caricature. It would be possible for an ill-natured critic to go through all his works and draw out in one long column a list of their chief characters, annexing in a parallel column the phrases or labels by which these characters are distinguished, and of which they are generalizations – the "There's some credit in being jolly here" of Mark Tapley; the "It isn't of the slightest consequence" of Toots; the "Something will turn up" of Mr. Micawber, etc., etc. Even this, however, is a mode of art legitimate, I believe, in principle, as it is certainly most effective in fact. There never was a Mr. Micawber in nature, exactly as he appears in the pages of Dickens; but Micawberism pervades nature through and through; and to have extracted this quality from nature, embodying the full essence of a thousand instances of it in one ideal monstrosity, is a feat of invention. From the incessant repetition by Mr. Dickens of this inventive process openly and without variation, except in the results, the public have caught what is called his mannerism or trick; and hence a certain recoil from his later writings among the cultivated and fastidious. But let any one observe our current table-talk or our current literature, and, despite this profession of dissatisfaction, and in the very circles where it most abounds, let him note how gladly Dickens is used, and how frequently his phrases, his fancies, and the names of his characters come in, as illustration, embellishment, proverb, and seasoning. Take any periodical in which there is a severe criticism of Dickens's last publication; and, ten to one, in the same periodical, and perhaps by the same hand, there will be a leading article, setting out with a quotation from Dickens that flashes on the mind of the reader the thought which the whole article is meant to convey, or containing some allusion to one of Dickens's characters which enriches the text in the middle and floods it an inch round with color and humor. Mr. Thackeray's writings also yield similar contributions of pithy sayings applicable to the occasions of common talk, and of typical characters serving the purpose of luminous metonymy – as witness his Becky Sharps, his Fokers, his Captain Costigans, and his Jeameses;[1] but, in his case, owing to his habit rather of close delineation of the complex and particular as nature presents it, than of rapid fictitious generalization, more of the total effect, whether of admiration or of ethical instruction, takes place in the art of reading him. . . .

There are no symptoms yet that the Novel is about to lose its popularity as a form of literature. On the contrary, there is every symptom, that in one shape or another it will continue to be popular for a long time, and that more and more of talent will flow into it. The very remarks which we have been making as to the recent tendencies and characteristics of our British novel-writing are proofs to this effect. The Novel, we have found, has been becoming more real and determinate, in so far as it can convey matter of fact, more earnest, in so far as it can be made a vehicle for matter of speculation, and more conscious, at the same time, of its ability in all matter of phantasy. What is this but saying that its capabilities have been increasing simultaneously as regards each of the three kinds of intellectual exercise which make up total literature – History, Philosophy, and Poetry; and what is this again but saying, that in future there may be either a greater disposition among those who naturally distribute themselves according to this threefold classification to employ it for their several purposes, or a greater desire among those who are peculiarly novelists to push its powers in the threefold service? On such a supposition, we may venture, in conclusion, on three hopes as to the Novel of the future, corresponding severally to the three tendencies which have been indicated as most conspicuous in the Novel of the present:

I. In the interest of the Novel considered in its relations to History, or as a form of literature representing the facts of human life, there might be a more general recognition than heretofore, both among Novelists and their readers, of the full theoretical capabilities of the Novel, as being the prose counterpart of the Epic. In other words, there might be more attention among our novelists of real life to epic breadth of interest.

I may illustrate my meaning by a particular instance of the defect I have in view. It will not be denied, I think, that, by the conversion of the Novel, in the hands of the majority of modern novelists, and especially of lady-novelists, into a mere love and marriage story, there has been a serious contraction of its capabilities. Of Love, as an influence in human affairs, it is impossible either for History or for Romance to exaggerate the importance. Over every portion of human society, from the beginning of the world till now, over every little hand's-breadth of British or of any other society at this moment, there has waved, there is waving, the white hand of Aphrodite. And what effects of the white hand wherever it waves – what sweet pain, what freaks and mischiefs, what trains of wild and unforeseen events, what derangements and convulsions, not confined to the spots where they begin, but sending forth circles of tremor, which agitate all interests, and ripple sometimes to the thrones of kings! Through love, as a portal, man and woman both pass, at one point or another, ere they are free of the corporation of the human race, acquainted with its laws and constitution, and partakers of its privileges. That this feeling, then, and all that appertains to it, should receive large recognition in literature, that representations of it should be multiplied, and that histories should be constructed to exhibit it, is right and necessary; nor can any history or fiction be accounted a complete rendering of all life in which this particular interest is omitted or made insignificant. But there are other human "interests" – if we may use that hacknied word – besides Love and Marriage. There are other deities in the Polytheistic Pantheon besides Aphrodite. There is Apollo, the physician and artist; there is Minerva, the wise and serene; there is Juno, the sumptuous and queenly; there is the red god, Mars; not far off sits green-haired Neptune; all around is Pan, the wood-rover; and down upon all, the resting bolt in his hand, looks the calm and great-browed Jove. It was the action and inter-action of these deities that, in the Pagan philosophy, produced life – Venus having only her characteristic part; and, if for deities we substitute principles, the same is true

yet. Exactly, therefore, as, in the Homeric Epic, the whole Pantheon
was engaged, and Venus appears but now and then to wave her hand
and have it wounded, so, to constitute a true modern epic, there must
be the like subordination, the like variety. And, indeed, in almost all
the greater novelists, whether of our own or of other countries, –
Richardson being one of the exceptions, – and certainly in all the
greatest narrative and dramatic poets, this breadth of interest, this
ranging of the mind over a wide surface of the phenomena of human
life, has been conspicuously characteristic. In Cervantes, we have all
Spain to range over. In Shakspeare's dramas we have love in abundance, and, at least, some thread or hint of love in each; but what a
play throughout of other interests, and in some how rare the gleam of
the white hand amid the spears of warriors and the deliberations of
senates! So in Scott; and so in almost every other very eminent
novelist. That so many of our inferior novels now should be love and
marriage novels, and nothing more, arises perhaps from the fact, that
the novel-reading age in the one sex falls generally between the
eighteenth and the twenty-fifth year, and that, with the other sex, in
the present state of our social arrangements, the 'white hand' remains,
directly or indirectly, the permanent human interest during the whole
of life.

II. In the interest of the Novel, considered as a vehicle for doctrine,
a very considerable influx into both of the speculative spirit and of the
best results of speculation, is yet to be desired.

The question of the proper limits within which a poet or other artist
may seek to inculcate doctrine through his works, is one on which
something has already been said in connection with those recent
novels which we have named Novels of Purpose. It is, however, a
question, the complete discussion of which would involve many
farther considerations.

On the one hand, the popular distaste for works of art evidently
manufactured to the order of some moral or dogma, is founded on a
right instinct. The art of Shakspeare in his dramas, as it is and always
has been more popular than the art of Ben Jonson in his, is also deeper
and truer in principle. Moreover, it may be said, there is a certain
incompatibility between the spirit in which an artist proceeds, and the
spirit in which a teacher or dogmatist ought to proceed, if he is true to
his calling. It is the supposed essence of a work of art that it shall give
pleasure; but perhaps it is the test of efficient doctrine that it shall give
pain. The artist may lawfully aspire to be popular; the teacher who
aspires to popularity does so at his peril. It might be a true testimony
to the power of an artist that the crowd were crowning him with laurel

in the market-place; but respecting a moralist, or spiritual reformer, a truer testimony might be that they were taking up stones to stone him. Works of art and imagination are such that those who produce them may live by their sale, and not necessarily be untrue to their function; the very worst feature in our modern organization of literature is that so many literary men must live by the sale of *doctrine*. When doctrine has to be sold to enable its producer to go on producing more, there is a grievous chance that the doctrine last sold, and the farther doctrine in preparation, will, more or less consciously, be of a kind to be salable. True, the laborer even in doctrine is worthy of his hire; but he will labour perhaps better if he is in circumstances not to require any. In the ancient Greek world it was the men who were called Sophists who took fees for their teaching; the philosopher Socrates had his bread otherwise. He earned his bread by sculpture, of the quality of which we do not hear much; by his philosophy, of the quality of which we can judge for ourselves, all that he got from the public in his life was a cup of hemlock. But, though we thus regard it as the distinction between the true Greek philosophers and the contemporary Sophists that the Sophists taught for hire and the philosophers gratuitously, we do not extend the inference to the Greek dramatists. They probably expected to be paid handsomely, as well as to be applauded for their dramas; and yet their dramas were such as we see. And so, in the case of the modern novel, what chance is there for the novelist of attaining his legitimate end as an artist, that of communicating and diffusing pleasure, if he aims also at reforming society by a strenuous inculcation of doctrine, which, in so far as it is good and calculated for the exigency, ought almost necessarily to irritate?

Now, without waiting to detect a certain amount of fallacy which mingles with the general truth of such an argument, it might be enough to fall back on the consideration already adduced – that every artist, poet, or novelist, is also a thinker, whether he chooses or not. The imagination is not a faculty working apart; it is the whole mind thrown into the act of imagining; and the value of any act of imagination, therefore, or of all the acts of imagination of any particular mind, will depend on the total strength and total furnishing of the mind, doctrinal contents and all, that is thrown into this form of exercise. Every artist is a thinker, whether he knows it or not; and ultimately no artist will be found greater as an artist than he was as a thinker. The novelist chooses a certain portion of life to be imaginatively represented; well, there is latent doctrine in the very choice. He is the providence of the mimic world he has framed; well, he must conduct it, consciously or unconsciously, according to *some* philosophy of life. He makes his characters reason and act in different situations and in modes calling for approbation or reprobation; well, he is, in spite of himself, a good or a bad moral casuist. Now, to the extent to which these obvious facts carry us, is it not to be wished that our novelists brought to their business a fair amount of scientific capital, a fair amount of acquaintance with the best thoughts that may be current on the subjects of greatest interest and importance? Is the wish unnecessary? It hardly appears to be so. If there is any kind of literary attempt to which a mind empty of all knowledge is apt, nevertheless, to think itself quite competent, is it not to writing a novel? And what havoc, in our actual novels, of the most simple and certain principles! The very element in which the novelist works is human nature; yet what sort of Psychology have we in the ordinary run of novels? A Psychology, if the truth must be spoken, such as would not hold good in a world of imaginary cats, not to speak of men; impossible conformations of character; actions determined by motives that never could have determined the like; sudden conversions brought about by logical means of such astounding simplicity that wonder itself is paralyzed in contemplating them; chains of events defying all laws of conceivable causation! How shaky, also, the Political Economy and the Social Science of a good many of our novelists – sciences in the matter of which they must work, if not also in that of some of the physical sciences, in framing their fictitious histories! Before novels or poems can stand the inspection of that higher criticism which every literary work must be able to pass ere it can rank in the first class, their authors must be at least abreast of the best speculation of their time. Not that what we want from novelists and poets is further matter of speculation. What we want from them is matter of imagination; but the imagination of a well-furnished mind is one thing, and that of a vacuum is another. Respecting some kinds of novels – those included, for example, in the more profound order of what we have called novels of purpose – our demands might be higher. That a writer may be fitted to frame imaginary histories illustrating the deeper problems of human education, and to be a sound casuist in the most difficult questions of human experience, it is necessary that he should bring to his task not only an average acquaintance with the body of good current doctrine, but also an original speculative faculty. In such cases, the desirable arrangement might be either that our novelists were philosophers, or that philosophers were our novelists.

III. In the interest of the Novel, considered as a variety of general Poetry, there might be a more decided assertion of its competency for the higher as well as for the lower exercises of the poetic faculty, of its fitness for representations of the grand, the elemental, the ideal, as well as for representations of the socially minute, varying, and real. In other words, there might, with advantage, be a protest, within certain limits, and especially at present, against the exclusive practice of what is called the novel of social reality. I have so often touched on this topic that it may be well here somewhat to vary my language in returning to it. Several times I have used the word "elemental" as synonymous, or nearly so, with the word "ideal," and as perhaps less objectionable, inasmuch as it avoids the notion of opposition to the "real," which this latter word is apt to suggest, and which is not intended. Let me now, therefore, confine myself to that word, and explain more distinctly what is meant by it.

The old doctrine of the Four Elements is now naught in Science; but there is a lingering validity in it, in respect that to the merely intuitive eye the four elements recognized in it still seem to compose the totality of nature, and yet to be distinct among themselves. There is the brown and stable Earth, mineral or organic; round its massive bulk roars and surges the fluid element of Water, here collected in oceans, there distributed in streams; over Earth and Water alike blows the fickle element of Air, deepening, as the eye ascends, from invisible transparency to the still blue of the heavenly dome; and finally, scattered through all, is the fiercer element of Fire, here tonguing over the earth wherever it may be kindled, there flashing through the ether, and, high over all, as natural vision fancies, collected permanently into points and orbs. Moreover, this distribution of external nature by the eye sinks inward into the mind, becomes a mode of universal thought, and affects our language respecting mind itself. Some souls, solid and strong, seem to have an affinity with the earth; some, more fluid, with the water; some, soft and supersubtle, with the air; some, hot and terrible, with the fires and the lightnings; while some there are – earthy-fiery, fiery-aërial, and the like – whose affinities must be represented as compound. Nay, more, it will be found that the element to which any mind is referred by those observing its operations, is also generally that for the sensible circumstance of which it shows, in its fancies, a marked affection. Shelley might be classed as an aërial spirit with a touch of fainter fire; and the circumstance with which Shelley's poetry abounds is that of Meteorology.

So much for the word "elemental" as it might be afforded to us out of the obsolete, but still significant, doctrine of the Four Elements. But we need not associate the word with any such doctrine. The elemental in nature or in life, may be defined as consisting simply of those objects or phenomena in each, which are recognized as most large, comprehensive, primitive, impressive, and enduring. There is an elemental of the physical world, and there is an elemental of the moral world. The elemental in the physical world consists of the more massive and enduring phenomena of that world, of those larger sights and sounds of nature that impressed men primevally, and that continue to impress powerfully now, – the wide expanse of earth, barren with moor or waving with corn and forest; the sea, restless to the horizon, and rolling its waves to the beach; the gusts of the raging tempest; the sun, majestic in the heavens, and the nocturnal glory of the stars; the clouds, the rains, the rocks, the vales, the mountains. To these more massive and permanent objects, or phenomena of the physical world, there correspond objects or phenomena of the moral world, distinguished from the rest as also more massive and enduring. Birth, Life, Death; Labor, Sorrow, Love, Revenge; the thought of the Whence, the thought of the Why, the thought of the Whither – these, in the moral world, are the considerations that are elemental. Men of old revolved them; we revolve them; those who come after us will revolve them. As in the physical world there are infinite myriads of phenomena, complex and minute, aggregated on the basis of the elemental, and into which the elemental may be decomposed, so on these fundamental feelings, facts, and thoughts of the moral world, are all the minuter facts of social experience piled, and over these as their basis they roll in varying whirl. These are the generalities; the rest are minutiæ. Now, to the hundred definitions that have been given of genius, let this one more be added – that that soul is a soul of genius which is in affinity with the elemental in nature and in life, and which, by the necessity of its constitution, tends always from the midst of the complex and minute to the simple and general.

... It may be that the representation of social reality is, on the whole, the proper business of the Novel; but even in the representation of social reality the spirit may be that of the far-surveying and the sublime. I believe, however, that there may be vindicated for the literature of prose phantasy the liberty of an order of fiction different from the usual Novel of Social Reality, and approaching more to what has always been allowed in metrical poesy, and that, accordingly, those occasional prose fictions are to be welcomed which deal with characters of heroic imaginary mould, and which remove us from cities and the crowded haunts of men.

George Eliot
(1819–1880)
'Silly Novels by Lady Novelists', 1856

In chapter 17 of George Eliot's first novel, *Adam Bede* (1859), there is a well-known digression on realism in verbal and visual art – what she calls 'this rare, precious quality of truthfulness' that gives 'delight in many Dutch paintings'. Two years earlier, in the first of her three *Scenes of Clerical Life*, 'The Sad Fortunes of the Reverend Amos Barton', she made a plea for the faithful presentation in fiction of decidedly ordinary people like her protagonist: 'Depend upon it, you would gain unspeakably if you would learn with me to see some of the poetry and the pathos, the tragedy and the comedy, lying in the experience of a human soul that looks out through dull grey eyes, and that speaks in quite ordinary tones' (ch. 5).

'Amos Barton' – the first work of Marian Evans to which she affixed her famous pen name – launched a remarkable career in fiction-writing, but it was by no means her first publication. During the preceding half-dozen years she had turned out, anonymously, a number of articles and reviews, principally for the *Leader* and the *Westminster Review*; of the latter highly respected quarterly she was editor in all but name between January 1852 and January 1854. In the best of this work, collected and edited by Thomas Pinney in *Essays of George Eliot* (1963), some central ideas that were to become fundamental principles for the novelist are prominently in evidence.

Nowhere is this more striking than in 'Silly Novels by Lady Novelists', which Eliot finished in September 1856, a few days before starting to write 'Amos Barton'. Complaining about 'the *white neck-cloth* species' of 'silly novels', featuring 'insipid' Evangelical curates from 'well-dressed and wealthy, if not fashionable society', she was moved to observe that 'The real drama of Evangelicalism ... lies among the middle and lower classes' and to ask: 'Are not Evangelical opinions understood to give an especial interest in the weak things of the earth, rather than in the mighty?' 'Amos Barton' and the next two *Scenes of Clerical Life*, 'Mr Gilfil's Love-Story' and especially 'Janet's Repentance' (both 1857), may be taken as Eliot's attempt to answer that question shortly after she posed it, at the threshold of her career as a novelist.

Implicit in Eliot's question is an essential ingredient of literary realism as she defines it: sympathy, which is especially called for and cultivated in the contemplation of 'the weak things of the earth'. Beginning with Hetty Sorrel in *Adam Bede*, her novels abound in frail creatures who arouse this response, one that affected and ignorant 'lady novelists' are incapable of evoking, any more than they can render a picture of the world in which credible men and women live, act, and speak. 'The greatest benefit we owe to the artist', she wrote in another 1856 *Westminster Review* essay, 'The Natural History of German Life,' 'is the extension of our sympathies.' In 'Silly Novels by Lady Novelists' she points out that 'the really cultured woman', unlike the one who persists in writing such trash, 'does not give you information, which is the raw material of culture, – she gives you sympathy, which is its subtlest essence'.

Preaching of the kind to be found in many 'silly novels' is not the way to bring about sympathy – or for that matter any other desirable effect; nor are 'lady novelists' alone in indulging in it. Reviewing Charles Kingsley's *Westward Ho!* in the *Leader* in 1855, Eliot found that

the preacher overcomes the painter often, which, though creditable to the writer's earnestness and honesty, injures his work as a mere work of art. It is as if a painter in colour were to write "Oh, you villain!" under his Jesuits or murderers; or to have a strip flowing from the hero's mouth, with "Imitate me, my man!" on it. No doubt the villain is to be hated, and the hero loved; but we ought to see that sufficiently in the figures of them. We don't want a man with a wand, going about the gallery and haranguing us. Art is art, and tells its own story.

Goethe, a much greater novelist than Kingsley, was aware of this truth. Dealing with 'The Morality of Wilhelm Meister' in the *Leader* later in 1855, Eliot described Goethe's practice in this way:

Everywhere he brings us into the presence of living, generous humanity – mixed and erring, and self-deluding, but saved from utter corruption by the salt of some noble impulse, some disinterested effort, some beam of good nature, even though grotesque or homely. And his mode of treatment seems to us precisely that which is really moral in its influence. It is without exaggeration; he is in no haste to alarm readers into virtue by melodramatic consequences; he quietly follows the stream of fact and of life; and waits patiently for the moral processes of nature as we all do for her material processes.

In 'Silly Novels by Lady Novelists' Eliot puts the same point more succinctly: what is at issue are 'those moral qualities that contribute to literary excellence – patient diligence, a sense of the responsibility involved in publication, and an appreciation of the sacredness of the writer's art'. The vocation of the novelist, male or female, is an exalted one, and no foolish dilettante can possibly be worthy of it.

'Silly Novels by Lady Novelists' first appeared in the *Westminster Review*, 66 (October 1856): 442–61.

SILLY Novels by Lady Novelists are a genus with many species, determined by the particular quality of silliness that predominates in them – the frothy, the prosy, the pious, or the pedantic. But it is a mixture of all these – a composite order of feminine fatuity, that produces the largest class of such novels, which we shall distinguish as the *mind-and-millinery* species. The heroine is usually an heiress, probably a peeress in her own right, with perhaps a vicious baronet, an amiable duke, and an irresistible younger son of a marquis as lovers in the foreground, a clergyman and a poet sighing for her in the middle distance, and a crowd of undefined adorers dimly indicated beyond. Her eyes and her wit are both dazzling; her nose and her morals are alike free from any tendency to irregularity; she has a superb *contralto* and a superb intellect; she is perfectly well-dressed and perfectly religious; she dances like a sylph, and reads the Bible in the original tongues. Or it may be that the heroine is not an heiress – that rank and wealth are the only things in which she is deficient; but she infallibly gets into high society, she has the triumph of refusing many matches and securing the best, and she wears some family jewels or other as a sort of crown of righteousness at the end. Rakish men either bite their lips in impotent confusion at her repartees, or are touched to penitence by her reproofs, which, on appropriate occasions, rise to a lofty strain of rhetoric; indeed, there is a general propensity in her to make speeches, and to rhapsodize at some length when she retires to her bedroom. In her recorded conversations she is amazingly eloquent, and in her unrecorded conversations, amazingly witty. She is understood to have a depth of insight that looks through and through the shallow theories of philosophers, and her superior instincts are a sort of dial by which men have only to set their clocks and watches, and all will go well. The men play a very subordinate part by her side. You are consoled now and then by a hint that they have affairs,[a] which keeps you in mind that the working-day business of the world is somehow being carried on, but ostensibly the final cause of their existence is that they may accompany the heroine on her "starring" expedition through life. They see her at a ball, and are dazzled; at a flower-show, and they are fascinated; on a riding excursion, and they are witched by her noble horsemanship; at church, and they are awed by the sweet solemnity of her demeanour. She is the ideal woman in feelings, faculties, and flounces. For all this, she as often as not marries the wrong person to begin with, and she suffers terribly from the plots and intrigues of the vicious baronet; but even death has a soft place in his heart for such a paragon, and remedies all mistakes for her just at the right moment. The vicious baronet is sure to be killed in a duel, and the tedious husband dies in his bed requesting his wife, as a particular favour to him, to marry the man she loves best, and having already dispatched a note to the lover informing him of the comfortable arrangement. Before matters arrive at this desirable issue our feelings are tried by seeing the noble, lovely, and gifted heroine pass through many *mauvais moments*, but we have the satisfaction of knowing that her sorrows are wept into embroidered pocket-

[a] Conduct business.

161

handkerchiefs, that her fainting form reclines on the very best uphol-
stery, and that whatever vicissitudes she may undergo, from being
dashed out of her carriage to having her head shaved in a fever, she
comes out of them all with a complexion more blooming and looks
more redundant than ever.

We may remark, by the way, that we have been relieved from a
serious scruple by discovering that silly novels by lady novelists rarely
introduce us into any other than very lofty and fashionable society.
We had imagined that destitute women turned novelists, as they
turned governesses, because they had no other "lady-like" means of
getting their bread. On this supposition, vacillating syntax and
improbable incident had a certain pathos for us, like the extremely
supererogatory pincushions and ill-devised nightcaps that are offered
for sale by a blind man. We felt the commodity to be a nuisance, but
we were glad to think that the money went to relieve the necessitous,
and we pictured to ourselves lonely women struggling for a maintenance, or wives and daughters devoting themselves to the production of "copy" out of pure heroism – perhaps to pay their
husband's debts, or to purchase luxuries for a sick father. Under these
impressions we shrank from criticising a lady's novel: her English
might be faulty, but, we said to ourselves, her motives are irreproach-
able; her imagination may be uninventive, but her patience is untir-
ing. Empty writing was excused by an empty stomach, and twaddle
was consecrated by tears. But no! This theory of ours, like many other
pretty theories, has had to give way before observation.

Women's silly novels, we are now convinced, are written under
totally different circumstances. The fair writers have evidently never
talked to a tradesman except from a carriage window; they have no
notion of the working-classes except as "dependents;" they think five
hundred a-year a miserable pittance; Belgravia[a] and "baronial halls"
are their primary truths; and they have no idea of feeling interest in
any man who is not at least a great landed proprietor, if not a prime
minister. It is clear that they write in elegant boudoirs, with violet-
coloured ink and a ruby pen; that they must be entirely indifferent to
publishers' accounts, and inexperienced in every form of poverty
except poverty of brains. It is true that we are constantly struck with
the want of verisimilitude in their representations of the high society
in which they seem to live; but then they betray no closer acquaintance
with any other form of life. If their peers and peeresses are improbable, their literary men, tradespeople, and cottagers are impossible;
and their intellect seems to have the peculiar impartiality of reproduc-

[a] Fashionable residential district in London.

ing both what they *have* seen and heard, and what they have *not* seen and heard, with equal unfaithfulness.

There are few women, we suppose, who have not seen something of children under five years of age, yet in "Compensation,"[1] a recent novel of the mind-and-millinery species, which calls itself a "story of real life," we have a child of four and a half years old talking in this Ossianic fashion[a] –

"Oh, I am so happy, dear gran'mamma; – I have seen, – I have seen such a delightful person: he is like everything beautiful, – like the smell of sweet flowers and the view from Ben Lomond; – or no, *better than that* – he is like what I think of and see when I am very very happy; and he is really like mamma, too, when she sings; and his forehead is like *that distant sea*," she continued, pointing to the blue Mediterranean; "there seems no end – no end; or like the clusters of stars I like best to look at on a warm fine night . . . Don't look so . . . your forehead is like Loch Lomond, when the wind is blowing and the sun is gone; I like the sunshine best when the lake is smooth . . . So now – I like it better than ever . . . it is more beautiful still from the dark cloud that has gone over it, *when the sun suddenly lights up all the colours of the forests and shining purple rocks, and it is all reflected in the waters below.*"

We are not surprised to learn that the mother of this infant phenomenon, who exhibits symptoms so alarmingly like those of adolescence repressed by gin, is herself a phoenix.[2] We are assured, again and again, that she had a remarkably original mind, that she was a genius, and "conscious of her originality," and she was fortunate enough to have a lover who was also a genius, and a man of "most original mind."

This lover, we read, though "wonderfully similar" to her "in powers and capacity," was "infinitely superior to her in faith and development," and she saw in him the "'Agape'[b] – so rare to find – of which she had read and admired the meaning in her Greek Testament; having, *from her great facility in learning languages*, read the Scriptures in their original *tongues*." Of course! Greek and Hebrew are mere play to a heroine; Sanscrit is no more than *a b c* to her; and she can talk with perfect correctness in any language except English. She is a polking[c] polyglott, a Creuzer[3] in crinoline. Poor men! There are so few of you who know even Hebrew; you think it something to boast of if, like Bolingbroke,[4] you only "understand that sort of learning, and what is writ about it;" and you are perhaps adoring women who can think slightingly of you in all the Semitic languages successively. But, then, as we are almost invariably told, that a heroine has a "beautifully small head," and as her intellect has probably been early invigorated by an

[a] In the high-flown style of the poems (1760–3) supposedly translated from the legendary Gaelic bard Ossian by James Macpherson.
[b] Christian love.
[c] I.e., dancing the polka.

attention to costume and deportment, we may conclude that she can pick up the Oriental tongues, to say nothing of their dialects, with the same aerial facility that the butterfly sips nectar. Besides, there can be no difficulty in conceiving the depth of the heroine's erudition, when that of the authoress is so evident.

In "Laura Gay,"[5] another novel of the same school, the heroine seems less at home in Greek and Hebrew, but she makes up for the deficiency by a quite playful familiarity with the Latin classics – with the "dear old Virgil," "the graceful Horace, the humane Cicero, and the pleasant Livy;" indeed, it is such a matter of course with her to quote Latin, that she does it at a pic-nic in a very mixed company of ladies and gentlemen, having, we are told, "no conception that the nobler sex were capable of jealousy on this subject. And if, indeed," continues the biographer of Laura Gay, "the wisest and noblest portion of that sex were in the majority, no such sentiment would exist; but while Miss Wyndhams and Mr. Redfords abound, great sacrifices must be made to their existence." Such sacrifices, we presume, as abstaining from Latin quotations, of extremely moderate interest and applicability, which the wise and noble minority of the other sex would be quite as willing to dispense with as the foolish and ignoble majority. It is as little the custom of well-bred men as of well-bred women to quote Latin in mixed parties; they can contain their familiarity with "the humane Cicero" without allowing it to boil over in ordinary conversation, and even references to "the pleasant Livy" are not absolutely irrepressible. But Ciceronian Latin is the mildest form of Miss Gay's conversation power. Being on the Palatine[a] with a party of sightseers, she falls into the following vein of well-rounded remark: – "Truth can only be pure objectively, for even in the creeds where it predominates, being subjective, and parcelled out into portions, each of these necessarily receives a hue of idiosyncrasy, that is, a taint of superstition more or less strong; while in such creeds as the Roman Catholic, ignorance, interest, the bias of ancient idolatries, and the force of authority, have gradually accumulated on the pure truth, and transformed it, at last, into a mass of superstition for the majority of its votaries; and how few are there, alas! whose zeal, courage, and intellectual energy are equal to the analysis of this accumulation, and to the discovery of the pearl of great price which lies hidden beneath this heap of rubbish." We have often met with women much more novel and profound in their observations than Laura Gay, but rarely with any so inopportunely long winded. A clerical lord, who is half in love with her, is alarmed by the daring

---

[a] Chief of the seven hills of Rome.

remarks just quoted, and begins to suspect that she is inclined to free-thinking. But he is mistaken; when in a moment of sorrow he delicately begs leave to "recal to her memory a *depôt* of strength and consolation under affliction, which, until we are hard pressed by the trials of life, we are too apt to forget," we learn that she really has "recurrence to that sacred depôt," together with the tea-pot. There is a certain flavour of orthodoxy mixed with the parade of fortunes and fine carriages in "Laura Gay," but it is an orthodoxy mitigated by study of "the humane Cicero," and by an "intellectual disposition to analyse."

"Compensation" is much more heavily dosed with doctrine, but then it has a treble amount of snobbish worldliness and absurd incident to tickle the palate of pious frivolity. Linda, the heroine, is still more speculative and spiritual than Laura Gay, but she has been "presented," and has more, and far grander, lovers; very wicked and fascinating women are introduced – even a French *lionne*;[a] and no expense is spared to get up as exciting a story as you will find in the most immoral novels. In fact, it is a wonderful *pot pourri* of Almack's, Scotch second-sight, Mr. Rogers's breakfasts,[6] Italian brigands, death-bed conversions, superior authoresses, Italian mistresses, and attempts at poisoning old ladies, the whole served up with a garnish of talk about "faith and development," and "most original minds." Even Miss Susan Barton, the superior authoress, whose pen moves in a "quick decided manner when she is composing," declines the finest opportunities of marriage; and though old enough to be Linda's mother (since we are told that she refused Linda's father), has her hand sought by a young earl, the heroine's rejected lover. Of course, genius and morality must be backed by eligible offers, or they would seem rather a dull affair; and piety, like other things, in order to be *comme il faut*, must be in "society," and have admittance to the best circles.

"Rank and Beauty"[7] is a more frothy and less religious variety of the mind-and-millinery species. The heroine, we are told, "if she inherited her father's pride of birth and her mother's beauty of person, had in herself a tone of enthusiastic feeling that perhaps belongs to her age even in the lowly born, but which is refined into the high spirit of wild romance only in the far descended, who feel that it is their best inheritance." This enthusiastic young lady, by dint of reading the newspaper to her father, falls in love with the *prime minister*, who, through the medium of leading articles and "the *resumé* of the debates," shines upon her imagination as a bright particular star,

[a] (Social) lioness.

which has no parallax for her, living in the country as simple Miss Wyndham. But she forthwith becomes Baroness Umfraville in her own right, astonishes the world with her beauty and accomplishments when she bursts upon it from her mansion in Spring Gardens,[a] and, as you foresee, will presently come into contact with the unseen *objet aimé*.[b] Perhaps the words "prime minister" suggest to you a wrinkled or obese sexagenarian; but pray dismiss the image. Lord Rupert Conway has been "called while still almost a youth to the first situation which a subject can hold in the *universe*," and even leading articles and a *resumé* of the debates have not conjured up a dream that surpasses the fact.

The door opened again, and Lord Rupert Conway entered. Evelyn gave one glance. It was enough; she was not disappointed. It seemed as if a picture on which she had long gazed was suddenly instinct with life, and had stepped from its frame before her. His tall figure, the distinguished simplicity of his air – it was a living Vandyke, a cavalier, one of his noble cavalier ancestors, or one to whom her fancy had always likened him, who long of yore had, with an Umfraville, fought the Paynim far beyond sea. Was this reality?

Very little like it, certainly.

By-and-by, it becomes evident that the ministerial heart is touched. Lady Umfraville is on a visit to the Queen at Windsor, and, –

The last evening of her stay, when they returned from riding, Mr. Wyndham took her and a large party to the top of the Keep, to see the view. She was leaning on the battlements, gazing from that "stately height" at the prospect beneath her, when Lord Rupert was by her side. "What an unrivalled view!" exclaimed she.

"Yes, it would have been wrong to go without having been up here. You are pleased with your visit?"

"Enchanted! 'A Queen to live and die under', to live and die for!"

"Ha!" cried he, with sudden emotion, and with a *eureka* expression of countenance, as if he had *indeed found a heart in unison with his own.*

The "*eureka* expression of countenance," you see at once to be prophetic of marriage at the end of the third volume; but before that desirable consummation, there are very complicated misunderstandings, arising chiefly from the vindictive plotting of Sir Luttrell Wycherley, who is a genius, a poet, and in every way a most remarkable character indeed. He is not only a romantic poet, but a hardened rake and a cynical wit; yet his deep passion for Lady Umfraville has so impoverished his epigrammatic talent, that he cuts an extremely poor figure in conversation. When she rejects him, he rushes into the shrubbery, and rolls himself in the dirt; and on recovering, devotes himself to the most diabolical and laborious schemes of vengeance, in the course of which he disguises himself as a

[a] Fashionable street in Westminster.   [b] Beloved object.

quack physician, and enters into general practice, foreseeing that Evelyn will fall ill, and that he shall be called in to attend her. At last, when all his schemes are frustrated, he takes leave of her in a long letter, written, as you will perceive from the following passage, entirely in the style of an eminent literary man: –

> Oh, lady, nursed in pomp and pleasure, will you ever cast one thought upon the miserable being who addresses you? Will you ever, as your gilded galley is floating down the unruffled stream of prosperity, will you ever, while lulled by the sweetest music – thine own praises, – hear the far-off sigh from that world to which I am going?

On the whole, however, frothy as it is, we rather prefer "Rank and Beauty" to the two other novels we have mentioned. The dialogue is more natural and spirited; there is some frank ignorance, and no pedantry; and you are allowed to take the heroine's astounding intellect upon trust, without being called on to read her conversational refutations of sceptics and philosophers, or her rhetorical solutions of the mysteries of the universe.

Writers of the mind-and-millinery school are remarkably unanimous in their choice of diction. In their novels, there is usually a lady or gentleman who is more or less of a upas tree:[a] the lover has a manly breast; minds are redolent of various things; hearts are hollow; events are utilized; friends are consigned to the tomb; infancy is an engaging period; the sun is a luminary that goes to his western couch, or gathers the rain-drops into his refulgent bosom; life is a melancholy boon; Albion and Scotia[b] are conversational epithets. There is a striking resemblance, too, in the character of their moral comments, such, for instance, as that "It is a fact, no less true than melancholy, that all people, more or less, richer or poorer, are swayed by bad example;" that "Books, however trivial, contain some subjects from which useful information may be drawn;" that "Vice can too often borrow the language of virtue;" that "Merit and nobility of nature must exist, to be accepted, for clamour and pretension cannot impose upon those too well read in human nature to be easily deceived;" and that, "In order to forgive, we must have been injured." There is, doubtless, a class of readers to whom these remarks appear peculiarly pointed and pungent; for we often find them doubly and trebly scored with the pencil, and delicate hands giving in their determined adhesion to these hardy novelties by a distinct *très vrai*, emphasized by many notes of exclamation. The colloquial style of these novels is often marked by much ingenious inversion, and a careful avoidance of such cheap phraseology as can be heard every day. Angry young gentlemen exclaim – "'Tis ever thus, methinks;" and in the half-hour before

[a] Tree yielding a poisonous juice.   [b] Literary names for Britain and Scotland, respectively.

dinner a young lady informs her next neighbour that the first day she read Shakspeare she "stole away into the park, and beneath the shadow of the greenwood tree, devoured with rapture the inspired page of the great magician." But the most remarkable efforts of the mind-and-millinery writers lie in their philosophic reflections. The authoress of "Laura Gay," for example, having married her hero and heroine, improves the event by observing that "if those sceptics, whose eyes have so long gazed on matter that they can no longer see aught else in man, could once enter with heart and soul into such bliss as this, they would come to say that the soul of man and the polypus are not of common origin, or of the same texture." Lady novelists, it appears, can see something else besides matter; they are not limited to phenomena, but can relieve their eyesight by occasional glimpses of the *noumenon*,[a] and are, therefore, naturally better able than any one else to confound sceptics, even of that remarkable, but to us unknown school, which maintains that the soul of man is of the same texture as the polypus.

The most pitiable of all silly novels by lady novelists are what we may call the *oracular* species – novels intended to expound the writer's religious, philosophical, or moral theories. There seems to be a notion abroad among women, rather akin to the superstition that the speech and actions of idiots are inspired, and that the human being most entirely exhausted of common sense is the fittest vehicle of revelation. To judge from their writings, there are certain ladies who think that an amazing ignorance, both of science and of life, is the best possible qualification for forming an opinion on the knottiest moral and speculative questions. Apparently, their recipe for solving all such difficulties is something like this: – Take a woman's head, stuff it with a smattering of philosophy and literature chopped small, and with false notions of society baked hard, let it hang over a desk a few hours every day, and serve up hot in feeble English, when not required. You will rarely meet with a lady novelist of the oracular class who is diffident of her ability to decide on theological questions, – who has any suspicion that she is not capable of discriminating with the nicest accuracy between the good and evil in all church parties, – who does not see precisely how it is that men have gone wrong hitherto, – and pity philosophers in general that they have not had the opportunity of consulting her. Great writers, who have modestly contented themselves with putting their experience into fiction, and have thought it quite a sufficient task to exhibit men and things as they are, she sighs

[a] An object apprehended by the intellect, a thing-in-itself, as opposed to a *phenomenon*, an object apprehended by the senses.

over as deplorably deficient in the application of their powers. "They have solved no great questions" – and she is ready to remedy their omission by setting before you a complete theory of life and manual of divinity, in a love story, where ladies and gentlemen of good family go through genteel vicissitudes, to the utter confusion of Deists, Puseyites,[8] and ultra-Protestants, and to the perfect establishment of that particular view of Christianity which either condenses itself into a sentence of small caps, or explodes into a cluster of stars on the three hundred and thirtieth page. It is true, the ladies and gentlemen will probably seem to you remarkably little like any you have had the fortune or misfortune to meet with, for, as a general rule, the ability of a lady novelist to describe actual life and her fellow-men, is in inverse proportion to her confident eloquence about God and the other world, and the means by which she usually chooses to conduct you to true ideas of the invisible is a totally false picture of the visible.

As typical a novel of the oracular kind as we can hope to meet with, is "The Engima: a Leaf from the Chronicles of the Wolchorley House."[9] The "enigma" which this novel is to solve, is certainly one that demands powers no less gigantic than those of a lady novelist, being neither more nor less than the existence of evil. The problem is stated, and the answer dimly foreshadowed on the very first page. The spirited young lady, with raven hair, says, "All life is an inextricable confusion;" and the meek young lady, with auburn hair, looks at the picture of the Madonna which she is copying, and – "*There* seemed the solution of that mighty enigma." The style of this novel is quite as lofty as its purpose; indeed, some passages on which we have spent much patient study are quite beyond our reach, in spite of the illustrative aid of italics and small caps; and we must await further "development" in order to understand them. Of Ernest, the model young clergyman, who sets every one right on all occasions, we read, that "he held not of marriage in the marketable kind, after a social desecration;" that, on one eventful night, "sleep had not visited his divided heart, where tumultuated, in varied type and combination, the aggregate feelings of grief and joy;" and that, "for the *marketable* human article he had no toleration, be it of what sort, or set for what value it might, whether for worship or class, his upright soul abhorred it, whose ultimatum, the self-deceiver, was to him THE *great spiritual lie*, 'living in a vain show, deceiving and being deceived;' since he did not suppose the phylactery and enlarged border on the garment to be *merely* a social trick." (The italics and small caps are the author's, and we hope they assist the reader's comprehension.) Of Sir Lionel, the model old gentleman, we are told that "the simple ideal of the middle age, apart from its anarchy and decadence, in him most truly seemed to live again, when the ties which knit men together were of heroic cast. The first-born colours of pristine faith and truth engraven on the common soul of man, and blent into the wide arch of brotherhood, where the primæval law of *order* grew and multiplied, each perfect after his kind, and mutually inter-dependent." You see clearly, of course, how colours are first engraven on a soul, and then blent into a wide arch, on which arch of colours – apparently a rainbow – the law of order grew and multiplied, each – apparently the arch and the law – perfect after his kind? If, after this, you can possibly want any further aid towards knowing what Sir Lionel was, we can tell you, that in his soul "the scientific combinations of thought could educe no fuller harmonies of the good and the true, than lay in the primæval pulses which floated as an atmosphere around it!" and that, when he was sealing a letter, "Lo! the responsive throb in that good man's bosom echoed back in simple truth the honest witness of a heart that condemned him not, as his eye, bedewed with love, rested, too, with something of ancestral pride, on the undimmed motto of the family – 'Loiauté.'"

The slightest matters have their vulgarity fumigated out of them by the same elevated style. Commonplace people would say that a copy of Shakspeare lay on a drawing-room table, but the authoress of "The Enigma," bent on edifying periphrasis, tells you that there lay on the table, "that fund of human thought and feeling, which teaches the heart through the little name, 'Shakspeare.'" A watchman sees a light burning in an upper window rather longer than usual, and thinks that people are foolish to sit up late when they have an opportunity of going to bed; but, lest this fact should seem too low and common, it is presented to us in the following striking and metaphysical manner: "He marvelled – as man *will* think for others in a necessarily separate personality, consequently (though disallowing it) in false mental premise, – how differently *he* should act, how gladly *he* should prize the rest so lightly held of within." A footman – an ordinary Jeames,[a] with large calves and aspirated vowels – answers the door-bell, and the opportunity is seized to tell you that he was a "type of the large class of pampered menials, who follow the curse of Cain – 'vagabonds' on the face of the earth, and whose estimate of the human class varies in the graduate scale of money and expenditure . . . . These, and such as these, O England, be the false lights of thy morbid civilization!" We have heard of various "false lights," from Dr. Cumming to Robert Owen, from Dr. Pusey to the Spirit-rappers,[10] but we never before heard of the false light that emanates from plush and powder.

[a] Cockney footman.

In the same way very ordinary events of civilized life are exalted into the most awful crises, and ladies in full skirts and *manches à la Chinoise*,[a] conduct themselves not unlike the heroines of sanguinary melodramas. Mrs. Percy, a shallow woman of the world, wishes her son Horace to marry the auburn-haired Grace, she being an heiress; but he, after the manner of sons, falls in love with the raven-haired Kate, the heiress's portionless cousin; and moreover, Grace herself shows every symptom of perfect indifference to Horace. In such cases, sons are often sulky or fiery, mothers are alternately manœuvring and waspish, and the portionless young lady often lies awake at night and cries a good deal. We are getting used to these things now, just as we are used to eclipses of the moon, which no longer set us howling and beating tin kettles. We never heard of a lady in a fashionable "front" behaving like Mrs. Percy under these circumstances. Happening one day to see Horace talking to Grace at a window, without in the least knowing what they are talking about, or having the least reason to believe that Grace, who is mistress of the house and a person of dignity, would accept her son if he were to offer himself, she suddenly rushes up to them and clasps them both, saying, "with a flushed countenance and in an excited manner" – "This is indeed happiness; for, may I not call you so, Grace? – my Grace – my Horace's Grace! – my dear children!" Her son tells her she is mistaken, and that he is engaged to Kate, whereupon we have the following scene and tableau: –

Gathering herself up to an unprecedented height, (!) her eyes lightning forth the fire of her anger:–

"Wretched boy!" she said, hoarsely and scornfully, and clenching her hand, "Take then the doom of your own choice! Bow down your miserable head and let a mother's–"

"Curse not!" spake a deep low voice from behind, and Mrs. Percy started, scared, as though she had seen a heavenly visitant appear, to break upon her in the midst of her sin.

Meantime, Horace had fallen on his knees at her feet, and hid his face in his hands.

Who, then, is she – who! Truly his "guardian spirit" hath stepped between him and the fearful words, which, however unmerited, must have hung as a pall over his future existence; – a spell which could not be unbound – which could not be unsaid.

Of an earthly paleness, but calm with the still, iron-bound calmness of death – the only calm one there, – Katherine stood; and her words smote on the ear in tones whose appallingly slow and separate intonation rung on the heart like the chill, isolated tolling of some fatal knell.

"He would have plighted me his faith, but I did not accept it; you cannot, therefore – you *dare* not curse him. And here", she continued, raising her hand to heaven, whither her large dark eyes also rose with a chastened glow, which, for the first time, *suffering* had lighted in those passionate orbs, – "here I promise, come weal, come woe, that Horace Wolchorley and I do never interchange vows without his mother's sanction – without his mother's blessing!"

[a] Sleeves in the Chinese style.

Here, and throughout the story, we see that confusion of purpose which is so characteristic of silly novels written by women. It is a story of quite modern drawing-room society – a society in which polkas are played and Puseyism discussed; yet we have characters, and incidents, and traits of manner introduced, which are mere shreds from the most heterogeneous romances. We have a blind Irish harper "relic of the picturesque bards of yore," startling us at a Sunday-school festival of tea and cake in an English village; we have a crazy gipsy, in a scarlet cloak singing snatches of romantic song, and revealing a secret on her deathbed which, with the testimony of a dwarfish miserly merchant, who salutes strangers with a curse and a devilish laugh, goes to prove that Ernest, the model young clergyman, is Kate's brother; and we have an ultra-virtuous Irish Barney, discovering that a document is forged, by comparing the date of the paper with the date of the alleged signature, although the same document has passed through a court of law, and occasioned a fatal decision. The "Hall" in which Sir Lionel lives is the venerable country-seat of an old family, and this, we suppose, sets the imagination of the authoress flying to donjons and battlements, where "lo! the warder blows his horn;" for, as the inhabitants are in their bedrooms on a night certainly within the recollection of Pleaceman X.,[11] and a breeze springs up, which we are at first told was faint, and then that it made the old cedars bow their branches to the greensward, she falls into this mediæval vein of description (the italics are ours): "The banner *unfurled it* at the sound, and shook its guardian wing above, while the startled owl *flapped her* in the ivy; the firmament looking down through her 'argus eyes,' –

Ministers of heaven's mute melodies.

And lo! two strokes tolled from out the warder tower, and 'Two o'clock' re-echoed its interpreter below."

Such stories as this of "The Enigma" remind us of the pictures clever children sometimes draw "out of their own head," where you will see a modern villa on the right, two knights in helmets fighting in the foreground, and a tiger grinning in a jungle on the left, and several objects being brought together because the artist thinks each pretty, and perhaps still more because he remembers seeing them in other pictures.

But we like the authoress much better on her mediæval stilts than on her oracular ones, – when she talks of the *Ich*[a] and of "subjective" and "objective," and lays down the exact line of Christian verity, between

---

[a] I, ego; in the recent German philosophy with which Eliot was familiar, the conscious, thinking subject.

"right-hand excesses and left-hand declensions." Persons who deviate from this line are introduced with a patronizing air of charity. Of a certain Miss Inshquine she informs us, with all the lucidity of italics and small caps, that *"function,* not *form,* AS *the inevitable outer expression of the spirit in this tabernacled age,* weakly engrossed her." And *à propos* of Miss Mayjar, an evangelical lady who is a little too apt to talk of her visits to sick women and the state of their souls, we are told that the model clergyman is "not one to disallow, through the *super* crust, the undercurrent towards good in the *subject,* or the positive benefits, nevertheless, to the *object."* We imagine the double-refined accent and protrusion of chin which are feebly represented by the italics in this lady's sentences! We abstain from quoting any of her oracular doctrinal passages, because they refer to matters too serious for our pages just now.

The epithet "silly" may seem impertinent, applied to a novel which indicates so much reading and intellectual activity as "The Enigma;" but we use this epithet advisedly. If, as the world has long agreed, a very great amount of instruction will not make a wise man, still less will a very mediocre amount of instruction make a wise woman. And the most mischievous form of feminine silliness is the literary form, because it tends to confirm the popular prejudice against the more solid education of woman. When men see girls wasting their time in consultations about bonnets and ball dresses, and in giggling or sentimental love-confidences, or middle-aged women mismanaging their children, and solacing themselves with acrid gossip, they can hardly help saying, "For Heaven's sake, let girls be better educated; let them have some better objects of thought – some more solid occupations." But after a few hours' conversation with an oracular literary woman, or a few hours' reading of her books, they are likely enough to say, "After all, when a woman gets some knowledge, see what use she makes of it! Her knowledge remains acquisition, instead of passing into culture; instead of being subdued into modesty and simplicity by a larger acquaintance with thought and fact, she has a feverish consciousness of her attainments; she keeps a sort of mental pocket-mirror, and is continually looking in it at her own 'intellectuality;' she spoils the taste of one's muffin by questions of metaphysics; 'puts down' men at a dinner table with her superior information; and seizes the opportunity of a *soirée* to catechise us on the vital question of the relation between mind and matter. And then, look at her writings! She mistakes vagueness for depth, bombast for eloquence, and affectation for originality; she struts on one page, rolls her eyes on another, grimaces in a third, and is hysterical in a fourth. She may have read many writings of great men, and a few writings of great women; but she is as unable to discern the difference between her own style and theirs as a Yorkshireman is to discern the difference between his own English and a Londoner's: rhodomontade[a] is the native accent of her intellect. No – the average nature of women is too shallow and feeble a soil to bear much tillage; it is only fit for the very lightest crops."

It is true that the men who come to such a decision on such very superficial and imperfect observation may not be among the wisest in the world; but we have not now to contest their opinion – we are only pointing out how it is unconsciously encouraged by many women who have volunteered themselves as representatives of the feminine intellect. We do not believe that a man was ever strengthened in such an opinion by associating with a woman of true culture, whose mind had absorbed her knowledge instead of being absorbed by it. A really cultured woman, like a really cultured man, is all the simpler and the less obtrusive for her knowledge; it has made her see herself and her opinions in something like just proportions; she does not make it a pedestal from which she flatters herself that she commands a complete view of men and things, but makes it a point of observation from which to form a right estimate of herself. She neither spouts poetry nor quotes Cicero on slight provocation; not because she thinks that a sacrifice must be made to the prejudices of men, but because that mode of exhibiting her memory and Latinity does not present itself to her as edifying or graceful. She does not write books to confound philosophers, perhaps because she is able to write books that delight them. In conversation she is the least formidable of women, because she understands you, without wanting to make you aware that you *can't* understand her. She does not give you information, which is the raw material of culture, – she gives you sympathy, which is its subtlest essence.

A more numerous class of silly novels than the oracular, (which are generally inspired by some form of High Church, or transcendental Christianity,) is what we may call the *white neck-cloth* species, which represent the tone of thought and feeling in the Evangelical party. This species is a kind of genteel tract on a large scale, intended as a sort of medicinal sweetmeat of Low Church young ladies; an Evangelical substitute for the fashionable novel, as the May Meetings[b] are a substitute for the Opera. Even Quaker children, one would think, can hardly have been denied the indulgence of a doll; but it must be a doll dressed in a drab gown and a coal-scuttle bonnet – not a worldly doll,

[a] Bluster.
[b] The Church of England Missionary Society's annual meeting.

in gauze and spangles. And there are no young ladies, we imagine, – unless they belong to the Church of the United Brethren, in which people are married without any love-making – who can dispense with love stories. Thus, for Evangelical young ladies there are Evangelical love stories, in which the vicissitudes of the tender passion are sanctified by saving views of Regeneration and the Atonement. These novels differ from the oracular ones, as a Low Churchwoman often differs from a High Churchwoman: they are a little less supercilious, and a great deal more ignorant, a little less correct in their syntax, and a great deal more vulgar.

The Orlando[12] of Evangelical literature is the young curate looked at from the point of view of the middle class, where cambric bands[a] are understood to have as thrilling an effect on the hearts of young ladies as epaulettes have in the classes above and below it. In the ordinary type of these novels, the hero is almost sure to be a young curate, frowned upon, perhaps, by worldly mammas, but carrying captive the hearts of their daughters, who can "never forget *that* sermon;" tender glances are seized from the pulpit stairs instead of the opera-box; *tête-à-têtes* are seasoned with quotations from Scripture, instead of quotations from the poets; and questions as to the state of the heroine's affections are mingled with anxieties as to the state of her soul. The young curate always has a background of well-dressed and wealthy, if not fashionable society; – for Evangelical silliness is as snobbish as any other kind of silliness; and the Evangelical lady novelist, while she explains to you the type of the scapegoat on one page, is ambitious on another to represent the manners and conversation of aristocratic people. Her pictures of fashionable society are often curious studies considered as efforts of the Evangelical imagination; but in one particular the novels of the White Neck-cloth School are meritoriously realistic, – their favourite hero, the Evangelical young curate is always rather an insipid personage.

The most recent novel of this species that we happen to have before us, is "The Old Grey Church."[13] It is utterly tame and feeble; there is no one set of objects on which the writer seems to have a stronger grasp than on any other; and we should be entirely at a loss to conjecture among what phases of life her experience has been gained, but for certain vulgarisms of style which sufficiently indicate that she has had the advantage, though she has been unable to use it, of mingling chiefly with men and women whose manners and characters have not had all their bosses and angles rubbed down by refined conventionalism. It is less excusable in an Evangelical novelist, than in any other,

---

[a] Linen strips hanging down the front of clerical garb.

gratuitously to seek her subjects among titles and carriages. The real drama of Evangelicalism – and it has abundance of fine drama for any one who has genius enough to discern and reproduce it – lies among the middle and lower classes; and are not Evangelical opinions understood to give an especial interest in the weak things of the earth, rather than in the mighty? Why then, cannot our Evangelical lady novelists show us the operation of their religious views among people (there really are many such in the world) who keep no carriage, "not so much as a brassbound gig," who even manage to eat their dinner without a silver fork, and in whose mouths the authoress's questionable English would be strictly consistent? Why can we not have pictures of religious life among the industrial classes in England, as interesting as Mrs. Stowe's pictures of religious life among the negroes?[14] Instead of this, pious ladies nauseate us with novels which remind us of what we sometimes see in a worldly woman recently "converted;" – she is as fond of a fine dinner table as before, but she invites clergymen instead of beaux; she thinks as much of her dress as before, but she adopts a more sober choice of colours and patterns; her conversation is as trivial as before, but the triviality is flavoured with gospel instead of gossip. In "The Old Grey Church," we have the same sort of Evangelical travesty of the fashionable novel, and of course the vicious, intriguing baronet is not wanting. It is worth while to give a sample of the style of conversation attributed to this high-born rake – a style that in its profuse italics and palpable innuendoes, is worthy of Miss Squeers.[15] In an evening visit to the ruins of the Colosseum, Eustace, the young clergyman, has been withdrawing the heroine, Miss Lushington, from the rest of the party, for the sake of a *tête-à-tête*. The baronet is jealous, and vents his pique in this way: –

There they are, and Miss Lushington, no doubt, quite safe; for she is under the holy guidance of Pope Eustace the First, who has, of course, been delivering to her an edifying homily on the wickedness of the heathens of yore, who, as tradition tells us, in this very place let loose the wild *beastises* on poor St. Paul! – Oh, no! by-the-bye, I believe I am wrong, and betraying my want of clergy, and that it was not at all St. Paul, nor was it here. But no matter, it would equally serve as a text to preach from, and from which to diverge to the degenerate *heathen* Christians of the present day, and all their naughty practices, and so end with an exhortation to 'come out from among them, and be separate;' – and I am sure, Miss Lushington, you have most scrupulously conformed to that injunction this evening, for we have seen nothing of you since our arrival. But every one seems agreed it has been a *charming party of pleasure*, and I am sure we all feel *much indebted* to Mr. Grey for having *suggested* it; and as he seems so capital a cicerone, I hope he will think of something else equally agreeable to *all*.

This drivelling kind of dialogue, and equally drivelling narrative, which, like a bad drawing, represents nothing, and barely indicates what is meant to be represented, runs through the book; and we have no doubt is considered by the amiable authoress to constitute an improving novel, which Christian mothers will do well to put into the hands of their daughters. But everything is relative; we have met with American vegetarians whose normal diet was dry meal, and who, when their appetite wanted stimulating, tickled it with *wet* meal; and so we can imagine that there are Evangelical circles in which "The Old Grey Church" is devoured as a powerful and interesting fiction.

But, perhaps, the least readable of silly women's novels, are the *modern-antique* species, which unfold to us the domestic life of Jannes and Jambres, the private love affairs of Sennacherib, or the mental struggles and ultimate conversion of Demetrius the silversmith.[16] From most silly novels we can at least extract a laugh; but those of the modern antique school have a ponderous, a leaden kind of fatuity, under which we groan. What can be more demonstrative of the inability of literary women to measure their own powers, than their frequent assumption of a task which can only be justified by the rarest concurrence of acquirement with genius? The finest effort to reanimate the past is of course only approximative – is always more or less an infusion of the modern spirit into the ancient form, –

> Was ihr den Geist der Zeiten heisst,
> Das ist im Grund der Herren eigner Geist,
> In dem die Zeiten sich bespiegeln.[a]

Admitting that genius which has familiarized itself with all the relics of an ancient period can sometimes, by the force of its sympathetic divination, restore the missing notes in the "music of humanity,"[17] and reconstruct the fragments into a whole which will really bring the remote past nearer to us, and interpret it to our duller apprehension, – this form of imaginative power must always be among the very rarest, because it demands as much accurate and minute knowledge as creative vigour. Yet we find ladies constantly choosing to make their mental mediocrity more conspicuous, by clothing it in a masquerade of ancient names; by putting their feeble sentimentality into the mouths of Roman vestals or Egyptian princesses, and attributing their rhetorical arguments to Jewish high-priests and Greek philosophers. A recent example of this heavy imbecility is, "Adonijah, a Tale of the Jewish Dispersion,"[18] which forms part of a series, "uniting," we are told, "taste, humour, and sound principles." "Adonijah," we presume,

---

[a] What you the spirit of the ages call
Is nothing but the spirit of you all,
Wherein the ages are reflected.
  Johann Wolfgang von Goethe, *Faust* I (1808), ll. 577–9

exemplifies the tale of "sound principles;"[19] the taste and humour are to be found in other members of the series. We are told on the cover, that the incidents of this tale are "fraught with unusual interest," and the preface winds up thus: "To those who feel interested in the dispersed of Israel and Judea, these pages may afford, perhaps, information on an important subject, as well as amusement." Since the "important subject" on which this book is to afford information is not specified, it may possibly lie in some esoteric meaning to which we have no key; but if it has relation to the dispersed of Israel and Judea at any period of their history, we believe a tolerably well-informed school-girl already knows much more of it than she will find in this "Tale of the Jewish Dispersion." "Adonijah" is simply the feeblest kind of love story, supposed to be instructive, we presume, because the hero is a Jewish captive, and the heroine a Roman vestal; because they and their friends are converted to Christianity after the shortest and easiest method approved by the "Society for Promoting the Conversion of the Jews;" and because, instead of being written in plain language, it is adorned with that peculiar style of grandiloquence which is held by some lady novelists to give an antique colouring, and which we recognise at once in such phrases as these: – "the splendid regnal talents undoubtedly possessed by the Emperor Nero" – "the expiring scion of a lofty stem" – "the virtuous partner of his couch" – "ah, by Vesta!" – and "I tell thee, Roman." Among the quotations which serve at once for instruction and ornament on the cover of this volume, there is one from Miss Sinclair,[20] which informs us that "Works of imagination are *avowedly* read by men of science, wisdom, and piety;" from which we suppose the reader is to gather the cheering inference that Dr. Daubeny, Mr. Mill, or Mr. Maurice,[21] may openly indulge himself with the perusal of "Adonijah," without being obliged to secrete it among the sofa cushions, or read it by snatches under the dinner table.

"Be not a baker if your head be made of butter," says a homely proverb, which, being interpreted, may mean, let no woman rush into print who is not prepared for the consequences. We are aware that our remarks are in a very different tone from that of the reviewers who, with a perennial recurrence of precisely similar emotions, only paralleled, we imagine, in the experience of monthly nurses, tell one lady novelist after another that they "hail" her productions "with delight." We are aware that the ladies at whom our criticism is pointed are accustomed to be told, in the choicest phraseology of puffery, that their pictures of life are brilliant, their characters well drawn, their style fascinating, and their sentiments lofty. But if they are inclined to resent our plainness of speech, we ask them to reflect for a moment on the chary praise, and often captious blame, which their panegyrists give to writers whose works are on the way to become classics. No sooner does a woman show that she has genius or effective talent, than she receives the tribute of being moderately praised and severely criticised. By a peculiar thermometric adjustment, when a woman's talent is at zero, journalistic approbation is at the boiling pitch; when she attains mediocrity, it is already at no more than summer heat; and if ever she reaches excellence, critical enthusiasm drops to the freezing point. Harriet Martineau, Currer Bell, and Mrs. Gaskell have been treated as cavalierly as if they had been men. And every critic who forms a high estimate of the share women may ultimately take in literature, will, on principle, abstain from any exceptional indulgence towards the productions of literary women. For it must be plain to every one who looks impartially and extensively into feminine literature, that its greatest deficiencies are due hardly more to the want of intellectual power than to the want of those moral qualities that contribute to literary excellence – patient diligence, a sense of the responsibility involved in publication, and an appreciation of the sacredness of the writer's art. In the majority of women's books you see that kind of facility which springs from the absence of any high standard; that fertility in imbecile combination or feeble imitation which a little self-criticism would check and reduce to barrenness; just as with a total want of musical ear people will sing out of tune, while a degree more melodic sensibility would suffice to render them silent. The foolish vanity of wishing to appear in print, instead of being counterbalanced by any consciousness of the intellectual or moral derogation implied in futile authorship, seems to be encouraged by the extremely false impression that to write *at all* is a proof of superiority in a woman. On this ground, we believe that the average intellect of women is unfairly represented by the mass of feminine literature, and that while the few women who write well are very far above the ordinary intellectual level of their sex, the many women who write ill are very far below it. So that, after all, the severer critics are fulfilling a chivalrous duty in depriving the mere fact of feminine authorship of any false prestige which may give it a delusive attraction, and in recommending women of mediocre faculties – as at least a negative service they can render their sex – to abstain from writing.

The standing apology for women who become writers without any special qualification is, that society shuts them out from other spheres of occupation. Society is a very culpable entity, and has to answer for the manufacture of many unwholesome commodities, from bad pickles to bad poetry. But society, like "matter," and Her Majesty's Government, and other lofty abstractions, has its share of excessive blame as well as excessive praise. Where there is one woman who writes from necessity, we believe there are three women who write from vanity; and, besides, there is something so antiseptic in the mere healthy fact of working for one's bread, that the most trashy and rotten kind of feminine literature is not likely to have been produced under such circumstances. "In all labour there is profit;"[22] but ladies' silly novels, we imagine, are less the result of labour than of busy idleness.

Happily, we are not dependent on argument to prove that Fiction is a department of literature in which women can, after their kind, fully equal men. A cluster of great names, both living and dead, rush to our memories in evidence that women can produce novels not only fine, but among the very finest; – novels, too, that have a precious speciality, lying quite apart from masculine aptitudes and experience. No educational restrictions can shut women out from the materials of fiction, and there is no species of art which is so free from rigid requirements. Like crystalline masses, it may take any form, and yet be beautiful; we have only to pour in the right elements – genuine observation, humour, and passion. But it is precisely this absence of rigid requirement which constitutes the fatal seduction of novel-writing to incompetent women. Ladies are not wont to be very grossly deceived as to their power of playing on the piano; here certain positive difficulties of execution have to be conquered, and incompetence inevitably breaks down. Every art which has its absolute *technique* is, to a certain extent, guarded from the intrusions of mere left-handed imbecility. But in novel-writing there are no barriers for incapacity to stumble against, no external criteria to prevent a writer from mistaking foolish facility for mastery. And so we have again and again the old story of La Fontaine's ass,[23] who puts his nose to the flute, and, finding that he elicits some sound, exclaims, 'Moi, aussi, je joue de la flute;'[a] – a fable which we commend, at parting, to the consideration of any feminine reader who is in danger of adding to the number of "silly novels by lady novelists."

[a] 'I too can play the flute.'

George Henry Lewes
(1817–1878)
'Criticism in Relation to Novels', 1865

Like so many of his mid-Victorian contemporaries, but even more than most of them, Georges Henry Lewes was blessed, or cursed, with a restlessly inquiring intellect that drew him into many fields of knowledge, among which he saw significant connections. Most of his encyclopedic learning he acquired on his own: his early education was irregular, he did not attend a university, and he had to earn his living from the time he was sixteen. Lewes's pen was as active as his mind was fertile, and he published substantial books on a variety of subjects. His two-volume *The Life and Works of Goethe* (1855) was widely acclaimed; his major works in philosophy include the four-volume *Biographical History of Philosophy* (1845–6) and *Comte's Philosophy of the Sciences* (1853); his scientific researches led to the writing of *Sea-side Studies at Ilfracombe, Tenby, the Scilly Isles, and Jersey* (1858), *The Physiology of Common Life* (1859–60), and *Studies in Animal Life* (1862); his life-long interest in the theatre (he had been both an actor and a playwright as well as a drama critic) was reflected in *On Actors and the Art of Acting* (1875); he wrote two novels; *Ranthorpe* (1847) and *Rose, Blanche, and Violet* (1848). For nearly a quarter-century (1854–78) Lewes and George Eliot lived together as husband and wife in a union that stimulated the creativity of each: it was she who after his death completed his five-volume *Problems of Life and Mind* (1874–9).

The lengthy list of Lewes's books, of which only some are mentioned above, includes none devoted to literary criticism. But he was constantly writing about belles-lettres, in such periodicals as the *British and Foreign Review*, the *Foreign Quarterly Review*, the *Edinburgh Review*, *Blackwood's Edinburgh Magazine*, the *British Quarterly Review*, the *Westminster Review*, the *Leader*, the *Cornhill Magazine*, and the *Fortnightly Review* (he edited each of the last three for brief periods during the 1850s and 1860s); and, though his ideas changed during his many years as a reviewer, he always brought to his reading the same intellectual rigour, the same refusal to accept fuzzy thinking or received opinions, the same insistence on a scrupulous examination of the evidence, that marked his writings about biology, psychology, or philosophy.

As Lewes makes clear at the beginning of 'Criticism in Relation to Novels', the widespread dismissal of fiction as 'light literature' is unacceptable, for not only do the lowered expectations of patronizing and 'contemptuous' critics excuse a lowered standard of performance by novelists but they actually contribute to 'the production of mediocrity'. This is lamentable because in Lewes's view the novel, like more respected literary genres, has a lofty aim: to enlarge the understanding of readers by making them intellectually and imaginatively aware of truth.

The serious novelist writing in an age of seemingly boundless activity in the natural, social, moral, and human sciences must be aware of current ideas and incorporate the best and most significant of them into his fiction. To be sure, his work must stir the emotions of his readers, bringing about delight, if it is to achieve the goals that Lewes sets for literature. But delight is not enough, and popular acclaim is not a valid criterion of merit for Lewes, the critic who writes of 'the intellectual feebleness of readers in general'. In Lewes's view, Dickens, the most popular novelist of the age, falls considerably short of his high standards. As Lewes argues in 'Dickens in Relation to Criticism' (*Fortnightly Review*, n.s. II (I February 1872): 141–54), Dickens cannot be called a realist, for he does not portray rounded characters of some complexity, nor is he an idealistic novelist in that he declines to concern himself with heroic men and women of some grandeur. Rather, in his frequent flights of imagination Dickens eschews the ideal but approaches or actually enters the realm of hallucination, which is the mark of a diseased mind. As for ideas, Dickens with his *'animal* intelligence' cannot grasp them, confining himself to 'perceptions' and 'sensations'.

For Lewes, 'Art always aims at the representation of Reality', but he ultimately refuses to oppose realistic to idealistic fiction: though realism is 'the basis of all Art', 'its antithesis is not Idealism, but *Falsism*'. In the review from which these quotations are taken – 'Realism in Art: Recent German Fiction' (*Westminster Review*, 70 (October 1858): 488–518) – he goes on to make the case that both the realistic and the idealistic artist must accurately apprehend and render whatever it is they strive to represent in their work, whether that be external fact or internal 'sentiment'.

The two new novels reviewed in 'Criticism in Relation to Novels' – *Sir Jasper's Tenant* by Mary Elizabeth Braddon and especially *Maxwell Drewitt* by Charlotte Riddell ('F. G. Trafford') – show all too plainly to what abuses the prevailing disregard of such criteria in the criticism of fiction has led. The essay appeared in the *Fortnightly Review* on 15 December 1865 (3: 352–61).

ALTHOUGH the fame of a great novelist is only something less than the fame of a great poet, and the reputation of a clever novelist is far superior to that of a respectable poet, the general estimation of prose fiction as a branch of Literature has something contemptuous in it. This is shown not only in the condescending tone in which critics speak, and the carelessness with which they praise, but also in the half-apologetic phrases in which very shallow readers confess that they have employed their leisured ignorance on such light literature. It is shown, moreover, in the rashness with which writers, confessedly incapable of success in far inferior efforts, will confidently attempt fiction, as if it were the easiest of literary tasks; and in the insolent assumption that "anything will do for a novel."

The reason of this fame, and the reason of this contempt, are not difficult to find. The fame is great because the influence of a fine novel is both extensive and subtle, and because the combination of high powers necessary for the production of a fine novel is excessively rare. The contempt is general, because the combination of powers necessary for the production of three volumes of Circulating Library reminiscences is very common; and because there is a large demand for the amusement which such reminiscences afford. The intellectual feebleness of readers in general prevents their forming a discriminating estimate of the worth of such works; and most of those who are capable of discrimination have had their standard of expectation so lowered by the profusion of mediocrity, that they languidly acquiesce in the implied assumption that novels are removed from the canons of common-sense criticism. Hence the activity of this commerce of trash. The sterile abundance casts a sort of opprobrium on the art itself. The lowered standard invites the incapable. Men and women who have shown no special aptitudes for this difficult art flatter themselves, and not unreasonably, that they may succeed as well as others whom openly they despise. And their friends are ready to urge them on this path. No one looking over the sketchbook of an amateur turns to him with the question – "Why not try your hand at a fresco?" But many men, on no better warrant, say to a writer – "Why not try your hand at a novel?" And there is great alacrity in trying the hand.

There is thus action and reaction: acquiescence in mediocrity increases the production of mediocrity and lowers the standard, which thus in turn admits of inferior production. We critics are greatly to blame. Instead of compensating for the inevitable evils of periodical criticism by doing our utmost to keep up the standard of public taste, too many of us help to debase it by taking a standard from the Circulating Library, and by a half-contemptuous, half-languid patronage of what we do not seriously admire. The lavish eulogies which welcome very trivial works as if they were masterpieces, are sometimes the genuine expression of very ignorant writers (for easy as it is to write a poor novel, to review it is easier still; and the very language of the reviews often betrays the intellectual condition of the writers); but sometimes they are judgments formed solely in reference to the degraded standard which the multitude of poor works has introduced. Thus although the same terms of commendation are applied to the last new novel which are applied to "Vanity Fair," or "Pride and Prejudice," the standard is nevertheless insensibly changed, and the critic who uses the same language respecting both never really thinks of placing both in the same class.

The general public knows nothing of this change of standards; and thus a foreigner, casting his eye over our advertisements, would suppose, from the "opinions of the press," that England boasted of two or three score writers of exquisite genius; but if, seduced by this supposition, he familiarised himself with the masterpieces thus extolled, he would perhaps conclude that England was suffering from a softened brain. One thing would certainly arouse his curiosity, and that would be to meet with a sample of what are everywhere called "the ordinary run of novels." He would hear that Mr. A's work was far superior to this ordinary run; that Mrs. B's exquisite story was carefully separated from the ordinary run; that Miss C's tale displayed a delicacy of conception, a depth of insight into character and passion, and a purity of moral tone sought for in vain in the ordinary run of novels. But he would appeal to Mudie[1] in vain for a novel which was acknowledged as one of the ordinary run.

Although I have a very high opinion of Fiction as a form of Literature, and read no kind of Literature with more delight and gratitude, I cannot pretend to an extensive acquaintance with recent novels; indeed there are writers of considerable reputation whose works I have never opened, either because they have not fallen in my way in hours of leisure, or because those whose judgment I respect have not by their praises induced me to make a trial. Nevertheless, living in a great literary centre, and naturally inclined to seek the immense gratification which a good novel always gives, I have become tolerably acquainted with the typical specimens, and come to the conclusion that if many of the novels of to-day are considerably better than those of twenty or thirty years ago, because they partake of the general advance in culture, and its wider diffusion; the vast increase of novels, mostly worthless, is a serious danger to public culture, a danger which tends to become more and more imminent, and can only be arrested by an energetic resolution on the part of the critics to do their duty with conscientious rigour. At present this duty is evaded, or performed fitfully. There is plenty of sarcasm and ill-nature; too much of it; there is little serious criticism which weighs considerably its praise and its blame. Even in the best journals poor novels are often praised in terms strictly applicable to works of genius alone. If a thoughtful reader opens one of these novels, he sees such violations of common sense and common knowledge, such style and such twaddle, as would never gain admission into the critical journals themselves, for these journals recommend to readers what they would refuse to print. The reason generally is that critics have ceased to regard novels as Literature, and do not think of applying to the style and sentiments of a fiction those ordinary canons which would be applied to a history, an article, or a pamphlet.

And there is sometimes a certain justification for this exception; only it should be always brought prominently forward. The distinctive element in Fiction is that of plot-interest. The rest is vehicle. If critics would carefully specify the qualities which distinguish the work they praise, and not confound plot-interest with other sources of interest, above all not confound together the various kinds of plot-interest, readers would be guided in their choice, and have their taste educated. For example, it is quite fair to praise Miss Braddon for the skill she undoubtedly displays in plot-interest of a certain kind – in selecting situations of crime and mystery which have a singular fascination for a large number of readers; and the success she has obtained is due to the skill with which she has prepared and presented these situations so as to excite the curiosity and sympathy of idle people. It is a special talent she possesses; and the critic is wrong who fails to recognise in it the source of her success. But he would be equally wrong, I think, if he confounded this merit with other merits, which her novels do not display. I have only read two of her works – "Lady Audley's Secret," and "Sir Jasper's Tenant" – but from those I have no hesitation in concluding that her grasp of character, her vision of realities, her regard for probabilities, and her theoretical views of human life, are very far from being on a level with her power over plot-interest. In praising stories there should be some discrimination of the kind of interest aimed at, and the means by which the aim is reached. A criminal trial will agitate all England, when another involving similar degrees of crime, but without certain adjuncts of interest, will be read only by the seekers of the very vulgarest stimulants. It is not the crime, but the attendant circumstances of horror and mystery, of pathetic interest, and of social suggestions, which give importance to a trial. In like manner the skill of the story-teller is displayed in selecting the attendant circumstances of horror, mystery, pathos, and social suggestion, bringing the events home to our experience and sympathy. And the critic should fix his attention on this mode of presentation, not demanding from the writer qualities incompatible with, or obviously disregarded by his method. In a story of wild and startling incidents, such as "Monte Christo,"[2] it is absurd to demand a minute attention to probabilities; provided our imaginative sympathy is not checked by a sense of the incongruous, we grant the author a large licence. But in proportion as the story lies among scenes and characters of familiar experience in proportion as the writer endeavours to engage our sympathy by pictures of concrete realities, and not by *abstractions* of passion and incident, the critic demands a closer adherence to truth and experience. Monte Christo may talk a language never heard off the stage, but Major Pendennis must speak as they speak in Pall Mall. It is obviously a much easier task to tell a story involving only the abstractions of life, than to tell one which moves amidst its realities. It is easier to disregard all those probabilities which would interfere with the symmetrical arrangement of incidents in a culminating progression, and all those truths of human character which in real life would complicate and thwart any scheme of prearranged events, than to tell a story which carries with it in every phase of its evolution a justification of what is felt, said, and done, so that the reader seems, as it were, to be the spectator of an actual drama. Nevertheless, both are legitimate forms of art; and although the latter is incomparably the more difficult, and the more valuable in its results, the former is and always will be popular with the mass of readers. A picture made up of improbable combinations and unreal elements may interest us once; but unless it be a pure play of fancy avowedly soaring away into regions beyond or beside this life of ours, it cannot sustain its interest, for it cannot withstand the inevitable scrutiny of deliberation. It will not bear re-reading. It cannot be thought of without misgiving. A picture made up of nature's sequences will interest for all time.

Plot-interest is, as I said, the distinctive element in Fiction; and the critic ought to mark plainly what the nature of the interest is no less than the skill with which it is presented. Having done this, if he speak of the historical, pictorial, moral, religious, or literary details, he should speak of them as amenable to the ordinary canons. Nonsense is not excusable because it forms part of the padding of a story. People ought to be ashamed of having written, or of having praised trash, wherever it may have appeared. And a little critical rigour exercised with respect to the descriptions, dialogues, and reflections which accompany a story, would act beneficially in two ways: first, in affording a test whereby the writer's pretensions might be estimated; secondly, by making writers more vigilant against avoidable mistakes.

As a test: You may have a very lively sense of the unreality with which a writer has conceived a character, or presented a situation, but it is by no means easy to make him see this, or to make his admirers see it. In vain would you refer to certain details as inaccurate; he cannot recognise their inaccuracy. In vain would you point to the general air of unreality, the conventional tone of the language, the absence of those subtle, individual traits which give verisimilitude to a conception; he cannot see it; to him the conception does seem lifelike; he may perhaps assure you that it is taken from the life. But failing on this ground, you may succeed by an indirect route. In cases so complex as those of human character and human affairs, the possibilities of misapprehension are numerous; and if we find a man liable to mistake sound for sense, to misapprehend the familiar relations of daily life, to describe vaguely or inaccurately the objects of common experience, or to write *insincerely* in the belief that he is writing eloquently, then we may *à fortiori* conclude that he will be still more liable to misapprehend the complexities of character, to misrepresent psychological subtleties, to put language into people's mouths which is not the language of real feeling, and to modify the course of events according to some conventional prejudice. In a word, if he is feeble and inaccurate in ordinary matters, he may be believed to be feeble and inaccurate in higher matters. If he writes nonsense, or extravagant sentimentality, in uttering his own comments, we may suspect his sense and truthfulness when his personages speak and act.

Before proceeding to the second result of critical rigour it will be desirable to apply the test in a specific instance, and I select "Maxwell Drewitt" for this purpose, rather than "Sir Jasper's Tenant," because the author has been specially lauded for powers of portraiture which I have been unable to recognise. It is but right to add that I have read none of this author's previous works; and to add further that there is much even in this work which I shall presently have to praise. If any of my remarks seem severe, let them be understood as at least implying the compliment of serious criticism. It is because I wish to treat her novel as Literature, and because she has an earnestness of purpose and a literary ability which challenge respect, that I make choice of her work for illustration; though at first sight any selection must seem invidious where so many examples abound.

"Maxwell Drewitt" is not a novel of incident, but a picture of life and character. Its interest is not meant to lie in the skilful combination of the abstractions of passion and situation, irrespective of concrete probabilities, irrespective of real human motives in the common transactions of life; in other words, it is not a romance, it is not a sensation story, trusting solely to the power of ideal presentation of abstractions, or to the appeal to our sympathies with mystery and crime. The obvious aim of the writer is to paint a picture of Irish life, and to inculcate a moral lesson. The aim is high; and being high, it challenges criticism as to its means. The aim is one which tasks a writer's powers; and success can only be proportionate to the verisimilitude with which the picture is painted. I do not think the degree of verisimilitude attained is such as to justify the praises which have been awarded it. There are excellent intentions; but the execution is approximative, inaccurate, wanting in the sharp individuality which comes from clear vision and dramatic insight. The first hazy conception of the characters is not condensed into distinctness. The careless, good-natured, indolent Irish landlord – always in difficulties, always cheery and improvident – is described, but not depicted. His energetic, clever, scheming, hard-hearted nephew is drawn with more detail, but nevertheless falls very short of a recognisable portrait. The rascally Irish lawyer, and the virtuous English lawyer, are pale, lifeless conventionalities. The reckless Harold and the vindictive but virtuous Brian, are shadows. The coquettish Lady Emeline, the loving Jenny Bourke, and the patient Mrs. Drewitt, are lay figures. The language has never that nice dramatic propriety which seems as if it could only come from the persons. None of the characters have the impress of creative genius. The same haziness and conventionality may be noted of the attempts to represent the fluctuations of feeling, and the combinations of motive, in the actors. We are informed at great length of what the people felt, we listen to their conversation and soliloquies, but we never seem to hear a real human voice, we never see a soul laid bare.

Such briefly is the impression produced on my mind by this novel as a picture of life and character. I do not really *see* the election riot, I do not feel myself ideally present at those scenes; I do not seem to know Archibald Drewitt's improvidence; nor does Maxwell's patient prosecution of his plans for improving the estate and making his fortune, although told at some length, come home to me like an experience. Both are described, neither is vividly painted. The scenes in Dublin and London are weak and shadowy. In fact, the execution is wanting in the sharpness of distinct vision, where it is not absolutely inaccurate. At the best it is but approximative, never lifelike.

But having said thus much, I should leave a false impression if I did not add that I have been judging 'Maxwell Drewitt' by a higher standard than that of the novels which are produced by the score. There is a certain gloomy earnestness in the writer, and a rhetorical power which carry you unwearied, though not unoffended, through the volumes. There is, moreover, a certain distinctiveness in the mode of treatment, and in the selection of the subjects. Without knowing anything of Ireland, I am quite sure that life at Connemara was not like what it appears in these pages; but then the fact that we are taken to unfamiliar scenes lightens our sense of the imperfect verisimilitude.

The *suggestions* of the novel are interesting. The obvious effort of the writer to depict the improvidence and ignorance of the Irish and the ready means by which the land may be immensely improved, gives it a more serious aim than if it were a mere love story, or story of incident. What I consider its gravest defects, are the absence of sufficient clearness of Vision, and of sufficient attention to the principle of Sincerity (as these have formerly been explained in this Review);[3] which defects might to a great extent be remedied by a resolute determination on her part not to write until her vision became clear, and only to write what she had distinctly in her mind.

Let us see what the application of our Test will do towards justifying such an impression. We find the hero, a young man of our own day, talking thus to himself: –

'Yes, yes,' he cried at last, halting suddenly, and looking away towards the hills that rose to heaven – 'yes, yes, Kincorth, you shall yet be mine – you and many a fair property beside; but you in especial, because I have sworn that neither man nor devil shall keep you from me. And shall a woman? No, before God.' And the veins came swelling up in his forehead as he stretched out one clenched hand towards Kincorth, and registered his oath.

It is difficult to suppose the author hearing her characters talk in this style, or believing it to be a representation of modern life, which could be accepted by a reflecting reader. Still worse is the rhapsody –

'I love the wind,' she thought; 'it is fresh and pure, and it comes from travelling over the great sea, instead of bringing the taint of large cities on its breath;' and she turned, even while she was thinking this, round Eversbeg Head, and the wide Atlantic and the full force of the western breeze burst upon her at once.

Thousands of miles! Millions upon millions of tossing billows! Oh! thou great God Almighty! who can look across the restless ocean and not think of Thee? Who can forget, while standing by the sea and watching the great waters come thundering upon the shore, that Thou hast set bounds to the waters and said, 'Here shall thy proud waves be stayed' – who, looking over the trackless expanse of ocean, but must feel that all unseen the feet of the Most High have traversed it?

When we see this work of the Lord, His wonders in the deep; when we perceive how at His command the floods arise, and how at His word the storm ceases; when we remember that though the waves of the sea are mighty and rage horribly, still that the Lord God who dwelleth on high is mightier; when we think that He holds the waters in the hollow of His hand, do we not seem for a moment, amid raging tempests and foaming billows, to catch a glimpse of the Infinite? Looking over the waste of waters, does not our weak mortality appear able to grasp for an instant the idea of immortality? Can we not imagine that no material horizon bounds our view – that we are gazing away and away across the ocean into eternity?

Thousands of miles, friends! Which of us has not at one time or other let his heart go free over the waters? Who has not stood by the shore silent, while his inner self – his self that never talks save to his God and his own soul – has gone out from his body and tossed with the billows, and answered the sullen roar of the waters, and risen and sunk with the waters as they rose and fell, rose and fell, and felt the breaking of the foam, the sobbing plash of the great ocean, as it rolls up on the sands and over the rocks and stones and shells of earth, while depth calleth unto depth, and the great floods clap their hands together?

And oh! with what a terrible sadness does that second self come back to us! It has been out listening to strange voices, hearing strange sounds, learning solemn truths. It has been out on the billows, on the foam, among the spray and the clouds and the tempest – out away to the very confines of the invisible world. It has been restless like the ocean, and it comes back to be set within the bounds of flesh; it has been free, and behold it must return to chains and fetters; it has been telling of its troubles to the ocean, and the ocean has lift up its mighty arms and mourned out its sorrowful reply.

Mourning – mourning – never silent, never still – now lashing itself up into fury – now tossing hither and thither as it seems to us without plan or purpose; now wave following after wave, as a man follows after man in the ranks of a vast army; now flinging its waters on the shore – now striving to climb the steep sides of some rugged rock; fretting itself as we fret ourselves – moaning as we moan – toiling as we toil – restless as we are; now receding – now advancing – but never at peace; in its strong moods wild and tumultuous – in its calmest moments stirred by the ground swell, ruffled by the lightest breeze! Well may man love this deep, inexplicable, unfathomable ocean, for as it through the ages has come on sobbing and mourning and struggling, so man through the years of his life goes mourning and struggling too.

Some thoughts like these passed through Mrs. Drewitt's mind as she stood at the base of Eversbeg Head, and looked out over the Atlantic.

This ambitious, but most injudicious passage is given as a representation of the thoughts which passed through the mind of a gentle, unhysterical, matter-of-fact woman! On reading it, every one will be able to form an estimate of the probability of a writer, who could present such a picture with a belief in its truthfulness being able to delineate truly the complexities of character under exceptional conditions. It is quite clear that she was led away by the temptation of 'fine writing' to substitute what she considered an eloquent passage about the sea, for what Mrs. Drewitt was likely to have felt by the sea-shore. This is what I have named insincerity; and it is one of the common vices of literature.

There is an unpleasant redundance of 'fine writing' and emphatic platitudes in these volumes. The desire to be eloquent, and the desire to sermonise, lead to pages upon pages which offend the taste, and which, if found out of a novel or a sermon, would provoke the critic's ridicule; but on the assumption that novels are not to be criticised as Literature, they pass without rebuke. Imagine any one of ordinary cleverness called upon to meditate on a truism thus ambitiously worded: –

Within a week Ryan took a house in Duranmore next to his office, and moved his furniture and himself and his sister away from the pretty cottage by the shore. *But the waves came rolling up the bay for all that*: though there was no human ear to listen to their music, they still rippled over the stones and sand – the shutters of the cottage windows were closed and fastened, *but the fuchsias bloomed the same as ever* – no Jenny now stood by the stream, singing her love songs, dreaming her love fantasies, *but the* stream went dancing over the stones to the sea none the less joyously – there were none to look up at the everlasting hills, *but the summer's sun shone on them*, and the winter's snows lay on them, as the sun had shone and the snow had lain since the beginning of time.

For whose instructions is this wisdom proffered? Was it a *possible* supposition that the removal of Jenny should cause the disappearance of the mountains and the cessation of the tides, or that fuchsias would cease to bloom because the window shutters were closed? Surely common sense ought not to be thus disregarded in the search for eloquence?

The truth seems to be that writing hastily, and unchecked by any sense of her responsibilities, never pausing to ask herself whether what she was setting down had truth or value, and would bear reflection, she indulged a propensity to vague moralising, feeling that anything was good enough for a novel. Thus, having killed her hero, she preaches a sermon on his career, in which we have remarks like this: –

Pitiful! most pitiful! In his prime this man was taken away from among his treasures – from the place he had longed to possess – from the country of his birth – from the scenes he had loved to gaze over. What did it matter, then, whether he had been rich or poor, wealthy or indigent, lofty or lowly, peer or peasant? – what did it matter? what even in life had the hands and the houses, had the silver and the gold, profited him?

And this –

Never more may he walk by the sea shore, or stand under the arching trees that shade the avenue, or ride by lake or river, past mountains and through the valleys – never more for ever.... The great mountains rear their blue summits to heaven, the lakes ripple and ripple, the rivers flow onward to the sea, and the boulders and the blocks of granite lie scattered about on the hill sides – the great Atlantic beats against the iron-bound coast, and up the thousand bays the waves steal gently as ever – on that strange country through which Maxwell rode when he was still young, when he had life all before him, the moon looks down with as cold a light, playing as many fantastic tricks, creeping up the hills, and lying in the waters just as she did then.

There are several other passages I had marked for comment,[4] but those already given will suffice to confirm both my opinion of the quality of "Maxwell Drewitt," and my opinion respecting the advantage of testing a writer's quality by a consideration of the way in which he handles minor points. If we find him wanting in truthfulness, insight, and good sense in these minor points, we may be prepared to find him inaccurate, inadequate, and conventional in the more difficult representation of life and character. He may make foolish remarks, and yet tell a story well; but if his remarks are deviations from common sense, his story will be a deviation from human experience; and the critic who detects this may avoid the appearance of arbitrariness in his judgment on higher matters less easily brought within the scope of ordinary recognition, by showing that a writer who is not to be trusted in the one case cannot be trusted in the other.

This leads me to the second benefit which would accrue from a more stringent criticism, especially applied to minor points. It would soon greatly purge novels of their insincerities and nonsense. If critics were vigilant and rigorous, they would somewhat check the presumptuous facility and *facundia*[a] of indolent novelists, by impressing on them a sense of danger in allowing the pen to wander at random. It would warn them that rhetoric without ideas would lead them into ridicule. It would teach them that what they wrote would not only be read, but reflected on; and if their glittering diction proved on inspection to be tinsel, they would suffer from the exposure. This would lead to a more serious conception of the art, and a more earnest effort to make their works in all respects conformable to sense and artistic truth. The man who begins to be vigilant as to the meaning of his phrases is already halfway towards becoming a good writer. The man who before passing on to his next sentence has already assured himself that the one just written expresses the thought actually in his mind, as well as he can express it, and declines to believe that insincere expressions or careless approximate phrases are good enough for a novel, will soon learn to apply the same vigilance to his conception of character and incident, and will strive to attain clearness of vision and sincerity of expression. Let criticism only exact from novels the same respect for truth and common sense which it exacts from other literary works; let it stringently mark where the approbation of a novel is given to it as Literature, and where it is given to plot-interest of a more or less attractive nature, and some good may be effected both on writers and readers.

[a] Eloquence.

Henry James
(1843–1916)
'The Art of Fiction', 1884

One may say that, like George Eliot, about whom he wrote perceptively, Henry James was a major novelist who was also a critic of the novel. But this simple factual statement hardly does justice either to the magnitude or to the significance of James's achievement in the latter capacity. In sheer bulk, his work in this line, which he began with some reviewing in his early twenties and carried on until he was well past sixty, easily outweighs hers. During James's lifetime, much of it was collected in *French Poets and Novelists* (1878), *Hawthorne* (1879), *Partial Portraits* (1888), *Essays in London and Elsewhere* (1893), and *Notes on Novelists* (1914); two other volumes appearing after his death contained essays on the novel that James himself did not gather for publication: *Notes and Reviews* (intro. Pierre de Chaignon la Rose, 1921) and *Literary Reviews and Essays* (ed. Albert Mordell, 1957). James's critical writings have been far more influential than Eliot's, especially the prefaces to the New York edition of his collected novels and stories (1907–9). His friend and disciple Percy Lubbock popularized their ideas in his widely read *The Craft of Fiction* (1921), and the American critic Richard P. Blackmur gave them academic respectability by publishing all eighteen, prefaced by an elegant and admiring introduction of his own, as *The Art of the Novel* (1934).

'The Art of Fiction' – first published in *Longman's Magazine* in September 1884 (4: 502–21) – is of course something quite different from the slight and respectful correction of Walter Besant's earnest lecture by the same title that it initially pretends to be, for in fact James not only destroys Besant's position but also sets forth an eloquent artistic credo of his own, one that has become famous. Though it is possible to see in it anticipations of much that was to come in both James's work and that of other critics, it will be more appropriate to consider here its relationship to Victorian criticism of the novel up to 1884.

A reading of the earlier selections in the present volume will suggest that James is hardly fair to his predecessors in saying that 'only a short time ago it might have been supposed that the English novel was not what the French called *discutable*'. On the contrary, for nearly half a century all of the critics represented here from Bulwer Lytton on had been insisting that fiction was an art that could and should be discussed by thoughtful men and women. What distinguishes James's position from theirs is not his assertion that the novel is 'as free and serious a branch of literature as any other' but rather the unapologetic tone of his argument and the boldness of the conclusions he draws.

A novel for James is a serious representation of life, so much so that it *does* compete with life – a remark with which Robert Louis Stevenson was to take issue a few weeks later in 'A Humble Remonstrance'. Because it is necessarily 'a personal impression of life', its success or failure is determined much less by the extent to which it adheres to literal surface fact – despite James's praise of 'solidity of specification' – than it is by the kind of mind out of which it grows. The novelist of 'genius', whose 'sensibility' is particularly keen, may well write interestingly – i.e., movingly and persuasively – of subjects that he or she has never experienced in any direct physical sense. So much for the old distinction between realistic and imaginative writing, between the novel and the romance. Nor will it do to assume that the various components of a novel – action, character, dialogue, description, and the like – can be distinguished from one another in any meaningful sense, for 'a novel is a living thing, all one and continuous, like every other organism, and in proportion as it lives will it be found, I think, that in each part there is something of the other parts'. (As Kenneth Graham has shown, James was by no means the first Victorian writer on the theory of fiction to refer to the organic unity of the novel.)[1] With regard to the supposed moral purpose of the novel, finally, James challenges the pious utterances of earlier critics with a series of unanswered, indeed unanswerable, questions, finally approaching ground very close to that occupied by the so-called Aesthetic Movement of the 1880s:

To what degree a purpose in a work of art is a source of corruption I shall not attempt to inquire; the one that seems to me least dangerous is the purpose of making a perfect work. . . .
  There is one point at which the moral sense and the artistic sense lie very near together; that is, in the light of the very obvious truth that the deepest quality of a work of art will always be the quality of the mind of the producer. In proportion as that mind is rich and noble will the novel, the picture, the statue, partake of the substance of beauty and truth. To be constituted of such elements is, to my vision, to have purpose enough.

I SHOULD not have affixed so comprehensive a title to these few remarks, necessarily wanting in any completeness, upon a subject the full consideration of which would carry us far, did I not seem to discover a pretext for my temerity in the interesting pamphlet lately published under this name by Mr. Walter Besant.[2] Mr. Besant's lecture at the Royal Institution – the original form of his pamphlet – appears to indicate that many persons are interested in the art of fiction and are not indifferent to such remarks as those who practise it may attempt to make about it. I am therefore anxious not to lose the benefit of this favourable association, and to edge in a few words under cover of the attention which Mr. Besant is sure to have excited. There is something very encouraging in his having put into form certain of his ideas on the mystery of story-telling.

  It is a proof of life and curiosity – curiosity on the part of the brotherhood of novelists, as well as on the part of their readers. Only a short time ago it might have been supposed that the English novel was not what the French called *discutable*.[a] It had no air of having a theory, a conviction, a consciousness of itself behind it – of being the expression of an artistic faith, the result of choice and comparison. I do not say it was necessarily the worse for that; it would take much more courage than I posssess to intimate that the form of the novel, as Dickens and Thackeray (for instance) saw it, had any taint of incompleteness. It was, however, *naïf* (if I may help myself out with another French word); and, evidently, if it is destined to suffer in any way for having lost its *naïveté*, it has now an idea of making sure of the corresponding advantages. During the period I have alluded to there was a comfortable, good-humoured feeling abroad that a novel is a novel, as a pudding is a pudding, and that this was the end of it. But within a year or two, for some reason or other, there have been signs of returning animation – the era of discussion would appear to have been to a certain extent opened. Art lives upon discussion, upon experiment, upon curiosity, upon variety of attempt, upon the exchanges of views and the comparison of standpoints; and there is a presumption that those times when no one has anything particular to say about it, and has no reason to give for practice or preference, though they may be times of genius, are not times of development, are times, possibly even, a little, of dulness. The successful application of any art is a delightful spectacle, but the theory, too, is interesting; and though there is a great deal of the latter without the former, I suspect there has never been a genuine success that has not had a latent core of conviction. Discussion, suggestion, formulation, these things are fertilizing when they are frank and sincere. Mr. Besant has set an excellent example in saying what he thinks, for his part, about the way in which fiction should be written, as well as about the way in which it should be published; for his view of the 'art,' carried on into an appendix, covers that too. Other labourers in the same field will doubtless take up the argument, they will give it the light of their experience, and the effect will surely be to make our interest in the novel a little more what it had for some time threatened to fail to be – a serious, active, inquiring interest, under protection of which this delightful study may, in moments of confidence, venture to say a little more what it thinks of itself.

It must take itself seriously for the public to take it so. The old superstition about fiction being 'wicked' has doubtless died out in England; but the spirit of it lingers in a certain oblique regard directed toward any story which does not more or less admit that it is only a

[a] Debatable.

joke. Even the most jocular novel feels in some degree the weight of the proscription that was formerly directed against literary levity; the jocularity does not always succeed in passing for gravity. It is still expected, though perhaps people are ashamed to say it, that a production which is after all only a 'make believe' (for what else is a 'story?') shall be in some degree apologetic – shall renounce the pretension of attempting really to compete with life. This, of course, any sensible wide-awake story declines to do, for it quickly perceives that the tolerance granted to it on such a condition is only an attempt to stifle it, disguised in the form of generosity. The old Evangelical hostility to the novel, which was as explicit as it was narrow, and which regarded it as little less favourable to our immortal part than a stage-play, was in reality far less insulting. The only reason for the existence of a novel is that it *does* compete with life. When it ceases to compete as the canvas of the painter competes, it will have arrived at a very strange pass. It is not expected of the picture that it will make itself humble in order to be forgiven; and the analogy between the art of the painter and the art of the novelist is, so far as I am able to see, complete. Their inspiration is the same, their process (allowing for the different quality of the vehicle) is the same, their success is the same. They may learn from each other, they may explain and sustain each other. Their cause is the same, and the honour of one is the honour of another. Peculiarities of manner, of execution, that correspond on either side, exist in each of them and contribute to their development. The Mahometans think a picture an unholy thing, but it is a long time since any Christian did, and it is therefore the more odd that in the Christian mind the traces (dissimulated though they may be) of a suspicion of the sister art should linger to this day. The only effectual way to lay it to rest is to emphasize the analogy to which I just alluded – to insist on the fact that as the picture is reality, so the novel is history. That is the only general description (which does it justice) that we may give of the novel. But history also is allowed to compete with life, as I say; it is not, any more than painting, expected to apologize. The subject-matter of fiction is stored up likewise in documents and records, and if it will not give itself away, as they say in California, it must speak with assurance, with the tone of the historian. Certain accomplished novelists have a habit of giving themselves away which must often bring tears to the eyes of people who take their fiction seriously. I was lately struck, in reading over many pages of Anthony Trollope,[3] with his want of discretion in this particular. In a digression, a parenthesis or an aside, he concedes to the reader that he and this trusting friend are only 'making believe.' He admits that the events he narrates have not really happened, and that he can give his narrative any turn the reader may like best. Such a betrayal of a sacred office seems to me, I confess, a terrible crime; it is what I mean by the attitude of apology, and it shocks me every whit as much in Trollope as it would have shocked me in Gibbon or Macaulay. It implies that the novelist is less occupied in looking for the truth than the historian, and in doing so it deprives him at a stroke of all his standing-room. To represent and illustrate the past, the actions of men, is the task of either writer, and the only difference that I can see is, in proportion as he succeeds, to the honour of the novelist, consisting as it does in his having more difficulty in collecting his evidence, which is so far from being purely literary. It seems to me to give him a great character, the fact that he has at once so much in common with the philosopher and the painter; this double analogy is a magnificent heritage.

It is of all this evidently that Mr. Besant is full when he insists upon the fact that the fiction is one of the *fine* arts, deserving in its turn of all the honours and emoluments that have hitherto been reserved for the successful profession of music, poetry, painting, architecture. It is impossible to insist too much on so important a truth, and the place that Mr. Besant demands for the work of the novelist may be represented, a trifle less abstractly, by saying that he demands not only that it shall be reputed artistic, but that it shall be reputed very artistic indeed. It is excellent that he should have struck this note, for his doing so indicates that there was need of it, that his proposition may be to many people a novelty. One rubs one's eyes at the thought; but the rest of Mr. Besant's essay confirms the revelation. I suspect, in truth, that it would be possible to confirm it still further, and that one would not be far wrong in saying that in addition to the people to whom it has never occurred that a novel ought to be artistic, there are a great many others who, if this principle were urged upon them, would be filled with an indefinable mistrust. They would find it difficult to explain their repugnance, but it would operate strongly to put them on their guard. 'Art,' in our Protestant communities, where so many things have got so strangely twisted about, is supposed, in certain circles, to have some vaguely injurious effect upon those who make it an important consideration, who let it weigh in the balance. It is assumed to be opposed in some mysterious manner to morality, to amusement, to instruction. When it is embodied in the work of the painter (the sculptor is another affair!) you know what it is; it stands there before you, in the honesty of pink and green and a gilt frame; you can see the worst of it at a glance, and you can be on your guard. But when it is introduced into literature it becomes more insidious –

there is danger of its hurting you before you know it. Literature should be either instructive or amusing, and there is in many minds an impression that these artistic preoccupations, the search for form, contribute to neither end, interfere indeed with both. They are too frivolous to be edifying, and too serious to be diverting; and they are, moreover, priggish and paradoxical and superfluous. That, I think, represents the manner in which the latent thought of many people who read novels as an exercise in skipping would explain itself if it were to become articulate. They would argue, of course, that a novel ought to be 'good,' but they would interpret this term in a fashion of their own, which, indeed, would vary considerably from one critic to another. One would say that being good means representing virtuous and aspiring characters, placed in prominent positions; another would say that it depends for a 'happy ending' on a distribution at the last of prizes, pensions, husbands, wives, babies, millions, appended paragraphs and cheerful remarks. Another still would say that it means being full of incident and movement, so that we shall wish to jump ahead, to see who was the mysterious stranger, and if the stolen will was ever found, and shall not be distracted from this pleasure by any tiresome analysis or 'description'. But they would all agree that the 'artistic' idea would spoil some of their fun. One would hold it accountable for all the description, another would see it revealed in the absence of sympathy. Its hostility to a happy ending would be evident, and it might even, in some cases, render any ending at all impossible. The 'ending' of a novel is, for many persons, like that of a good dinner, a course of dessert and ices, and the artist in fiction is regarded as a sort of meddlesome doctor who forbids agreeable aftertastes. It is therefore true that this conception of Mr. Besant's, of the novel as a superior form, encounters not only a negative but a positive indifference. It matters little that, as a work of art, it should really be as little or as much concerned to supply happy endings, sympathetic characters, and an objective tone, as if it were a work of mechanics; the association of ideas, however incongruous, might easily be too much for it if an eloquent voice were not sometimes raised to call attention to the fact that it is at once as free and as serious a branch of literature as any other.

Certainly, this might sometimes be doubted in presence of the enormous number of works of fiction that appeal to the credulity of our generation, for it might easily seem that there could be no great substance in a commodity so quickly and easily produced. It must be admitted that good novels are somewhat compromised by bad ones, and that the field, at large, suffers discredit from overcrowding. I think, however, that this injury is only superficial, and that the superabundance of written fiction proves nothing against the principle itself. It has been vulgarised, like all other kinds of literature, like everything else, to-day, and it has proved more than some kinds accessible to vulgarisation. But there is as much difference as there ever was between a good novel and a bad one: the bad is swept, with all the daubed canvases and spoiled marble, into some unvisited limbo or infinite rubbish-yard, beneath the back-windows of the world, and the good subsists and emits its light and stimulates our desire for perfection. As I shall take the liberty of making but a single criticism of Mr. Besant, whose tone is so full of the love of his art, I may as well have done with it at once. He seems to me to mistake in attempting to say so definitely beforehand what sort of an affair the good novel will be. To indicate the danger of such an error as that has been the purpose of these few pages; to suggest that certain traditions on the subject, applied *a priori*, have already had much to answer for, and that the good health of an art which undertakes so immediately to reproduce life must demand that it be perfectly free. It lives upon exercise, and the very meaning of exercise is freedom. The only obligation to which in advance we may hold a novel without incurring the accusation of being arbitrary, is that it be interesting. That general responsibility rests upon it, but it is the only one I can think of. The ways in which it is at liberty to accomplish this result (of interesting us) strike me as innumerable and such as can only suffer from being marked out, or fenced in, by prescription. They are as various as the temperament of man, and they are successful in proportion as they reveal a particular mind, different from others. A novel is in its broadest definition a personal impression of life; that, to begin with, constitutes its value, which is greater or less according to the intensity of the impression. But there will be no intensity at all, and therefore no value, unless there is freedom to feel and say. The tracing of a line to be followed, of a tone to be taken, of a form to be filled out, is a limitation of that freedom and a suppression of the very thing that we are most curious about. The form, it seems to me, is to be appreciated after the fact; then the author's choice has been made, his standard has been indicated; then we can follow lines and directions and compare tones. Then, in a word, we can enjoy one of the most charming of pleasures, we can estimate quality, we can apply the test of execution. The execution belongs to the author alone; it is what is most personal to him, and we measure him by that. The advantage, the luxury, as well as the torment and responsibility of the novelist, is that there is no limit to what he may attempt as an executant – no limit to his possible experiments, efforts, discoveries, successes. Here it is especially that he works, step by step, like his brother of the brush, of whom we may always say that he has painted his picture in a manner best known to himself. His manner is his secret, not necessarily a deliberate one. He cannot disclose it, as a general thing, if he would; he would be at a loss to teach it to others. I say this with a due recollection of having insisted on the community of method of the artist who paints a picture and the artist who writes a novel. The painter *is* able to teach the rudiments of his practice, and it is possible, from the study of good work (granted the aptitude), both to learn how to paint and how to write. Yet it remains true, without injury to the *rapprochement*, that the literary artist would be obliged to say to his pupil much more than the other, 'Ah, well, you must do it as you can!' It is a question of degree, a matter of delicacy. If there are exact sciences there are also exact arts, and the grammar of painting is so much more definite that it makes the difference.

I ought to add, however, that if Mr. Besant says at the beginning of his essay that the 'laws of fiction may be laid down and taught with as much precision and exactness as the laws of harmony, perspective, and proportion,' he mitigates what might appear to be an over-statement by applying his remark to 'general' laws, and by expressing most of these rules in a manner with which it would certainly be unaccommodating to disagree. That the novelist must write from experience, that his 'characters must be real and such as might be met with in actual life;' that 'a young lady brought up in a quiet country village should avoid descriptions of garrison life,' and 'a writer whose friends and personal experiences belong to the lower middle-class should carefully avoid introducing his characters into Society;' that one should enter one's notes in a common-place book; that one's figures should be clear in outline; that making them clear by some trick of speech or of carriage is a bad method, and 'describing them at length' is a worse one; that English Fiction should have a 'conscious moral purpose;' that 'it is almost impossible to estimate too highly the value of careful workmanship – that is, of style;' that 'the most important point of all is the story,' that 'the story is everything' – these are principles with most of which it is surely impossible not to sympathise. That remark about the lower-middle-class writer and his knowing his place is perhaps rather chilling; but for the rest, I should find it difficult to dissent from any one of these recommendations. At the same time I should find it difficult positively to assent to them, with the exception, perhaps, of the injunction as to entering one's notes in a common-place book. They scarcely seem to me to have the quality that Mr. Besant attributes to the rules of the novelist – the 'precision and exactness' of 'the laws of harmony, perspective, and proportion.' They are suggestive, they are even inspiring, but they are not exact, though they are doubtless as much so as the case admits of; which is a proof of that liberty of interpretation for which I just contended. For the value of these different injunctions – so beautiful and so vague – is wholly in the meaning one attaches to them. The characters, the situation, which strike one as real will be those that touch and interest one most, but the measure of reality is very difficult to fix. The reality of Don Quixote or of Mr. Micawber is a very delicate shade; it is a reality so coloured by the author's vision that, vivid as it may be, one would hesitate to propose it as a model; one would expose one's self to some very embarrassing questions on the part of a pupil. It goes without saying that you will not write a good novel unless you possess the sense of reality; but it will be difficult to give you a recipe for calling that sense into being. Humanity is immense and reality has a myriad forms; the most one can affirm is that some of the flowers of fiction have the odour of it, and others have not; as for telling you in advance how your nosegay should be composed, that is another affair. It is equally excellent and inconclusive to say that one must write from experience; to our suppositious aspirant such a declaration might savour of mockery. What kind of experience is intended, and where does it begin and end? Experience is never limited and it is never complete; it is an immense sensibility, a kind of huge spider-web, of the finest silken threads, suspended in the chamber of consciousness and catching every air-borne particle in its tissue. It is the very atmosphere of the mind; and when the mind is imaginative – much more when it happens to be that of a man of genius – it takes to itself the faintest hints of life, it converts the very pulses of the air into revelations. The young lady living in a village has only to be a damsel upon whom nothing is lost to make it quite unfair (as it seems to me) to declare to her that she shall have nothing to say about the military. Greater miracles have been seen than that, imagination assisting, she should speak the truth about some of these gentlemen. I remember an English novelist, a woman of genius, telling me that she was much commended for the impression she had managed to give in one of her tales of the nature and way of life of the French Protestant youth. She had been asked where she learned so much about this recondite being, she had been congratulated on her peculiar opportunities. These opportunities consisted in her having once, in Paris, as she ascended a staircase, passed an open door where, in the household of a *pasteur*,[a]

---

[a] Pastor, Protestant minister.

some of the young Protestants were seated at table round a finished meal. The glimpse made a picture; it lasted only a moment, but that moment was experience. She had got her impression, and she evolved her type. She knew what youth was, and what Protestantism; she also had the advantage of having seen what it was to be French; so that she converted these ideas into a concrete image and produced a reality. Above all, however, she was blessed with the faculty which when you give it an inch takes an ell, and which for the artist is a much greater source of strength than any accident of residence or of place in the social scale. The power to guess the unseen from the seen, to trace the implication of things, to judge the whole piece by the pattern, the condition of feeling life, in general, so completely that you are well on your way to knowing any particular corner of it – this cluster of gifts may almost be said to constitute experience, and they occur in country and in town, and in the most differing stages of education. If experience consists of impressions, it may be said that the impressions *are* experience, just as (have we not seen it?) they are the very air we breathe. Therefore, if I should certainly say to a novice, 'Write from experience, and experience only,' I should feel that this was a rather tantalising monition if I were not careful immediately to add, 'Try to be one of the people on whom nothing is lost!'

I am far from intending by this to minimise the importance of exactness – of truth in detail. One can speak best from one's own taste, and I may therefore venture to say that the air of reality (solidity of specification) seems to me to be the supreme virtue of a novel – the merit in which all its other merits (including that conscious moral purpose of which Mr. Besant speaks) helplessly and submissively depend. If it be not there, they are all as nothing, and if these be there, they owe their effect to the success with which the author has produced the illusion of life. The cultivation of this success, the study of this exquisite process, form, to my taste, the beginning and the end of the art of the novelist. They are his inspiration, his despair, his reward, his torment, his delight. It is here, in very truth, that he competes with life; it is here that he competes with his brother the painter, in *his* attempt to render the look of things, the look that conveys their meaning, to catch the colour, the relief, the expression, the surface, the substance of the human spectacle. It is in regard to this that Mr. Besant is well inspired when he bids him take notes. He cannot possibly take too many, he cannot possibly take enough. All life solicits him, and to 'render' the simplest surface, to produce the most momentary illusion, is a very complicated business. His case would be easier, and the rule would be more exact, if Mr. Besant had been able to tell him what notes to take. But this I fear he can never learn in any hand-book; it is the business of his life. He has to take a great many in order to select a few, he has to work them up as he can, and even the guides and philosophers who might have most to say to him must leave him alone when it comes to the application of precepts, as we leave the painter in communion with his palette. That his characters 'must be clear in outline,' as Mr. Besant says – he feels that down to his boots; but how he shall make them so is a secret between his good angel and himself. It would be absurdly simple if he could be taught that a great deal of 'description' would make them so, or that, on the contrary, the absence of description and the cultivation of dialogue, or the absence of dialogue and the multiplication of 'incident,' would rescue him from his difficulties. Nothing, for instance, is more possible than that he be of a turn of mind for which this odd, literal opposition of description and dialogue, incident and description, has little meaning and light. People often talk of these things as if they had a kind of internecine distinctness, instead of melting into each other at every breath and being intimately associated parts of one general effort of expression. I cannot imagine composition existing in a series of blocks, nor conceive, in any novel worth discussing at all, of a passage of description that is not in its intention narrative, a passage of dialogue that is not in its intention descriptive, a touch of truth of any sort that does not partake of the nature of incident, and an incident that derives its interest from any other source than the general and only source of the success of a work of art – that of being illustrative. A novel is a living thing, all one and continuous, like every other organism, and in proportion as it lives will it be found, I think, that in each of the parts there is something of each of the other parts. The critic who over the close texture of a finished work will pretend to trace a geography of items will mark some frontiers as artificial, I fear, as any that have been known to history. There is an old-fashioned distinction between the novel of character and the novel of incident, which must have cost many a smile to the intending romancer who was keen about his work. It appears to me as little to the point as the equally celebrated distinction between the novel and the romance – to answer as little to any reality. There are bad novels and good novels, as there are bad pictures and good pictures; but that is the only distinction in which I see any meaning, and I can as little imagine speaking of a novel of character as I can imagine speaking of a picture of character. When one says picture, one says of character, when one says novel, one says of incident, and the terms may be transposed. What is character but the determination of

incident? What is incident but the illustration of character? What is a
picture or a novel that is *not* of character? What else do we seek in it
and find in it? It is an incident for a woman to stand up with her hand
resting on a table and look out at you in a certain way; or if it be not an
incident, I think it will be hard to say what is. At the same time it is an
expression of character. If you say you don't see it (character in *that –
allons donc!*[a]) this is exactly what the artist who has reasons of his own
for thinking he *does* see it undertakes to show you. When a young man
makes up his mind that he has not faith enough, after all, to enter the
Church, as he intended, that is an incident, though you may not hurry
to the end of the chapter to see whether perhaps he doesn't change
once more. I do not say that these are extraordinary or startling
incidents. I do not pretend to estimate the degree of interest proceeding from them, for this will depend upon the skill of the painter. It
sounds almost puerile to say that some incidents are intrinsically much
more important than others, and I need not take this precaution after
having professed my sympathy for the major ones in remarking that
the only classification of the novel that I can understand is into the
interesting and the uninteresting.

The novel and the romance, the novel of incident and that of
character – these separations appear to me to have been made by
critics and readers for their own convenience, and to help them out of
some of their difficulties, but to have little reality or interest for the
producer, from whose point of view it is, of course, that we are
attempting to consider the art of fiction. The case is the same with
another shadowy category, which Mr. Besant apparently is disposed
to set up – that of the 'modern English novel;' unless, indeed, it be that
in this matter he has fallen into an accidental confusion of standpoints.
It is not quite clear whether he intends the remarks in which he alludes
to it to be didactic or historical. It is as difficult to suppose a person
intending to write a modern English, as to suppose him writing an
ancient English, novel; that is a label which begs the question. One
writes the novel, one paints the picture, of one's language and of one's
time, and calling it modern English will not, alas! make the difficult
task any easier. No more, unfortunately, will calling this or that work
of one's fellow artist a romance – unless it be, of course, simply for the
pleasantness of the thing, as for instance, when Hawthorne gave this
heading to his story of Blithedale. The French, who have brought the
theory of fiction to remarkable completeness, have but one word for
the novel, and have not attempted smaller things in it, that I can see,
for that. I can think of no obligation to which the 'romancer' would

[a] Come on! Nonsense!

not be held equally with the novelist; the standard of execution is equally high for each. Of course it is of execution that we are talking – that being the only point of a novel that is open to contention. This is perhaps too often lost sight of, only to produce interminable confusions and cross-purposes. We must grant the artist his subject, his idea, what the French all his *donnée*; our criticism is applied only to what he makes of it. Naturally I do not mean that we are bound to like it or find it interesting: in case we do not our course is perfectly simple – to let it alone. We may believe that of a certain idea even the most sincere novelist can make nothing at all, and the event may perfectly justify our belief; but the failure will have been a failure to execute, and it is in the execution that the fatal weakness is recorded. If we pretend to respect the artist at all we must allow him his freedom of choice, in the face, in particular cases, of innumerable presumptions that the choice will not fructify. Art derives a considerable part of its beneficial exercise from flying in the face of presumptions, and some of the most interesting experiments of which it is capable are hidden in the bosom of common things. Gustave Flaubert has written a story about the devotion of a servant-girl to a parrot,[4] and the production, highly finished as it is, cannot on the whole be called a success. We are perfectly free to find it flat, but I think it might have been interesting; and I, for my part, am extremely glad he should have written it; it is a contribution to our knowledge of what can be done – or what cannot. Ivan Turgénieff has written a tale about a deaf and dumb serf and a lap-dog,[5] and the thing is touching, loving, a little masterpiece. He struck the note of life where Gustave Flaubert missed it – he flew in the face of a presumption and achieved a victory.

Nothing, of course, will ever take the place of the good old fashion of 'liking' a work of art or not liking it; the more improved criticism will not abolish that primitive, that ultimate, test. I mention this to guard myself from the accusation of intimating that the idea, the subject, of a novel or a picture, does not matter. It matters, to my sense, in the highest degree, and if I might put up a prayer it would be that artists should select none but the richest. Some, as I have already hastened to admit, are much more substantial than others, and it would be a happily arranged world in which persons intending to treat them should be exempt from confusions and mistakes. This fortunate condition will arive only, I fear, on the same day that critics become purged from error. Meanwhile, I repeat, we do not judge the artist with fairness unless we say to him, 'Oh, I grant you your starting-point, because if I did not I should seem to prescribe to you, and heaven forbid I should take that responsibility. If I pretend to tell you what you must not take, you will call upon me to tell you then what you must take; in which case I shall be nicely caught! Moreover, it isn't till I have accepted your data that I can begin to measure you. I have the standard; I judge you by what you propose, and you must look out for me there. Of course I may not care for your idea at all; I may think it silly, or stale, or unclean; in which case I wash my hands of you altogether. I may content myself with believing that you will not have succeeded in being interesting, but I shall of course not attempt to demonstrate it, and you will be as indifferent to me as I am to you. I needn't remind you that there are all sorts of tastes: who can know it better? Some people, for excellent reasons, don't like to read about carpenters; others, for reasons even better, don't like to read about courtesans. Many object to Americans. Others (I believe they are mainly editors and publishers) won't look at Italians. Some readers don't like quiet subjects; others don't like bustling ones. Some enjoy a complete illusion; others revel in a complete deception. They choose their novels accordingly, and if they don't care about your idea they won't, *a fortiori*, care about your treatment.'

So that it comes back very quickly, as I have said, to the liking; in spite of M. Zola,[6] who reasons less powerfully than he represents, and who will not reconcile himself to this absoluteness of taste, thinking that there are certain things that people ought to like, and that they can be made to like. I am quite at a loss to imagine anything (at any rate in this matter of fiction) that people *ought* to like or to dislike. Selection will be sure to take care of itself, for it has a constant motive behind it. That motive is simply experience. As people feel life, so they feel the art that is most closely related to it. This closeness of relation is what we should never forget in talking of the effort of a novel. Many people speak of it as a factitious, artificial form, a product of ingenuity, the business of which is to alter and arrange the things that surround us, to translate them into conventional, traditional moulds. This, however, is a view of the matter which carries us but a very short way, condemns the art to an eternal repetition of a few familiar *clichés*, cuts short its development, and leads us straight up to a dead wall. Catching the very note and trick, the strange irregular rhythm of life, that is the attempt whose strenuous force keeps Fiction upon her feet. In proportion as in what she offers us we see life *without* rearrangement do we feel that we are touching the truth; in proportion as we see it *with* rearrangement do we feel that we are being put off with a substitute, a compromise and convention. It is not uncommon to hear an extraordinary assurance of remark in regard to this matter of rearranging, which is often spoken of as if it were the last word of art. Mr. Besant seems to me in danger of falling into this great error with his rather unguarded talk about 'selection.' Art is essentially selection, but it is a selection whose main care is to be typical, to be inclusive. For many people art means rose-coloured windows, and selection means picking a bouquet for Mrs. Grundy.[7] They will tell you glibly that artistic considerations have nothing to do with the disagreeable, with the ugly; they will rattle off shallow commonplaces about the province of art and the limits of art, till you are moved to some wonder in return as to the province and the limits of ignorance. It appears to me that no one can ever have made a seriously artistic attempt without being conscious of an immense increase – a kind of revelation – of freedom. One perceives, in that case – by the light of a heavenly ray – that the province of art is all life, all feeling, all observation, all vision. As Mr. Besant so justly intimates, it is all experience. That is a sufficient answer to those who maintain that it must not touch the painful, who stick into its divine unconscious bosom little prohibitory inscriptions on the end of sticks, such as we see in public gardens – 'It is forbidden to walk on the grass; it is forbidden to touch the flowers; it is not allowed to introduce dogs, or to remain after dark; it is requested to keep to the right.' The young aspirant in the line of fiction, whom we continue to imagine, will do nothing without taste, for in that case his freedom would be of little use to him; but the first advantage of his taste will be to reveal to him the absurdity of the little sticks and tickets. If he have taste, I must add, of course he will have ingenuity, and my disrespectful reference to that quality just now was not meant to imply that it is useless in fiction. But it is only a secondary aid; the first is a vivid sense of reality.

Mr Besant has some remarks on the question of 'the story,' which I shall not attempt to criticise, though they seem to me to contain a singular ambiguity, because I do not think I understand them. I cannot see what is meant by talking as if there were a part of a novel which is the story and part of it which for mystical reasons is not – unless indeed the distinction be made in a sense in which it is difficult to suppose that anyone should attempt to convey anything. 'The story,' if it represents anything, represents the subject, the idea, the data of the novel; and there is surely no 'school' – Mr. Besant speaks of a school – which urges that a novel should be all treatment and no subject. There must assuredly be something to treat; every school is intimately conscious of that. This sense of the story being the idea, the starting-point, of the novel is the only one that I see in which it can be spoken of as something different from its organic whole; and since, in proportion as the work is successful, the idea permeates and pene-

trates it, informs and animates it, so that every word and every punc-
tuation-point contribute directly to the expression, in that proportion
do we lose our sense of the story being a blade which may be drawn
more or less out of its sheath. The story and the novel, the idea and the
form, are the needle and thread, and I never heard of a guild of tailors
who recommended the use of the thread without the needle or the
needle without the thread. Mr. Besant is not the only critic who may
be observed to have spoken as if there were certain things in life which
constitute stories and certain others which do not. I find the same odd
implication in an entertaining article in the *Pall Mall Gazette*,[8]
devoted, as it happens, to Mr. Besant's lecture. 'The story is the thing!'
says his graceful writer, as if with a tone of opposition to another idea.
I should think it was, as every painter who, as the time for 'sending in'
his picture looms in the distance, finds himself still in quest of a subject
– as every belated artist, not fixed about his *donnée*, will heartily agree.
There are some subjects which speak to us and others which do not,
but he would be a clever man who should undertake to give a rule by
which the story and the no-story should be known apart. It is
impossible (to me at least) to imagine any such rule which shall not be
altogether arbitrary. The writer in the *Pall Mall* opposes the delightful
(as I suppose) novel of 'Margot la Balafrée'[9] to certain tales in which
'Bostonian nymphs' appear to have 'rejected English dukes for
psychological reasons.'[10] I am not acquainted with the romance just
designated, and can scarcely forgive the *Pall Mall* critic for not
mentioning the name of the author, but the title appears to refer to a
lady who may have received a scar in some heroic adventure. I am
inconsolable at not being acquainted with this episode, but am utterly
at a loss to see why it is a story when the rejection (or acceptance) of a
duke is not, and why a reason, psychological or other, is not a subject
when a cicatrix is. They are all particles of the multitudinous life with
which the novel deals, and surely no dogma which pretends to make it
lawful to touch the one and unlawful to touch the other will stand for a
moment on its feet. It is the special picture that must stand or fall,
according as it seems to possess truth or to lack it. Mr. Besant does
not, to my sense, light up the subject by intimating that a story must,
under penalty of not being a story, consist of 'adventures.' Why of
adventures more than of green spectacles? He mentions a category of
impossible things, and among them he places 'fiction without adventure.' Why without adventure, more than without matrimony, or
celibacy, or parturition, or cholera, or hydropathy, or Jansenism?[11]
This seems to me to bring the novel back to the hapless little *rôle* of
being an artificial, ingenious thing – bring it down from its large, free

character of an immense and exquisite correspondence with life. And what *is* adventure, when it comes to that, and by what sign is the listening pupil to recognise it? It is an adventure – an immense one – for me to write this little article; and for a Bostonian nymph to reject an English duke is an adventure only less stirring, I should say, than for an English duke to be rejected by a Bostonian nymph. I see dramas within dramas in that, and innumerable points of view. A psychological reason is, to my imagination, an object adorably pictorial; to catch the tint of its complexion – I feel as if that idea might inspire one to Titianesque efforts. There are few things more exciting to me, in short, than a psychological reason, and yet, I protest, the novel seems to me the most magnificent form of art. I have just been reading, at the same time, the delightful story of 'Treasure Island,' by Mr. Robert Louis Stevenson, and the last tale from M. Edmond de Goncourt, which is entitled 'Chérie.'[12] One of these works treats of murders, mysteries, islands of dreadful renown, hairbreadth escapes, miraculous coincidences and buried doubloons. The other treats of a little French girl who lived in a fine house in Paris and died of wounded sensibility because no one would marry her. I call 'Treasure Island' delightful, because it appears to me to have succeeded wonderfully in what it attempts; and I venture to bestow no epithet upon 'Chérie,' which strikes me as having failed in what it attempts – that is, in tracing the development of the moral consciousness of a child. But one of these productions strikes me as exactly as much of a novel as the other, and as having a 'story' quite as much. The moral consciousness of a child is as much a part of life as the islands of the Spanish Main, and the one sort of geography seems to me to have those 'surprises' of which Mr. Besant speaks quite as much as the other. For myself (since it comes back in the last resort, as I say, to the preference of the individual), the picture of the child's experience has the advantage that I can at successive steps (an immense luxury, near to the 'sensual pleasure' of which Mr. Besant's critic in the *Pall Mall* speaks) say Yes or No, as it may be, to what the artist puts before me. I have been a child, but I have never been on a quest for a buried treasure, and it is a simple accident that with M. de Goncourt I should have for the most part to say No. With George Eliot, when she painted that country, I always said Yes.

The most interesting part of Mr. Besant's lecture is unfortunately the briefest passage – his very cursory allusion to the 'conscious moral purpose' of the novel. Here again it is not very clear whether he is recording a fact or laying down a principle; it is a great pity that in the latter case he should not have developed his idea. This branch of the subject is of immense importance, and Mr. Besant's few words point to considerations of the widest reach, not to be lightly disposed of. He will have treated the art of fiction but superficially who is not prepared to go every inch of the way that these considerations will carry him. It is for this reason that at the beginning of these remarks I was careful to notify the reader that my reflections on so large a theme have no pretension to be exhaustive. Like Mr. Besant, I have left the question of the morality of the novel till the last, and at the last I find I have used up my space. It is a question surrounded with difficulties, as witness the very first that meets us, in the form of a definite question, on the threshold. Vagueness, in such a discussion, is fatal, and what is the meaning of your morality and your conscious moral purpose? Will you not define your terms and explain how (a novel being a picture) a picture can be either moral or immoral? You wish to paint a moral picture or carve a moral statue; will you not tell us how you would set about it? We are discussing the Art of Fiction; questions of art are questions (in the widest sense) of execution; questions of morality are quite another affair, and will you not let us see how it is that you find it so easy to mix them up? These things are so clear to Mr. Besant that he has deduced from them a law which he sees embodied in English Fiction and which is 'a truly admirable thing and a great cause for congratulation.' It is a great cause for congratulation, indeed, when such thorny problems become as smooth as silk. I may add that, in so far as Mr Besant perceives that in point of fact English Fiction has addressed itself preponderantly to these delicate questions, he will appear to many people to have made a vain discovery. They will have been positively struck, on the contrary, with the moral timidity of the usual English novelist; with his (or with her) aversion to face the difficulties with which, on every side, the treatment of reality bristles. He is apt to be extremely shy (whereas the picture that Mr. Besant draws is a picture of boldness), and the sign of his work, for the most part, is a cautious silence on certain subjects. In the English novel (by which I mean the American as well), more than in any other, there is a traditional difference between that which people know and that which they agree to admit that they know, that which they see and that which they speak of, that which they feel to be a part of life and that which they allow to enter into literature. There is the great difference, in short, between what they talk of in conversation and what they talk of in print. The essence of moral energy is to survey the whole field, and I should directly reverse Mr. Besant's remark, and say not that the English novel has a purpose, but that is has a diffidence. To what degree a purpose in a work of art is a source of corruption I shall not attempt to inquire; the one that seems to me least dangerous is the purpose of making a perfect work. As for our novel, I may say, lastly, on this score, that, as we find it in England to-day, it strikes me as addressed in a large degree to 'young people,' and that this in itself constitutes a presumption that it will be rather shy. There are certain things which it is generally agreed not to discuss, not even to mention, before young people. That is very well, but the absence of discussion is not a symptom of the moral passion. The purpose of the English novel – 'a truly admirable thing, and a great cause for congratulation' – strikes me, therefore, as rather negative.

There is one point at which the moral sense and the artistic sense lie very near together; that is, in the light of the very obvious truth that the deepest quality of a work of art will always be the quality of the mind of the producer. In proportion as that mind is rich and noble will the novel, the picture, the statue, partake of the substance of beauty and truth. To be constituted of such elements is, to my vision, to have purpose enough. No good novel will ever proceed from a superficial mind; that seems to me an axiom which, for the artist in fiction, will cover all needful moral ground; if the youthful aspirant take it to heart it will illuminate for him many of the mysteries of 'purpose.' There are many other useful things that might be said to him, but I have come to the end of my article, and can only touch them as I pass. The critic in the *Pall Mall Gazette*, whom I have already quoted, draws attention to the danger, in speaking of the art of fiction, of generalizing. The danger that he has in mind is rather, I imagine, that of particularizing, for there are some comprehensive remarks which, in addition to those embodied in Mr. Besant's suggestive lecture, might, without fear of misleading him, be addressed to the ingenuous student. I should remind him first of the magnificence of the form that is open to him, which offers to sight so few restrictions and such innumerable opportunities. The other arts, in comparison, appear confined and hampered; the various conditions under which they are exercised are so rigid and definite. But the only condition that I can think of attaching to the composition of the novel is, as I have already said, that it be interesting. This freedom is a splendid privilege, and the first lesson of the young novelist is to learn to be worthy of it. 'Enjoy it as it deserves,' I should say to him; 'take possession of it, explore it to its utmost extent, reveal it, rejoice in it. All life belongs to you, and don't listen either to those who would shut you up into corners of it and tell you that it is only here and there that art inhabits, or to those who would persuade you that this heavenly messenger wings her way outside of life altogether, breathing a superfine air and turning away her head from the truth of things. There is no impression of life, no manner of seeing it and feeling it, to which the plan of the novelist may not offer a place; you have only to remember that talents so dissimilar as those of Alexandre Dumas and Jane Austen, Charles Dickens and Gustave Flaubert, have worked in this field with equal glory. Don't think too much about optimism and pessimism; try and catch the colour of life itself. In France to-day we see a prodigious effort (that of Emile Zola, to whose solid and serious work no explorer of the capacity of the novel can allude without respect), we see an extraordinary effort vitiated by a spirit of pessimism on a narrow basis. M. Zola is magnificent, but he strikes an English reader as ignorant; he has an air of working in the dark; if he had as much light as energy his results would be of the highest value. As for the aberrations of a shallow optimism, the ground (of English fiction especially) is strewn with their brittle particles as with broken glass. If you must indulge in conclusions let them have the taste of a wide knowledge. Remember that your first duty is to be as complete as possible – to make as perfect a work. Be generous and delicate, and then, in the vulgar phrase, go in!'

Robert Louis Stevenson
(1850–1894)
'A Humble Remonstrance', 1884

Robert Louis Stevenson was the elected champion of romance in the late Victorian period. His novels, beginning with *Treasure Island* (1881), but including such adult works as *The Master of Ballantrae* (1888–9) and *Weir of Hermiston* (1896), led what many hoped would develop into successful revolt against realism – against French naturalism on the one hand and the American novel of character on the other. Novelists as different from him as Kipling, Haggard, Wilde, and Anthony Hope belonged roughly to the same movement. Although he joined 'The Art of Fiction' argument late, he had really been in it from the beginning: both Walter Besant, in his lecture, and Stevenson's friend Andrew Lang, in his review of the lecture (*The Pall Mall Gazette*, 34 (30 April 1884): 1–2), had mentioned him as a promising writer and, of course, Henry James makes reference to *Treasure Island*. Moreover, Stevenson had been arguing similar positions to those he takes in 'A Humble Remonstrance' in such earlier essays as 'Victor Hugo's Romances' (1874), 'A Gossip on Romance' (1882), and 'A Note on Realism' (1883), where he had written, 'The immediate danger of the realist is to sacrifice the beauty and significance of the whole to local dexterity, or, in the insane pursuit of completion to immolate his readers under the facts; but he comes in the last resort, and as his energy declines, to discard all design, abjure all choice, and with scientific thoroughness, steadily to communicate matter which is not worth learning.' Indeed Lang saved Robert Louis Stevenson a place in the argument when he wrote, 'Mr Besant stood up as lustily as Mr Louis Stevenson for the excellence of stories.'

'A Humble Remonstrance' was first published in *Longman's Magazine* in December 1884, three months after James's 'The Art of Fiction' had appeared there. Of the debate which began with Besant's lecture, it was the last word intended for publication, but since it led to a life-long friendship between James and Stevenson, the discussion was continued in letters and, no doubt, in many conversations.

The editors have chosen to use the text which Stevenson reprinted in *Memories and Portraits* (1887) and to which he added the final paragraph on W. D. Howells. It is unlikely that in 1884 Robert Louis Stevenson was as ignorant of Howells as he implies, for it was Howells, much more than James, who epitomized to both Besant and Lang the so-called American position on the novel of character, and who had outraged British critics when he wrote that 'In one manner or other the stories were all told long ago; and now we want merely to know what the novelist thinks about persons and situations' (*Century Magazine*, November 1882).

I

WE have recently enjoyed a quite peculiar pleasure: hearing, in some detail, the opinions, about the art they practise, of Mr. Walter Besant and Mr. Henry James; two men certainly of very different calibre: Mr. James so precise of outline, so cunning of fence, so scrupulous of finish, and Mr. Besant so genial, so friendly, with so persuasive and humorous a vein of whim: Mr. James[1] the very type of the deliberate artist, Mr. Besant the impersonation of good nature. That such doctors should differ will excite no great surprise; but one point in which they seem to agree fills me, I confess, with wonder. For they are both content to talk about the "art of fiction"; and Mr. Besant, waxing exceedingly bold, goes on to oppose this so-called "art of fiction" to the "art of poetry." By the art of poetry he can mean nothing but the art of verse, an art of handicraft, and only comparable with the art of prose. For that heat and height of sane emotion which we agree to call by the name of poetry, is but a libertine and vagrant quality; present, at times, in any art, more often absent from them all; too seldom present in the prose novel, too frequently absent from the ode and epic. Fiction is in the same case; it is no substantive art, but an element which enters largely into all the arts but architecture. Homer, Wordsworth, Phidias, Hogarth, and Salvini,[2] all deal in fiction; and yet I do not suppose that either Hogarth or Salvini, to mention but these two, entered in any degree into the scope of Mr. Besant's interesting lecture or Mr. James's charming essay. The art of fiction, then, regarded as a definition, is both too ample and too scanty. Let me suggest another; let me suggest that what both Mr. James and Mr. Besant had in view was neither more nor less than the art of narrative.[3]

But Mr. Besant is anxious to speak solely of "the modern English novel," the stay and bread-winner of Mr. Mudie[4]; and in the author of the most pleasing novel on that roll, *All Sorts and Conditions of Men*, the desire is natural enough. I can conceive then, that he would hasten to propose two additions, and read thus: the art of *fictitious* narrative *in prose*.

Now the fact of the existence of the modern English novel is not to be denied; materially, with its three volumes, leaded type, and gilded lettering, it is easily distinguishable from other forms of literature; but to talk at all fruitfully of any branch of art, it is needful to build our definitions on some more fundamental ground than binding. Why, then, are we to add "in prose"? *The Odyssey* appears to me the best of romances; *The Lady of the Lake* to stand high in the second order; and Chaucer's tales and prologues to contain more of the matter and art of the modern English novel than the whole treasury of Mr. Mudie. Whether a narrative be written in blank verse or the Spenserian stanza, in the long period of Gibbon or the chipped phrase of Charles Reade, the principles of the art of narrative must be equally observed. The choice of a noble and swelling style in prose affects the problem of narration in the same way, if not to the same degree, as the choice of measured verse; for both imply a closer synthesis of events, a higher key of dialogue, and a more picked and stately strain of words. If you are to refuse *Don Juan*, it is hard to see why you should include *Zanoni*[5] or (to bracket works of very different value) *The Scarlet Letter*; and by what discrimination are you to open your doors to *The Pilgrim's Progress* and close them on *The Faery Queen*? To bring things closer home, I will here propound to Mr. Besant a conundrum. A narrative called *Paradise Lost* was written in English verse by one John Milton; what was it then? It was next translated by Chateaubriand[6] into French prose; and what was it then? Lastly, the French translation was, by some inspired compatriot of George Gilfillan[7] (and of mine) turned bodily into an English novel[8]; and, in the name of clearness, what was it then?

But, once more, why should we add "fictitious"? The reason why is obvious. The reason why not, if something more recondite, does not want for weight. The art of narrative, in fact, is the same, whether it is applied to the selection and illustration of a real series of events or of an imaginary series. Boswell's *Life of Johnson* (a work of cunning and inimitable art) owes its success to the same technical manœuvres as (let us say) *Tom Jones*: the clear conception of certain characters of man, the choice and presentation of certain incidents out of a great number that offered, and the invention (yes, invention) and preservation of a certain key in dialogue. In which these things are done with the more art – in which with the greater air of nature – readers will differently judge. Boswell's is, indeed, a very special case, and almost a generic; but it is not only in Boswell, it is in every biography with any salt of life, it is in every history where events and men, rather than ideas, are presented – in Tacitus, in Carlyle, in Michelet, in Macaulay – that the novelist will find many of his own methods most conspicuously and adroitly handled. He will find besides that he, who is free – who has the right to invent or steal a missing incident, who has the right, more precious still, of wholesale omission – is frequently defeated, and, with all his advantages, leaves a less strong impression of reality and passion. Mr. James utters his mind with a becoming fervour on the sanctity of truth to the novelist; on a more careful examination truth will seem a word of very debatable propriety[9], not only for the labours of the novelist, but for those of the historian. No art – to use the daring phrase of Mr. James – can successfully "compete with life"; and the art that seeks to do so is condemned to perish *montibus aviis.*[a] Life goes before us, infinite in complication; attended by the most various and surprising meteors; appealing at once to the eye, to the ear, to the mind – the seat of wonder, to the touch – so thrillingly delicate, and to the belly – so imperious when starved. It combines and employs in its manifestation the method and material, not of one art only, but of all the arts. Music is but an arbitrary trifling with a few of life's majestic chords; painting is but a shadow of its pageantry of light and colour; literature does but drily indicate that wealth of incident, of moral obligation, of virtue, vice, action, rapture and agony, with which it teems. To "compete with life," whose sun we cannot look upon, whose passions and diseases waste and slay us – to compete with the flavour of wine, the beauty of the dawn, the scorching of fire, the bitterness of death and separation – here is, indeed, a projected escalade of heaven; here are, indeed, labours for a Hercules in a dress coat, armed with a pen and a dictionary to depict the passions, armed with a tube of superior flake-white to paint the portrait of the insufferable sun. No art is true in this sense: none can "compete with life": not even history, built indeed of indisputable facts, but these facts robbed of their vivacity and sting; so that even when we read of the sack of a city or the fall of an empire, we are surprised, and justly commend the author's talent, if our pulse be quickened. And mark, for a last differentia, that this quickening of the pulse is, in almost every case, purely agreeable; that these phantom reproductions of experience, even at their most acute, convey decided pleasure; while experience itself, in the cockpit of life, can torture and slay.

What, then, is the object, what the method, of an art, and what the source of its power? The whole secret is that no art does "compete with life." Man's one method, whether he reasons or creates, is to half-shut his eyes against the dazzle and confusion of reality. The arts, like arithmetic and geometry, turn away their eyes from the gross, coloured and mobile nature at our feet, and regard instead a certain figmentary abstraction. Geometry will tell us of a circle, a thing never seen in nature; asked about a green circle or an iron circle, it lays its

[a] In the trackless mountains; Horace, Bk I, Ode XXIII, l. 2.

hand upon its mouth. So with the arts. Painting, ruefully comparing sunshine and flake-white, gives up truth of colour, as it had already given up relief and movement; and instead of vying with nature, arranges a scheme of harmonious tints. Literature, above all in its most typical mood, the mood of narrative, similarly flees the direct challenge and pursues instead an independent and creative aim. So far as it imitates at all, it imitates not life but speech: not the facts of human destiny, but the emphasis and the suppressions with which the human actor tells of them. The real art that dealt with life directly was that of the first men who told their stories round the savage camp-fire. Our art is occupied, and bound to be occupied, not so much in making stories true as in making them typical; not so much in capturing the lineaments of each fact, as in marshalling all of them towards a common end. For the welter of impressions, all forcible but all discreet, which life presents, it substitutes a certain artificial series of impressions, all indeed most feebly represented, but all aiming at the same effect, all eloquent of the same ideas, all chiming together like consonant notes in music or like the graduated tints in a good picture. From all its chapters, from all its pages, from all its sentences, the well-written novel echoes and re-echoes its one creative and control- ling thought; to this must every incident and character contribute; the style must have been pitched in unison with this; and if there is anywhere a word that looks another way, the book would be stronger, clearer, and (I had almost said) fuller without it. Life is monstrous, infinite, illogical, abrupt and poignant; a work of art, in comparison, is neat, finite, self-contained, rational, flowing and emasculate. Life imposes by brute energy, like inarticulate thunder; art catches the ear, among the far louder noises of experience, like an air artificially made by a discreet musician. A proposition of geometry does not compete with life; and a proposition of geometry is a fair and luminous parallel for a work of art. Both are reasonable, both untrue to the crude fact; both inhere in nature, neither represents it. The novel, which is a work of art, exists, not by its resemblances to life, which are forced and material, as a shoe must still consist of leather, but by its immeasurable difference from life, which is designed and significant, and is both the method and the meaning of the work.

The life of man is not the subject of novels, but the inexhaustible magazine from which subjects are to be selected; the name of these is legion; and with each new subject – for here again I must differ by the whole width of heaven from Mr. James – the true artist will vary his method and change the point of attack. That which was in one case an excellence, will become a defect in another; what was the making of one book, will in the next be impertinent or dull. First each novel, and then each class of novels, exists by and for itself.[10] I will take, for instance, three main classes, which are fairly distinct: first, the novel of adventure, which appeals to certain almost sensual and quite illogical tendencies in man; second, the novel of character, which appeals to our intellectual appreciation of man's foibles and mingled and inconstant motives; and third, the dramatic novel, which deals with the same stuff as the serious theatre, and appeals to our emotional nature and moral judgment.

And first for the novel of adventure. Mr. James refers, with singular generosity of praise, to a little book about a quest for hidden treasure;[11] but he lets fall, by the way, some rather startling words. In this book he misses what he calls the "immense luxury" of being able to quarrel with his author. The luxury, to most of us, is to lay by our judgment, to be submerged by the tale as by a billow, and only to awake, and begin to distinguish and find fault, when the piece is over and the volume laid aside. Still more remarkable is Mr. James's reason. He cannot criticise the author, as he goes, "because," says he, comparing it with another work, "*I have been a child, but I have never been on a quest for buried treasure.*" Here is, indeed, a wilful paradox; for if he has never been on a quest for buried treasure, it can be demonstrated that he has never been a child. There never was a child (unless Master James) but has hunted gold, and been a pirate, and a military commander, and a bandit of the mountains; but has fought, and suffered shipwreck and prison, and imbrued its little hands in gore, and gallantly retrieved the lost battle, and triumphantly protected innocence and beauty. Elsewhere in his essay Mr. James has protested with excellent reason against too narrow a conception of experience; for the born artist, he contends, the "faintest hints of life" are converted into revelations; and it will be found true, I believe, in a majority of cases, that the artist writes with more gusto and effect of those things which he has only wished to do, than of those which he has done. Desire is a wonderful telescope, and Pisgah[a] the best observatory. Now, while it is true that neither Mr. James nor the author of the work in question has ever, in the fleshly sense, gone questing after gold, it is probable that both have ardently desired and fondly imagined the details of such a life in youthful daydreams; and the author, counting upon that, and well aware (cunning and low-minded man!) that this class of interest, having been frequently treated, finds a readily accessible and beaten road to the sympathies of the reader, addressed himself throughout to the building up and circumstantiation of this

[a] Mountain from which Moses saw the Promised Land; Deuteronomy 34.

boyish dream. Character to the boy is a sealed book; for him, a pirate is a beard, a pair of wide trousers and a liberal complement of pistols. The author, for the sake of circumstantiation and because he was himself more or less grown up, admitted character, within certain limits, into his design; but only within certain limits. Had the same puppets figured in a scheme of another sort, they had been drawn to very different purpose; for in this elementary novel of adventure, the characters need to be presented with but one class of qualities – the warlike and formidable. So as they appear insidious in deceit and fatal in the combat, they have served their end. Danger is the matter with which this class of novel deals; fear, the passion with which it idly trifles; and the characters are portrayed only so far as they realise the sense of danger and provoke the sympathy of fear. To add more traits, to be too clever, to start the hare of moral or intellectual interest while we are running the fox of material interest, is not to enrich but to stultify your tale. The stupid reader will only be offended, and the clever reader lose the scent.

The novel of character has this difference from all others: that it requires no coherency of plot, and for this reason, as in the case of *Gil Blas*,[12] it is sometimes called the novel of adventure. It turns on the humours of the persons represented; these are, to be sure, embodied in incidents, but the incidents themselves, being tributary, need not march in a progression; and the characters may be statically shown. As they enter, so they may go out; they must be consistent, but they need not grow. Here Mr. James will recognise the note of much of his own work: he treats, for the most part, the statics of character, studying it at rest or only gently moved; and, with his usual delicate and just artistic instinct, he avoids those stronger passions which would deform the attitudes he loves to study, and change his sitters from the humorists of ordinary life to the brute forces and bare types of more emotional moments. In his recent *Author of Beltraffio*, so just in conception, so nimble and neat in workmanship, strong passion is indeed employed; but observe that it is not displayed. Even in the heroine the working of the passion is suppressed; and the great struggle, the true tragedy, the *scène-à-faire*,[a] passes unseen behind the panels of a locked door. The delectable invention of the young visitor is introduced, consciously or not, to this end: that Mr. James, true to his method, might avoid the scene of passion. I trust no reader will suppose me guilty of undervaluing this little masterpiece. I mean merely that it belongs to one marked class of novel, and that it would

---

[a] The big scene.

have been very differently conceived and treated had it belonged to that other marked class, of which I now proceed to speak.

I take pleasure in calling the dramatic novel by that name, because it enables me to point out by the way a strange and peculiarly English misconception. It is sometimes supposed that the drama consists of incident. It consists of passion, which gives the actor his opportunity; and that passion must progressively increase, or the actor, as the piece proceeded, would be unable to carry the audience from a lower to a higher pitch of interest and emotion.[13] A good serious play must therefore be founded on one of the passionate *cruces* of life, where duty and inclination come nobly to the grapple; and the same is true of what I call, for that reason, the dramatic novel. I will instance a few worthy specimens, all of our own day and language: Meredith's *Rhoda Fleming*, that wonderful and painful book, long out of print, and hunted for at bookstalls like an Aldine;[a] Hardy's *Pair of Blue Eyes*; and two of Charles Reade's *Griffith Gaunt* and *The Double Marriage*, originally called *White Lies*, and founded (by an accident quaintly favourable to my nomenclature) on a play by Maquet,[14] the partner of the great Dumas. In this kind of novel the closed door of *The Author of Beltraffio* must be broken open; passion must appear upon the scene and utter its last word; passion is the be-all and the end-all, the plot and the solution, the protagonist and the *deus ex machinâ* in one. The characters may come anyhow upon the stage: we do not care; the point is, that, before they leave it, they shall become transfigured and raised out of themselves by passion. It may be part of the design to draw them with detail; to depict a full-length character, and then behold it melt and change in the furnace of emotion. But there is no obligation of the sort; nice portraiture is not required; and we are content to accept mere abstract types, so they be strongly and sincerely moved. A novel of this class may be even great, and yet contain no individual figure; it may be great, because it displays the workings of the perturbed heart and the impersonal utterance of passion; and with an artist of the second class it is, indeed, even more likely to be great, when the issue has thus been narrowed and the whole force of the writer's mind directed to passion alone. Cleverness again, which has its fair field in the novel of character, is debarred all entry upon this more solemn theatre. A far-fetched motive, an ingenious evasion of the issue, a witty instead of a passionate turn, offend us like an insincerity. All should be plain, all straightforward to the end. Hence it is that, in *Rhoda Fleming*, Mrs. Lovel raises such resentment in the reader; her motives are too flimsy, her ways are too equivocal, for the

[a] Rare, sixteenth-century edition of the classics.

weight and strength of her surroundings. Hence the hot indignation
of the reader when Balzac, after having begun the *Duchesse de Langeais*
in terms of strong if somewhat swollen passion, cuts the knot by the
derangement of the hero's clock. Such personages and incidents
belong to the novel of character; they are out of place in the high
society of the passions; when the passions are introduced in art at their
full height, we look to see them, not baffled and impotently striving,
as in life, but towering above circumstance and acting substitutes for
fate.

And here I can imagine Mr. James, with his lucid sense, to
intervene. To much of what I have said he would apparently demur; in
much he would, somewhat impatiently, acquiesce. It may be true; but
it is not what he desired to say or to hear said. He spoke of the finished
picture and its worth when done; I, of the brushes, the palette, and the
north light. He uttered his views in the tone and for the ear of good
society; I, with the emphasis and technicalities of the obtrusive
student. But the point, I may reply, is not merely to amuse the public,
but to offer helpful advice to the young writer. And the young writer
will not so much be helped by genial pictures of what an art may aspire
to at its highest, as by a true idea of what it must be on the lowest
terms. The best that we can say to him is this: Let him choose a
motive, whether of character or passion; carefully construct his plot so
that every incident is an illustration of the motive, and every property
employed shall bear to it a near relation of congruity or contrast; avoid
a sub-plot, unless, as sometimes in Shakespeare, the sub-plot be a
reversion or complement of the main intrigue; suffer not his style to
flag below the level of the argument; pitch the key of conversation,
not with any thought of how men talk in parlours, but with a single
eye to the degree of passion he may be called on to express; and allow
neither himself in the narrative, nor any character in the course of the
dialogue, to utter one sentence that is not part and parcel of the
business of the story or the discussion of the problem involved. Let
him not regret if this shortens his book; it will be better so; for to add
irrelevant matter is not to lengthen but to bury. Let him not mind if he
miss a thousand qualities, so that he keeps unflaggingly in pursuit of
the one he has chosen. Let him not care particularly if he miss the tone
of conversation, the pungent material detail of the day's manners, the
reproduction of the atmosphere and the environment. These elements
are not essential: a novel may be excellent, and yet have none of them;
a passion or a character is so much the better depicted as it rises clearer
from material circumstance. In this age of the particular, let him
remember the ages of the abstract, the great books of the past, the

brave men that lived before Shakespeare and before Balzac. And as the root of the whole matter, let him bear in mind that his novel is not a transcript of life, to be judged by its exactitude; but a simplification of some side or point of life, to stand or fall by its significant simplicity. For although, in great men, working upon great motives, what we observe and admire is often their complexity, yet underneath appearances the truth remains unchanged: that simplification was their method, and that simplicity is their excellence.

II

Since the above was written another novelist has entered repeatedly the lists of theory: one well worthy of mention, Mr. W. D. Howells; and none ever couched a lance with narrower convictions.[15] His own work and those of his pupils and masters singly occupy his mind; he is the bond-slave, the zealot of his school; he dreams of an advance in art like what there is in science; he thinks of past things as radically dead; he thinks a form can be outlived: a strange immersion in his own history; a strange forgetfulness of the history of the race! Meanwhile, by a glance at his own works (could he see them with the eager eyes of his readers) much of this illusion would be dispelled. For while he holds all the poor little orthodoxies of the day – no poorer and no smaller than those of yesterday or to-morrow, poor and small, indeed, only so far as they are exclusive – the living quality of much that he has done is of a contrary, I had almost said of a heretical, complexion. A man, as I read him, of an originally strong romantic bent – a certain glow of romance still resides in many of his books, and lends them their distinction. As by accident he runs out and revels in the exceptional; and it is then, as often as not, that his reader rejoices – justly, as I contend. For in all this excessive eagerness to be centrally human, is there not one central human thing that Mr. Howells is too often temped to neglect: I mean himself? A poet, a finished artist, a man in love with the appearances of life, a cunning reader of the mind, he has other passions and aspirations than those he loves to draw. And why should he suppress himself and do such reverence to the Lemuel Barkers?[16] The obvious is not of necessity the normal; fashion rules and deforms; the majority fall tamely into the contemporary shape, and thus attain, in the eyes of the true observer, only a higher power of insignificance; and the danger is lest, in seeking to draw the normal, a man should draw the null, and write the novel of society instead of the romance of man.

Vernon Lee
(1856–1935)
From 'A Dialogue on Novels', 1885

Vernon Lee was the pen name of Violet Paget, who was born in France to a
Welsh mother and an English father, received her early education in Germany
and Switzerland, and spent most of her long life in Florence. Her forty books
included travel sketches and collections of essays, as well as fiction and
historical, aesthetic, and philosophical studies. These, and her brilliant and
forthright conversation, gained her the respect and the often rather uneasy
friendship of such illustrious contemporaries as the writers John Addington
Symonds, Henry James, Walter Pater, Robert Browning, Edith Wharton,
and H. G. Wells, the painter John Singer Sargent, the art connoisseur Bernard
Berenson, and the composer Ethel Smyth. Reviewing one of her books in
1920, George Bernard Shaw went so far as to call her 'the noblest Briton of
them all'. Four years later the University of Durham conferred on her the
honorary degree of Doctor of Letters.

In 1884, the year of 'The Art of Fiction', Vernon Lee dedicated her first
novel, *Miss Brown*, to Henry James (who disliked it intensely). Like James, she
was keenly interested at the time in 'the aesthetics of fiction' – the title of one
of several penetrating essays on this subject that she contributed to English
periodicals during the 1880s and 1890s. A number of them were collected in
The Handling of Words and Other Studies in Literary Psychology (1923), in the
introduction to which she declared herself to be a proponent of what has
come to be called reader-response criticism.

'A Dialogue on Novels', which is not included in *The Handling of Words*,
was published in the *Contemporary Review* for September 1885
(48:378–401). Like James's *Daniel Deronda: A Conversation* (1876), it is
literary criticism in the form of drama, but with the characters more fully
developed and with the setting more closely related to the argument. Vernon
Lee has a spokesman in 'A Dialogue on Novels' as James did in the person of
Constantius in his piece on George Eliot's last novel: Baldwin makes the
longest speeches, develops the most coherent position, and gets the last word.
He returns as the protagonist – if that is the right word for the central figure in
such an unusual work that is neither fiction nor non-fiction – of Vernon Lee's
Baldwin: Being Dialogues on Views and Aspirations (1886), where 'A Dialogue
on Novels' reappears, with an augmented conclusion, as 'On Novels'
(pp. 187–245).

In Baldwin's view, the modern novel cannot be considered as an art because
it does not appeal exclusively to our sense of beauty as art must. Rather, 'it

trains us to feel and comprehend – that is to say, to live'. In the second part of 'A Dialogue on Novels' (pp. 390–401 in the September 1885 *Contemporary Review*), a comparison between the French novel and the English that is not reprinted here, Baldwin goes on to argue that fiction cannot carry out this teaching function if it merely reproduces discrete bits of reality without arranging them or relating them to those 'essences, types, lessons, generalizations' (p. 393) that the human intellect, of which the ethical sense is a part, is prepared to register and store.

Recent French fiction is reprehensible not because it depicts vicious conduct but rather because it fails to set such behaviour into an appropriate context and therefore misrepresents life. Recent English fiction, on the other hand, fails to take due cognizance of the darker aspects of human existence and so is equally unsatisfactory. Unlike those nineteenth-century critics who view the didactic role of fiction in narrowly moralistic terms, however, Baldwin (i.e., Vernon Lee) does not advocate a restriction of the writer's liberty to explore certain kinds of subjects; on the contrary, the English novelist must be as free to handle any material, even the most unsavoury, as poets and playwrights are, so long as his or her treatment of it contributes to the teaching mission of the novel in question. 'Is the novel', he asks, 'the one great literary form produced by our age, as the drama and the epic were produced by other ages, to appeal to a public of which we are to take for granted that it is so infinitely less mature, so infinitely less intelligent, and less clean-minded than the public of the poet?' (p. 398). If that question is answered as Vernon Lee would have it be, 'A Dialogue on Novels' is yet another Victorian plea, though one couched in somewhat unconventional terms, that the novel not be dismissed as 'light literature' but rather be accorded its due place of honour among literary genres.

"AFTER all," said Mrs. Blake, the eminent novelist, "with the exception of very few touches, there is nothing human in 'Wuthering Heights;' those people with their sullenness and coldness and frenzy are none of them real men and women, such as Charlotte Brontë would have given us had she written the book instead of her sister. You can't deny that, Monsieur Marcel."

They had clambered through the steep, bleak Yorkshire village, which trickles, a water-course of rough black masonry, down the green hillside; past the inn where Branwell Brontë drank and raved; through the churchyard, a grim, grassless garden of blackened tombstones; under the windows of the Brontës' parsonage; and still higher, up the slippery slope of coarse, sere grass, on to the undulating flatness of Haworth Moor.[1]

André Marcel, the subtle young French critic and novelist, who had come to Yorkshire in order to study the Brontës, listened to Mrs. Blake with disappointed pensiveness. Knowing more of English things than most Frenchmen, and with a natural preference for the exotic of all kinds, it was part of his mission to make known to the world that England really was what, in the days of Goethe, Italy had falsely been supposed to be – a sort of exceptional and esoteric country, whence æsthetic and critical natures might get weird and exquisite moral impressions as they got orchids and porcelain and lacquer from Japan. Such being the case, this clever woman with her clever novels, both so narrow and so normal, so full at once of scepticism and of respect for precedent, gave him as much of a sense of annoyance and hostility almost as his placid, pessimistic, purely artistic and speculative nature could experience.

They walked on in some minutes in silence, Marcel and Mrs. Blake behind, Baldwin and his cousin Dorothy in front, trampling the rough carpet of lilac and black heather matted with long withered grass and speckled with the bright scarlet of sere bilberry leaves; the valleys gradually closing up all around; the green pasture slopes, ribbed with black stone fences, gradually meeting one another, uniting, disappearing, absorbed in the undulating sea of moorland, spreading solitary, face to face with the low, purplish-grey sky. As Mrs. Blake spoke, Dorothy turned round eagerly.

"They are not real men and women, the people in 'Wuthering Heights,'" she said; "but they are real all the same. Don't you feel that they are real, Monsieur Marcel, when you look about you now? Don't you feel that they are these moors and the sunshine, the clouds, the winds, the storms upon them?"

"All the moors and all the storms upon them put together haven't the importance for a human being that has one well-understood real character of Charlotte Brontë's or George Eliot's," answered Mrs. Blake, coldly.

"I quite understand your point of view," said Marcel; "but, for all my admiration for Charlotte Brontë and George Eliot, I can't agree that either of them, or any writer of their school, can give us anything of the value of 'Wuthering Heights.' After all, what do we gain by their immense powers of psychological analysis and reconstruction? Merely a partial insight into a certain number of characters – characters which, whatever the genius of the novelist, can be only approximations to reality, because they are the result of the study of something of which we can never completely understand the nature – because it is outside ourselves."

Mrs. Blake, who could understand of Marcel's theories only the fact they were extremely distasteful to herself, began to laugh.

"If we are never to understand anything except ourselves, I think

225

we had better leave off novel-writing at once, Monsieur Marcel," she said.

"I don't think that would suit Marcel at all," put in Baldwin, "and he does not by any means condemn the ordinary novel for being what he considers a mere approximation to reality. All he says is, that he prefers books where there is no attempt at completely solving what he considers the inscrutable – namely, the character of every one not oneself. He perceives, more than most people, perhaps even too much, the complexity of human nature; and what to you or me is a complete moral portrait is to him a mere partial representation. I personally think that it is all the better for us if we are unable to see every little moral nerve and muscle in our neighbours: there are in all of us remains of machinery which belongs to something baser, and is little or not at all put in movement. If we could see all the incipient thoughts and incipient feelings of even the best people, we should probably form a much less really just estimate of them than we do at present. It is not morally correct, any more than it is artistically correct, to see the microscopic and the hidden."

"I don't know about that," said Marcel. "But I know that, by the fatality of heredity on one hand, a human being contains within himself a number of different tendencies, all moulded, it is true, into one character, but existing none the less each in its special nature, ready to respond to its special stimulus from without; on the other hand, by the fatality of environment every human being is modified in many different ways: he is rammed into a place until he fits it, and absorbs fragments of all the other personalities with whom he is crushed together. So that there must be, in all of us, even in the most homogeneous, tendencies which, from not having met their appropriate stimulus, may be lying unsuspected at the very bottom of our nature, far below the level of consciousness; but which, on the approach of the specific stimulus, or merely on the occasion of any violent shaking of the whole nature, will suddenly come to the surface. Now it seems to me that such complications of main and minor characteristics, such complications inherited or induced, of half-perceived or dormant qualities, can be disentangled, made intelligible, when the writer is speaking of himself, may be shown even unconsciously to himself; but they cannot be got at in a third person. Therefore, I give infinitely less value to one of your writers with universal intuition and sympathy, writing of approximate realities neither himself nor yourself, than to one who like Emily Brontë simply shows us men, women, nature, passion, life, all seen through the medium of her own personality. It is this sense of coming really and absolutely in contact with a real soul which gives such a poignancy to a certain very small class of books – books, to my mind the most precious we have – such as the Memoirs of St. Augustine, the 'Vita Nuova,'[2] the 'Confessions' of Jean-Jacques Rousseau; and 'Wuthering Heights,' although an infinitely non-imaginative book, seems to me worthy to be ranked with these."

Dorothy Orme had been walking silently in front, her hat slung on her arm, her light curly hair flying in the wind, filling her arms with pale lilac heather; and seeming to the Frenchman a kind of outcome of the moor, an illustration of 'Wuthering Heights;' something akin to Emily Brontë's heroine, nay, rather to Emily Brontë herself, as she existed for his imagination. She turned round as he spoke, and said, with a curious mixture of surprise, pain, and reproach:

"I am glad you put 'Wuthering Heights' with the 'Vita Nuova;' but how can you mention in the same breath those disgusting, degraded 'Confessions' of Rousseau? I once tried to read them, and they made me feel sick."

Marcel looked at her with grave admiration. "Mademoiselle," he said, "the 'Confessions' are not a book for you; a diseased soul like Jean-Jacques ought never to be obtruded upon your notice: you ought to read only things like 'Wuthering Heights' and the 'Vita Nuova,' just as you ought to walk on these moors, but not among the squalor and confusion of a big town; you fit into the one, and not into the other. But I put the 'Confessions' by the side of these other books because they belong, in their deeply troubling way, as the 'Vita Nuova,' is in its perfect serenity, to that very small class of scarcely self-conscious revelations of personality which may teach us what the novel should aim at."

Dorothy did not answer. This young man, with his keen appreciation, his delicate enthusiasm alike for purity and impurity, puzzled her and made her unhappy. She felt sure he was good himself, yet his notions were so very strange.

"At that rate," put in Mrs. Blake, "there is an end of the novel as a work of art, if we are to make it into a study of the mere psychology of a single individual. As it is, the perpetual pre-occupation of psychology has pretty well got rid of all real interest of plot and incident, and is rapidly getting rid of all humour; a comic character like those of Dickens, and even those of Thackeray, will soon be out of the question. Did you read an extraordinarily suggestive article by Mr Hillebrand, which appeared in THE CONTEMPORARY last year,[3] contrasting the modern novel with the old one? It was very one-sided, of course; but in many things wonderfully correct. I felt that he must condemn my novels along with the others, but I was pleased; it was as if Fielding's ghost had told us his opinion of modern novelists."

Dorothy Orme was not addicted to literary discussions; but the recollection of this article seemed suddenly to transform her.

"I read it," she cried eagerly; "I hated it. He was very angry with George Eliot because she had made the story of Dorothea and Casaubon tragic, instead of making it farcical, as I suppose Fielding or some such creature would have done; he would have liked some disgusting, ridiculous comedy of an old pedant, a sort of Don Bartolo,[4] and a girl whom he bored and who made fun of him. Did he never ask himself whether the reality of a situation such as that of Dorothea and Casaubon would be more comic or tragic, whether we should be entering more into the feelings of the people themselves, whether we should be placing ourselves more in the position to help, to diminish unhappiness, by laughing at Dorothea and Casaubon, or be crying at their story? I am sure we are far too apt to laugh at things already. I dare say that the sense of the ridiculous is a very useful thing; I dare say it helps to make the world more supportable; but not when the sense of the ridiculous makes us see things as they are not, or as they are merely superficially; when it makes us feel pleased and passive where we ought to be pained and active. People have a way of talking about the tendency which the wish for nobility and beauty has to make us see things in the wrong light; but there is much more danger, surely, of that sort of falsification from our desire for the comic. There's Don Quixote – we have laughed at him quite long enough. I wish some one would write a book now about the reverse of Don Quixote, about a good and kind and helpful man who is made unjust, unkind, and useless by his habit of seeking for the ridiculous, by his habit of seeing windmills where there are real giants, and coarse peasants where there are really princesses. The history of that man, absurd though it may seem as a whole, would yet be, in its part, the history of some little bit of the life of all of us; a bit which might be amusing enough to novelists of the old school, but is sad enough, I think, in all conscience, when we look back upon it in ourselves."

Marcel looked up. To him the weirdest and most exotic flowers of this moral and intellectual Japan called England, were its young women, wonderful it seemed to him in delicacy, in brilliancy of colour, in *bizarre* outline, in imaginatively stimulating and yet reviving perfume; and ever since he had met her a few days ago, this cousin of his old friend Baldwin, this Dorothy Orme, painter, sculptor, philanthropist, and mystic, with the sea-blue eyes, and the light hair that seemed always caught up by the breeze, this creature at once so mature and so immature, so full of enthusiasm, so unconscious of passion, so boldly conversant with evil in the abstract, so pathetically ignorant of evil in the concrete, had appeared to him as almost the strangest of all these strange English girls who fascinated him as a poet and a critic.

Baldwin had affectionately taken his cousin's arm and passed it through his own.

"You are quite right, Dorothy," he said; "you have put into words what I myself felt while reading that paper; but then, you know, unfortunately, as one grows older – and I am a good bit older than you – one is apt to let oneself drift into looking at people only from the comic side; it is so much easier, and saves one such a deal of useless pain and rage. But you are quite right all the same. A substitution of psychological sympathetic interest for the comic interest of former days has certainly taken place in the novel; and is taking place more and more every day. But I don't think, with Mrs. Blake and Hillebrand, that this is at all a matter for lamentation. Few things strike me more in old fiction, especially if we go back a century, than the curious callousness which many of its incidents reveal; a callousness not merely to many impressions of disgust and shame, which to the modern mind would counter-balance the pleasure of mere droll contrast, as is so constantly the case in Rabelais (where we can't laugh because we have to hold our nose), but also to impressions of actual pain at the pain, moral or physical, endured by the person at whom we are laughing; of indignation at the baseness or cruelty of those through whose agency that comic person is made comic. After all, a great deal of what people are pleased to call the healthy sense of fun of former days is merely the sense of fun of the boy who pours a glass of water down his companion's back, of the young brutes who worry an honest woman in the street, of the ragamuffins who tie a saucepan to a cat's tail and hunt it along. Sometimes it is even more deliberately wanton and cruel; it is the spiritual equivalent of the cock-fighting and bull-baiting, of the amusement at what Michelet[5] reckons among the three great jokes of the Middle Ages: 'La grimace du pendu.'[a] It is possible that we may at some future period be in danger of becoming too serious, too sympathizing, of losing our animal spirits; but I don't see any such danger in the present. And I do see that it is a gain, not only in our souls, but in the actual influence on the amount of good and bad in the world, that certain things which amused our ancestors, the grimace of the dupe, of the betrayed husband, or the kicked

[a] The grimace of one who has been hanged.

servant, should no longer amuse, but merely make us sorry or indignant. Let us laugh by all means, but not when others are crying.'

"I perfectly agree with you," said Marcel. "What people call the comic is a lower form of art; legitimate, but only in so far as it does not interfere with the higher. Complete beauty in sculpture, in painting, and in music has never been compatible with the laughable, and I think it will prove to be the same in fiction. To begin with, all great art carries with it a poignancy which is incompatible with the desire to laugh."

"The French have strangely changed," exclaimed Mrs. Blake. "It is difficult to imagine that you belong to the country which produced Rabelais, and Molière, and Voltaire, Monsieur Marcel."

Marcel sighed. "I know it is," he said; "it is sad, perhaps, as it is always sad to see that one is no longer a child, but a man. Our childhood, at least as artists, is over; we have lost our laughter, our pleasure in romping. But we can understand and feel; we are men."

Mrs. Blake looked shrewdly at the young man. "It seems to me that they were men also, those of the past," she answered. "They laughed; but they also suffered, and hoped, and hated; and the laugh seemed to fit in with the rest. Your modern French literature seems to me no longer French; it all somehow comes out of Rousseau. Balzac, Flaubert, Zola, Baudelaire, all that comes out of those 'Confessions' which you choose to place by the side of the 'Vita Nuova.' And as Rousseau, who certainly was not a true Frenchman, has never seemed to be a genuine man either, but a sickly, morbid piece of half-developed precocity, so I cannot admit that the present phase of French literature represents manhood as opposed the French literature of the past. Had there remained in France more of the old power of laughter, we should not have had your Zolas and Baudelaires, or rather the genius of your Zolas and Baudelaires would have been healthy and useful. Don't wish to lose that laugh of yours, Monsieur Marcel; our mortal health here, in England, where evil is brutish, depends upon seriousness; yours, in France, where evil immediately becomes intellectual, depends upon laughter. I am an old woman, so you must not be offended with me."

"There is a deal of truth in what you say," said Baldwin. "The time will come, I am sure, when Frenchmen will look back upon the literature of the last twenty-five years, not as a product of maturity, but rather as a symptom of a particular sort of humourless morbidness which is one of the unbeautiful phases of growth."

Marcel shook his head. "You are merely falling foul of a new form of art because it does not answer to the critical standards which you have deduced from an old one. The art which deals with human emotions real and really appreciated is a growth of our century, and mainly a growth of my country; and you are criticizing it from the standpoint of quite a different art, which made use of only an approximation to psychological reality, for the sake of a tragic or comic effect; it is as if you criticized a landscape by Corot, where beauty is extracted out of the quality of the light, of the soil, and the dampness or dryness of the air, without a thought of the human figure, because it is not like the little bits of conventional landscape which Titian used to complete the scheme of his groups of Saints or Nymphs. Shakespeare and Cervantes are legitimate; but we moderns are legitimate also: they sought for artistic effects new in their day; we seek for artistic effects new in ours."

Baldwin was twisting a long brown rush between his fingers meditatively, looking straight before him upon the endless, grey and purple, thundercloud-coloured undulations of heather.

"I think," he said, "that you imagine you are seeking new artistic effects; but I think, also, that you are mistaken, simply because I feel daily more persuaded that artistic aims are only partially compatible with psychological aims, and that the more the novel becomes psychological the less also will it become artistic. The aim of art, of painting, sculpture, music, and architecture, is, if we put aside the mere display of technical skill, which, as a rule, appears only to the technically initiated – the aim of art is the production of something which shall give us the particular kind of pleasure associated with the word *beautiful*, pleasure given to our æsthetic faculties, which have a mode of action and necessities as special and as impossible to translate into the mode of action and necessities of our logical and animal faculties as it is impossible to translate the impressions of sight into the impressions of hearing. All art addresses itself, however unconsciously and however much hampered by extraneous necessities, to a desire belonging to these æsthetic faculties, to a desire for the beautiful. Now, to postulate such a predominant desire for the beautiful in a literary work dealing exclusively with human emotion and action seems to me utterly absurd. First, because mere beauty, the thing which gives us the specific æsthetic impression, exists, I believe, in its absolute reality only in the domain of the senses and of the sensuous impressions recalled and reconstructed by the intellect; and because I believe that it is merely by analogy, and because we perceive that such a pleasure is neither unreasoning and animal nor intellectual and utilitarian, that we apply to pleasing moral impressions the adjective beautiful. The beautiful, therefore, according to my view, can exist in literature only inasmuch as literature reproduces and reconstructs certain sensuous impressions which we name beautiful, or as it deals with such moral effects as give us an unmixed, direct unutilitarian pleasure analogous to that produced by these sensuous impressions of beauty. Now, human character, emotion, and action not merely present us with a host of impressions which, applying an æsthetical word to moral phenomena, are more or less ugly; but, by the very fatility of things, nearly always require for the production of what we call moral beauty a certain proportion of moral ugliness to make it visible. It is not so in art. A dark background, necessary to throw a figure into full light, is as much part of the beautiful whole as the figure in the light; whereas moral beauty – namely, virtue – can scarcely be conceived as existing, except in a passive and almost invisible condition, unless it be brought out by a struggle with vice; so that we can't get rid of ugliness in this department. On the other hand, while the desire for beauty can never be paramount in a work dealing with human character and emotion, at least in anything like the sense in which it is paramount in a work dealing with lines, colours, or sounds; there are connected with this work, dealing with human character and emotion, desires special to itself, independent of, and usually hostile to, the desire of beauty – such desires are those for psychological truth and for dramatic excitement. You may say that these are themselves, inasmuch as they are desires without any proximate practical object, artistic; and that, in this sense, every work that caters for them is subject to artistic necessities. So far you may call them artistic, if you like; but then we must call artistic also every other non-practical desire of our nature; the desire which is gratified by a piece of scientific information, divested of all practical value, will also be artistic, and the man who presents an abstract logical argument in the best order, so that the unimportant be always subordinate to the important, will have to be called an artist. The satisfaction we have in following the workings of a character, when these workings do not awaken sympathy or aversion, is as purely scientific as the satisfaction in following a mathematical demonstration or a physiological experiment; and when these workings of character do awaken sympathy or aversion, this sympathy or aversion is a moral emotion, to which we can apply the æsthetical terms 'beautiful' and 'ugly' only by a metaphor, only in the same way that we apply adjectives of temperature to character, or adjectives belonging to music to qualities of painting. The beautiful, as such, has a far smaller share in the poem, novel, or the drama than in painting, sculpture, or music; and, what is more, the ugly has an immeasurably larger one, both in the actual sense of physical ugliness and in the metaphorical sense of moral deformity. I wonder how much of the desire which makes a painter seek for a peculiar scheme of colour, or a peculiar arrangement of hands, enters into the production of such characters as Regan and Goneril and Cousin Bette and Emma Bovary;[6] into the production of the Pension Vauquer dining-room[7] and the Dissenting chapel in Browning's 'Christmas Eve and Easter Day'?[8] To compare a man who works with such materials, who, every now and then at least, carefully elaborates descriptions of hideous places and odious people, with an artist like Corot, seeking for absolute loveliness in those less showy effects which previous painters have neglected, is simply an absurdity. The arts which deal with man and his passions, and especially the novel, which does so far more exclusively and completely than poetry or the drama, are, compared with painting, or sculpture, or architecture, or music, only half-arts. They can scarcely attain unmixed, absolute beauty; and they are perpetually obliged to deal with unmixed, absolute ugliness."

There was a moment's silence.

"I can't make out our friend Baldwin," said Mrs. Blake; "he is too strangely compounded of a scientific thinker, a moralist, and an æsthete; and each of the three component parts is always starting up when you expect one of the others. Yesterday he was descanting on the sublime superiority of literature over art; now he suddenly tells us that, compared with art, literature is an ugly hybrid."

Dorothy Orme had been listening attentively, and her face wore an expression of vague pain and perplexity.

"I can't understand," she said. "What you say seems dreadfully true; it is what I have often vaguely felt, and what has made me wretched. Human nature does not seem to give one that complete, perfect satisfaction which we get from physical beauty; it is always mixed up, or in conflict with, something that gives pain. And yet one feels, one knows, that it is something much higher and nobler than mere combinations of lines, or sounds, or colours. Oh, why should art that deals with these things be the only real, the only thoroughly perfect art? Why should art that deals with human beings be a mistake? Don't you feel that there is something very wrong and very humiliating in such an admission? – in the admission that an artist is less well employed in showing us real men and women than in showing us a certain amount of heather and cloud and rock like that?"

And Dorothy pointed to the moor which spread, with immediately beneath them a sudden dip, a deep pool of rough, spray-like, blackish-purple heather round half-buried fragments of black rock, for what might be yards or miles or scores of miles; not a house, not a tree, not a track, nothing but the tufts of black and lilac heather and wind-bent rushes being there by which to measure the chain of moors: a sort of second sky, folds and folds and rolls and rolls of grey and purple and black-splashed cloud, swelling out and going in, beneath the folds and folds and rolls and rolls of the real sky, black-splashed, purple and grey, into which the moorland melted, with scarcely a line of division, on the low horizon.

"I make no such admission, my dear Dorothy," answered Baldwin. "Nay, I think that the artist who shows us real men and women in their emotion and action is a far more important person than the artist who shows us trees and skies, and clouds and rocks; although the one may always give us beauty, and the other may often give us ugliness. I was saying just now that the art dealing with human character and emotion is only half an art, that it cannot fulfil the complete æsthetic purposes of the other arts, and cannot be judged entirely by their standard; but while fiction – let us say at once, the novel – falls short of absolute achievement on one side, it is able to achieve much more, something quite unknown to the rest of the arts, on the other; but while it evades some of the laws of the merely æsthetical, it becomes liable to another set of necessities, the necessities of ethics. The novel has less value in art, but more importance in life. Let me explain my idea. We have seen that there enter into the novel a proportion of interests which are not artistic, interests which are emotional and scientific; desire for the excitement of sympathy and aversion, and desire for the comprehension of psychological problems. Now one of the main differences between these emotional and scientific interests and the merely æsthetic ones is, I think, that the experience accumulated, the sensitiveness increased, by æsthetic stimulation serves merely (except we go hunting for most remote consequences) to fit us for the reception of more æsthetic experiences, for the putting out of more æsthetic sensitiveness, familiarity with beauty training us only for further familiarity with beauty; whereas, on the contrary, our emotional and scientific experiences obtained from art, however distant all practical object may have been while obtaining them, mingle with other emotional and scientific experiences obtained, with no desire of pleasure, in the course of events; and thus become part of our *viaticum*[a] for life.

Emotional and scientific art, or rather emotional and scientific play (for I don't see why the word art should always be used when we do a thing merely to gratify our higher faculties without practical pur-

[a] Supplies for a journey.

poses), trains us to feel and comprehend – that is to say, to live. It trains us well or ill; and, the thing done as mere play becoming thus connected with practical matters, it is evident that it must submit to the exigencies of practical matters. From this passive acquiescence in the interests of our lives to an active influence therein is but one step; for the mere play desires receive a strange additional strength from the half-conscious sense that the play has practical results: it is the difference, in point of excitement, between gambling with markers and gambling with money. There is a kind of literature, both in verse and in prose, in which the human figure is but a mere accessory – a doll on which to arrange beautiful brocades and ornaments. But wherever the human figure becomes the central interest, there literature begins to diverge from art; other interests, foreign to those of art, conflicting with the desire for beauty, arise; and these interests, psychological and sympathetic, in mankind, create new powers and necessities. Hence, I say, that although the novel, for instance, is not as artistically valuable as painting, or sculpture, or music, it is practically more important and more noble."

"It is extraordinary," mused Marcel, "how æsthetical questions invariably end in ethical ones when treated by English people: and yet in practice you have given the world as great an artistic literature as any other nation, perhaps even greater."

"I think," answered Mrs. Blake, who was always sceptical even when she assented, and who represented that portion of reasoning mankind which carries a belief in spontaneous action to the length of disbelief in all action at all – "I think that, like most speculative thinkers, our friend Baldwin always exaggerates the practical result of everything."

They had turned, after a last look at the grey and purple and blackish undulations of the moors, and were slowly walking back over the matted sere grass and the stiff short heather in the direction of Haworth; the apparently continuous table-land beginning to divide once more, the tops of the green pasture-slopes to reappear, the valleys separating hill from hill to become apparent; and a greyness, different from the greyness of the sky, to tell, on one side, of the neighbourhood down below, of grim, smoky manufacturing towns and villages, from which, in one's fancy, these wild, uncultivated hill-top solitudes seemed separated by hundreds of miles.

"I don't think I exaggerate the practical effects in this case," answered Baldwin. "When we think of the difference in what I must call secular, as distinguished from religious, inner life, between our-selves and our ancestors of two or three centuries, nay, of only one century, ago, the question must come to us: Whence this difference? Social differences, due to political and economical ones, will explain a great deal; but they will not explain all. Much is a question of mere development. Nothing external has altered, only time has passed. Now what has developed in us such a number and variety of moral notes which did not exist in the gamut of our fathers? What has enabled us to follow consonances and dissonances for which their moral ear was still too coarse? Development? Doubtless; just as development has enabled us to execute, nay, to hear, music which would have escaped the comprehension of the men of former days. But what is development? A mere word, a mere shibboleth, unless we attach to it the conception of a succession of acts which have constituted or produced the change. Now, what, in a case such as this, is that succession of acts? We have little by little become conscious of new harmonies and dissonances, have felt new feelings? But whence came these new harmonies and dissonances, those new feelings. Out of their predecessors: the power of to-day's perception arising out of the fact of yesterday's. But what are such perceptions; and would mere real life suffice to give them? I doubt it. In real life there would be mere dumb, inarticulate, unconscious feeling, at least for the immense majority of humanity, if certain specially gifted individuals did not pick out, isolate, those feelings of real life, show them to us in an ideal condition where they have a merely intellectual value, where we could assimilate them into our conscious ideas. This is done by the moralist, by the preacher, by the poet, by the dramatist; people who have taught mankind to see the broad channels along which its feelings move, who have dug those channels. But in all those things, those finer details of feeling which separate us from the people of the time of Elizabeth, nay, from the people of the time of Fielding, who have been those that have discovered, made familiar, placed within the reach of the immense majority, subtleties of feeling barely known to the minority some hundred years before? The novelists, I think. They have, by playing upon our emotions, immensely increased the sensitiveness, the richness, of this living keyboard; even as a singing-master, by playing on his pupil's throat, increases the number of the musical intervals which he can intone."

"I ask you," went on Baldwin, after a minute, "do you think that our great-grandfathers and great-grandmothers would have been able to understand such situations as those of Dorothea and Casaubon, of the husband and wife in Howells' 'Modern Instance,'[9] as that of the young widow in a novel which I think we must all have read a couple of years ago, Lucas Malet's 'Mrs. Lorimer'?[10] Such situations may have existed, but their very heroes and heroines must have been unconscious of them. I ask you again, Mrs. Blake – for you know the book – could you conceive a modern girl of eighteen, pure and charming and loving, as Fielding represents his Sophia Western, learning the connection between her lover and a creature like Molly Seagrim,[11] without becoming quite morally ill at the discovery? But in the eighteenth century a nice girl had not the feelings, the ideal of repugnances, of a nice girl of our day. In the face of such things it is absurd to pretend, as some people do, that the feelings of mankind and womankind are always the same. Well, to return to my argument. Believing, as I do, in the power of directing human feeling into certain channels rather than into certain others; believing, especially, in the power of reiteration of emotion in constituting our emotional selves, in digging by a constant drop, drop, such moral channels as have already been traced; I must necessarily also believe that the modern human being has been largely fashioned, in all his more delicate peculiarities, by those who have written about him; and most of all, therefore, by the novelist. I believe that were the majority of us, educated and sensitive men and women, able to analyze what we consider our almost inborn, nay, automatic, views of life, character, and feeling; that could we scientifically assign its origin to each and trace its modifications; I believe that, were this possible, we should find that a good third of what we take to be instinctive knowledge, or knowledge vaguely acquired from personal experience, is really obtained from the novels which we or our friends have read."

Joseph Conrad
(1857–1924)
'Preface' to
'The Nigger of the "Narcissus"', 1897

Joseph Conrad came late to the art of fiction, and his present position of eminence among late Victorian and early-twentieth-century novelists is the outcome of what can now be seen as a series of happy accidents, though Conrad himself could not have thought of his early life as fundamentally a happy one. Born Józef Teodor Konrad Korzeniowski in the Polish Ukraine, then chafing under Russian rule, he lost both his parents before he was twelve. After a boyhood during which he experienced much suffering and observed much frustrated nationalist plotting in which his father had been a leader, he left Poland for Marseilles shortly before his seventeenth birthday and spent most of the next two decades as a sailor aboard French and English vessels, travelling to many remote parts of the world, incurring illness and other physical and mental hardships, and rising in the British merchant service to the rank of master. Settling down in England at the age of thirty-six, in 1894, Conrad turned to writing as a career, using as raw material many of his own adventures and the insights they had given him about human nature and the role of the artist in making our often lonely and dangerous lives both comprehensible and bearable.

It did not take Conrad long after this late beginning to achieve either publication or critical acclaim; popularity came later. *Almayer's Folly*, his first novel, appeared in 1895; *An Outcast of the Islands* followed the next year; and *The Nigger of the 'Narcissus'* was serialized in the *New Review* from August through December 1897, coming out in book form in the latter month. (An American edition, under the title *The Children of the Sea*, was published a few days earlier.) Of the works that followed in rapid succession over the next quarter-century, *Heart of Darkness* (1899), *Lord Jim* (1900), *Nostromo* (1904), *The Secret Agent* (1907), 'The Secret Sharer' (1910), and *Under Western Eyes* (1911) are generally recognized as his masterpieces, though it was not until *Chance* (1913) that a new novel by Conrad brought the author a considerable financial return. As a mark of the esteem he came to enjoy in his adopted homeland, he was offered a knighthood, which he declined, three months before his death.

It is arguable that *The Nigger of the 'Narcissus'*, his third novel, marked a turning point in Conrad's life and in the view he took of the role of writing fiction in that life. As he later put it in 'To My Readers in America' – the preface to the original Preface, and to the novel, in an edition brought out by Doubleday, Page, in Garden City, New York, in 1914 – 'After writing the last words of that book … I understood that I had done with the sea, and that henceforth I had to be a writer.' As to the Preface itself, Conrad made it clear in 'To My Readers in America' that it was written after the novel was finished, in an effort 'to express the spirit in which I was entering on the task of my new life'.

Though often quoted from, the Preface to *The Nigger of the 'Narcissus'* is, as Conrad's own comment suggests, more a quiet, personal, after-the-fact justification of his decision to devote himself to literature than the ringing manifesto it is sometimes held to be. Those who have studied the Preface most closely – for example, David Goldknopf, Ian Watt, and John Howard Weston – have pointed to its lack of coherence and its imperfect applicability to either *The Nigger of the 'Narcissus'* or anything else in Conrad's fiction. Certainly he never again wrote anything like it: the Author's Notes to his later books, unlike Henry James's prefaces, tend to be autobiographical rather than critical. And yet anyone tracing the criticism of the novel throughout the Victorian period, which was nearly over when the Preface first appeared, is bound to be struck by the way in which certain nineteenth-century preoccupations made themselves felt in its few paragraphs.

A novel is a painstakingly wrought work of art and not a mere piece of light entertainment. The novelist works with and through the senses and is therefore a realist (or an impressionist); he employs and appeals to those internal capacities that unite him and his readers in human 'solidarity' and is therefore a romantic, in a tradition that goes all the way back to Wordsworth's 1800 Preface to the *Lyrical Ballads*; he does not avert his eyes from any 'dark corner of the earth' and is therefore a naturalist. But in the end such 'temporary formulas of his craft' as realism, romanticism, and naturalism, and even the 'Art for Art itself' slogan of the recent Aesthetic Movement, cannot guide the practitioner of the art of fiction as he undertakes his solitary and difficult task.

The complicated textual history of Conrad's Preface is traced by Thomas Lavoie in the Norton Critical Edition of *The Nigger of the 'Narcissus'* (1979), pp. 148–50. Our text is the only version printed during the period treated in this book: the 'Author's Note' appended to the final instalment of the serialized version of the novel in the *New Review*, 17 (December 1897): 628–31.

Any work that aspires, however humbly, to the condition of art should carry its justification in every line. And art itself may be defined as a single-minded attempt to render the highest kind of justice to the visible universe, by bringing to light the truth, manifold and one, underlying its every aspect. It is an attempt to find in its forms, in its colours, in its light, in its shadows, in the aspects of matter and in the facts of life, what of each is fundamental, what is enduring and essential – their one illuminating and convincing quality – the very truth of their existence. The artist, then, like the thinker or the man of science, seeks the truth and makes his appeal. Impressed by the aspect of the world the thinker plunges into ideas, the scientist into facts – whence, presently, emerging they make their appeal to those qualities of our being that fit us best for the hazardous enterprise of living. They speak authoritatively to our common-sense, to our intelligence, to our desire of peace or to our desire of unrest; not seldom to our prejudices, sometimes to our fears, often to our egoism – but always to our credulity. And their words are heard with reverence, for their concern is with weighty matters: with the cultivation of our minds and the proper care of our bodies: with the attainment of our ambitions; with the perfection of the means and the glorification of our precious aims.

It is otherwise with the artist. Confronted by the same enigmatical spectacle the artist descends within himself, and in that lonely region of stress and strife, if he be deserving and fortunate, he finds the terms of his appeal. His appeal is made to our less obvious capacities: to that part of our nature which, because of the warlike conditions of existence, is necessarily kept out of sight within the more resisting and hard qualities – like the vulnerable body within the steel armour. His appeal is less loud, more profound, less distinct, more stirring – and sooner forgotten. Yet its effect endures for ever. The changing wisdom of successive generations discards ideas, questions facts, demolishes theories. But the artist appeals to that part of our being which is not dependent on wisdom: to that in us which is a gift and not an acquisition – and, therefore, more permanently enduring. He appeals to temperament, and he speaks to our capacity for delight and wonder, to the sense of mystery surrounding our lives; to our sense of pity, and beauty, and pain; to the latent feeling of fellowship with all creation – and to the subtle, but invincible, conviction of solidarity that knits together the loneliness of innumerable hearts: to the solidarity in dreams, in joy, in sorrow, in aspirations, in illusions, in hope, in fear, which binds men to each other, which binds all humanity – the dead to the living and the living to the unborn.

Thus, fiction – if it at all aspires to be art – appeals to temperament. And in truth it must be, like painting, like music, like all art, the appeal of one temperament to all the other innumerable temperaments whose subtle and resistless power endows passing events with their true meaning and creates the moral, the emotional atmosphere of the place and time. Such an appeal to be effective must be an impression conveyed through the senses; and, in fact, it cannot be made in any other way, because temperament, whether individual or collective, is not amenable to persuasion. All art, therefore, appeals primarily to the senses, and the artistic aim when expressing itself in written words must also make its appeal through the senses, if its high desire is to reach the secret spring of responsive emotions. It must strenuously aspire to the plasticity of sculpture, to the colour of painting, and to the magic suggestiveness of music – which is the art of arts. And it is only through complete, unswerving devotion to the perfect blending of form and substance; it is only through an unremitting, never-discouraged care for the shape and ring of sentences that an approach can be made to plasticity, to colour; and the light of magic sugges-tiveness may be brought to play for an evanescent instant over the commonplace surface of words: of the old, old words, worn thin, defaced by ages of careless usage.

The sincere endeavour to accomplish that creative task, to go as far on that road as his strength will carry him, to go undeterred by faltering, weariness, or reproach, is the only valid justification for the worker in prose. And if his conscience is clear, his answer to those who, in the fulness of a wisdom which looks for immediate profit, demand specifically to be edified, consoled, amused, to be promptly improved, or encouraged, or frightened, or shocked, or charmed, must run thus: – "My task which I am trying to achieve is, by the power of the written word, to make you hear, to make you feel – it is, before all, to make you *see*. That – and no more, and it is everything. If I succeed, you shall find there according to the need of your hearts: encouragement, consolation, fear, charm – all you demand; and, perhaps, also that glimpse of truth for which you have forgotten to ask."

To snatch in a moment of courage, from the remorseless rush of time, a passing phase of life is only the beginning of the task. The task approached in tenderness and faith is to hold up unquestioningly, without choice and without fear, the rescued fragment before all eyes and in the light of a sincere mood. It is to show its vibration, its colour, its form; and through its movement, its form, and its colour, reveal the substance of its truth – disclose its inspiring secret: the stress and passion within the core of each convincing moment. In a single-minded attempt of that kind, if one be deserving and fortunate, one may perchance attain to such clearness of sincerity that at last the presented vision of regret or pity, of terror or mirth, shall awaken in the hearts of the beholders that feeling of unavoidable solidarity; of the solidarity in mysterious origin, in toil, in joy, in hope, in uncertain fate, which binds men to each other and all mankind to the visible world.

It is evident that he who, rightly or wrongly, holds by the convictions expressed above cannot be faithful to any one of the temporary formulas of his craft. The enduring part of them – the truth which each only imperfectly veils – should abide with him as the most precious of his possessions, but they all: Realism, Romanticism, Naturalism, even the unofficial sentimentalism (which, like the poor, is exceedingly difficult to get rid of), all these gods must, after a short period of fellowship, abandon him: even on the very threshold of the temple, to the stammerings of his conscience and to the outspoken consciousness of the difficulties of his work. In that uneasy solitude the supreme cry of Art for Art itself loses the exciting ring of its apparent immorality. It sounds far off. It has ceased to be a cry, and when it is heard, it is only as a whisper, often incomprehensible, but at times, and faintly, encouraging.

When, stretched at ease in the shade of a roadside tree, we watch in a distant field the motions of a labourer, we being, after a time, to wonder languidly as to what he may be at. We watch the movements of his body, the waving of his arms, we see him bend down, stand up, hesitate, begin again. It may add to the charm of an idle hour to be told the purpose of his exertions. If we know he is trying to lift a stone, or dig a ditch, or uproot a stump, we look with a more real interest at his efforts: we are disposed to condone the jar of his agitation upon the restfulness of the landscape; and even, if in a brotherly frame of mind, we may bring ourselves to forgive his failure. We understood his object, and, after all, the fellow has tried – and perhaps he had not the strength – and perhaps he had not the knowledge. We forgive, go on our way – and forget.

And so it is with the workman of art. Art is long, and life is short, and success is very far off. And thus, doubtful of strength to travel so far, we talk a little about the aim – the aim of art, which, like life itself, is inspiring, difficult, obscured by mists. It is not in the clear logic of a triumphant conclusion; it is not in the unveiling of one of those heartless secrets which are called the Laws of Nature. It is not less great, but only more difficult.

To arrest, for the space of a breath, the hands busy about the work of the earth, and compel men entranced by the sight of distant goals to glance for a moment at the surrounding vision of form and colour, of sunshine and shadows; to make them pause for a look, for a sigh, for a smile – such is the aim, difficult and evanescent, and reserved only for a very few to achieve. But sometimes, by the deserving and the fortunate, even that task is accomplished. And when it is accomplished – behold! – all the truth of life is there: a moment of vision, a sigh, a smile – and the return to an eternal rest.

Notes

INTRODUCTORY ESSAY

1 'Aspects of English Criticism of the Novel, 1830–1850', unpublished dissertation, Indiana University, 1970, p. 156.
2 *The Evangelical and Oxford Movements*, 1983, p. 15.
3 'Aspects of English Criticism', p. 75.
4 *Ibid.*, p. 126.
5 'English Criticism of Technique in Fiction, 1880–1900', unpublished dissertation, Harvard University, 1957, p. 200.
6 *The Theory of the Novel in England, 1850–1870*, 1959, p. xii.
7 *English Criticism of the Novel, 1865–1900*, 1965, p. 62.

EDWARD BULWER LYTTON

1 *British Novelists and Their Styles*, 1859, pp. 228–9.
2 Runzo, 'Aspects of English Criticism', pp. 6–7.
3 Count Vittorio Alfieri, Italian dramatist. Bulwer Lytton's reference is probably to Alfieri's *Filippo* (1783), in which Don Carlos is a principal character.
4 This distinction between writers who plan and those who improvise was to establish one of the principal differences later in the century between the novel and the romance.
5 *The Mysteries of Udolpho* (1794), by Ann Radcliffe.
6 *Anastasius: or Memoirs of a Modern Greek, Written at the end of the Eighteenth Century* (1819), by Thomas Hope.
7 The background for these remarks and those of the next section are significant. Bulwer, Ainsworth, Dickens, and others were currently under attack for their sensational Newgate novels, which were understood by enemies and sometimes advertised by friends as attempts to revive the gothic novel and to give it an urban setting and English criminal heroes.
8 Bulwer was later to adopt this principle of Schiller's, restricting it to long novels with which the reader has lived on intimate terms for a considerable time. It forms the basis of his criticism of *The Mill on the Floss*, expressed in a letter to John Blackwood (25 January 1858), and it may have been the reason he urged Dickens to change the original unhappy ending of *Great Expectations*.
9 Novel by Bulwer Lytton himself, 1832.
10 William Godwin (1756–1836), English novelist and political philosopher.
11 In Bulwer Lytton's own plays he tried to take care to observe the unities, especially that of action. An unpublished preface to his version of *Oedipus Rex* takes even Sophocles to task for digressive materials, and he wrote a special acting version of his historical drama *Richelieu*, in which the digressions of the reading version were eliminated. His novels, on the other hand, usually observe only a thematic unity.

12 Bulwer Lytton footnotes this passage as follows: '"The nature of the Drama," observes Schiller, in his preface to Fiesco [*Die Verschwerung des Fiesco zu Genua*, 1784] and in excuse for his corruption of history, "does not admit the hand of Chance."'

13 Bulwer Lytton footnotes this passage as follows: '"Why is it that a successful novelist has never been a successful play-writer?" This is a question that has been so often put, that we have been frightened out of considering whether the premises involved in the question are true or not. It is something like the schoolboy question, "Why is a pound of feathers heavier than a pound of lead?" It is long before Tom or Jack ask, "Is it heavier?" *Is* it true that a successful novelist has never been a successful play-writer? We will not insist on Goldsmith, whose comedy of "She Stoops to Conquer," and whose novel of the "Vicar of Wakefield," are alike among the greatest ornaments of our language. But was not Göthe a great play-writer and a great novelist? Who will decide whether the palm of genius should be given to the "Tasso" or the "Wilhelm Meister" of that all-sided genius? Is not the "Ghost-seer" a successful novel? Does it not afford the highest and most certain testimony of what Schiller could have done as a writer of narrative fiction, and are not the "Wallerstein," and "Fiesco," and "Don Carlos," great plays by the same author? Are not "Candide" and "Zadig" [novels by Voltaire] imperishable masterpieces in the art of the novelist? And are not "Zaire" and "Mahomet" [plays by Voltaire] equally immortal? The three greatest geniuses that, in modern times, the Continent has produced, were both novelists and dramatists – equally great in each department. In France, at this day, Victor Hugo, who with all his faults, is immeasurably the first writer in the school he has sought to found, is both the best novelist and the most powerful dramatist. That it has not happened *oftener* that the same man has achieved equal honour in the novel and the play is another question. But we might just as well ask why it has not happened oftener that the same man has been equally successful in tragedy and epic – in the ode and the didactic – why he who is sublime as a poet is often tame as a prose writer, and *vice versá* – why the same artist who painted the "Transfiguration" [Raphael] did not paint the "Last Day" [Michelangelo]. Nature, circumstance, and education have not fitted many men to be great, except in one line. And least of all are they commonly great in two lines, which, though seemingly close to each other, run in parallel directions. The more subtle the distinctions between the novel and the play, the more likely are they to be overlooked by him who attempts both. It is the same with all departments of art; the closer the approximation of the boundary, the more difficult the blending.'

14 In his famous speech, *De Corona*.

15 Le Sage's picaresque novel, *Gil Blas* (1715–35), was considered by Bulwer Lytton and many other nineteenth-century authorities as one of the major achievements of prose fiction. Bulwer Lytton regarded it as an outstanding example of the first of the two forms of philosophical fiction: the satirical and the metaphysical. See his 'On the Different Kinds of Prose Fiction with Some Apology for the Fiction of the Author', published with *The Disowned* (1835).

16 Novel by Dr John Moore, 1786.

17 By Bulwer Lytton himself, 1838.

18 With this final statement Bulwer Lytton disavows the kind of didactic fiction towards which his insistence on the importance of thematic statement might have been supposed to be tending. His truths are emotional rather than intellectual, the result, more frequently, of mystical visions than of rational conclusions.

GEORGE MOIR

1   These definitions occur in the first paragraph of the article on 'Romance' by Sir Walter Scott, originally written for the supplement to the 1824 edition of the *Encyclopaedia Britannica* and appearing in the 1842 edition immediately before 'Modern Romance and Novel' (vol. 19, pp. 318–34). Scott's account has little to say about anything later than the medieval romance; Moir's essay brings the history of prose fiction up to date.

2   'See some valuable papers on Art in Fiction, ascribed, we believe with justice, to Sir L. Bulwer. *Monthly Chronicle*, Nos. i and ii' (Moir's note). See pp. 22–38 in the present volume.

3   Reference to Defoe's 'A True Relation of the Apparition of One Mrs Veal' (1706), considered until the end of the nineteenth century to be an invention of Defoe's rather than a piece of factual reporting.

4   Protagonists of Spanish picaresque (from *pícaro* = rogue) novels. The authorship of *Lazarillo de Tormes* (1554) cannot be established with certainty; *Marcos de Obregon* (1618) is by Vicente Martínez Espinel and *Guzmán de Alfarache* (1599–1604) by Matéo Aleman.

5   Waterside district of east London.

6   William Dampier, buccaneer and explorer; author of *Voyages* (1607), *Voyages and Descriptions* (1699), and *A Voyage to New Holland* (1703–9).

7   *The Newgate Calendar, or Malefactors' Bloody Register*, brought out in several late-eighteenth-century and early-nineteenth-century series, described notorious crimes and criminals.

8   Boswell's *Life of Johnson*, 6 April 1772: 'Why, Sir, if you were to read Richardson for the story, your impatience would be so much fretted that you would hang yourself.'

9   Scott, 'Samuel Richardson'; in *Lives of the Novelists* (1825).

10   Isaac D'Israeli called Richardson 'the Shakespeare of novelists' in the opening sentence of 'Richardson'; *Curiosities of Literature*, 5th edn (1807).

11   Heartless libertine in *The Fair Penitent* (1703) by Nicholas Rowe.

12   Philip Massinger, author, with Nathaniel Field, of *The Fatal Dowry* (1632), the tragedy on which Rowe's *The Fair Penitent* was based.

13   Anna Letitia Barbauld, 'Life of Samuel Richardson, With Remarks on His Writings'; preface to *The Correspondence of Samuel Richardson* (1804).

14   Pierre Carlet de Chamblain de Marivaux (1688–1763), French author of prose comedies and romances, known especially for his analyses of sentiment.

15   A reference to the precise and loving rendering of ordinary, even humble, subjects characteristic of sevententh-century Dutch painting, often taken as a hallmark of realism in literature as well as in the visual arts. See, e.g., George Eliot's admiring comment in ch. 17 of *Adam Bede*, quoted on p. 159. In that same passage, she went on to point out that 'lofty-minded people despise' Dutch realism; one of these was Archibald Alison, whose scornful references to 'the Boors of Ostade' and 'the Village Wakes of Teniers' appear on p. 62.

16   Paraphrase of a famous definition of the effect of tragedy in Aristotle's *Poetics*, 6.

17   Milton, 'L'Allegro', l. 32.

18   Characters in Smollett's *The Adventures of Peregrine Pickle* (1751).

19   John Benbow (1653–1702), English admiral.

20   English painter in *Peregrine Pickle*.

21   Character in Fielding's *Joseph Andrews* (1742).

22   *Peregrine Pickle*, chs. 44, 7, 47, and 56–7, respectively.

23 *Tom Jones* (1749), Bk IX, ch. 5.

24 *The Adventures of Ferdinand Count Fathom* (1753), ch. 21.

25 *The Adventures of Roderick Random* (1748), ch. 29.

26 Character based on John Dryden in *The Rehearsal* (1672), a satiric play by George Villiers, second Duke of Buckingham, and others. Bayes's words are: 'Why, what a devil is the plot good for but to bring in fine things?' (III. i).

27 In *Tristram Shandy* (1760–7), vol. 5, ch. 1, a sentence reading 'Shall we for ever make new books, as apothecaries make new mixtures, by pouring only out of one vessel into another?' was 'stolen', according to Scott (*Lives of the Novelists*), from Robert Burton's *The Anatomy of Melancholy* (1621), where it appears in this form: 'As Apothecaries we make new mixtures every day, pour out of one vessel into another…' ('Democritus Junior to the Reader'). In *Tristram Shandy*, Sterne's sentence precedes an attack on plagiarism.

28 *Tristram Shandy*, vol. 9, ch. 24. Maria reappears near the end of Sterne's *A Sentimental Journey through France and Italy* (1768).

29 *Tristram Shandy*, vol. 6, ch. 8.

30 Goldsmith's 'The Deserted Village' (1770), l. 180 ('fools, who came to scoff, remain'd to pray').

31 *The Recess*, by Sophia Lee, was published in 1785, *The Scottish Chiefs*, by Jane Porter, in 1810.

32 *Lives of the Novelists*.

ARCHIBALD ALISON

1 Samuel Johnson's dictum, in the *Journey to the Western Islands of Scotland* (1775), reads: 'Whatever withdraws us from the power of our senses; whatever makes the past, the distant, or the future predominate over the present, advances us in the dignity of thinking beings' ('Inch Kenneth'). The concept of 'the distant', so important to Alison, does appear in Johnson's original.

2 *Romeo and Juliet*, IV.i.III–12.

3 Adriaen van Ostade (1610–85) or possibly his brother Isaac (1621–49); David Teniers the Younger (1610–90); Guido Reni (1575–1642); Raphael Santi (1483–1520). Alison is here contrasting the realistic painting of the first two with the sacred painting that may be said to 'elevate and purify' of the last two.

4 Voltaire objected to the bombast and 'barbarism' of Shakespeare, especially when combined with the unselective verisimilitude that he considered characteristic of English drama before Addison. Of *Hamlet*, for all its 'sublime' features, he said that 'one would think the whole piece was the product of the imagination of a drunken savage' ('Dissertation sur la tragédie ancienne et moderne', 1750).

5 The collected *Discourses* of Reynolds were published in 1794. These ideas appear most prominently in Nos. III and VII.

6 Claude Gelée (1600–82), called Lorraine after the province where he was born; Salvator(e) Rosa (1615–73). Though Rosa was more versatile than Claude, both were important landscape painters.

7 Scott called Charlotte Smith, whose work is little known today, 'one of our most distinguished novelists' (*Lives of the Novelists*); her fiction – including *Emmeline* (1788), *Celistina* (1791), *Desmond* (1792), and *The Old Manor House* (1793) – is highly romantic, featuring heroines whose emotional suffering reflects Smith's own disastrous experience with marriage and embodying her close observations of physical nature. Ann Radcliffe, best known for *The Mysteries of Udolpho* (1794), also wrote *A Sicilian Romance* (1790), *The Romance of the Forest* (1791), and *The Italian*

(1797); Frances (Fanny) Burney was the author of *Evelina* (1778), *Cecilia* (1782), *Camilla* (1796), and *The Wanderer* (1814).

8 In the final chapter of his *Decline and Fall of the Roman Empire* (1776–87), completed shortly before the outbreak of the French Revolution in 1789, Edward Gibbon referred to his distant subject as 'the greatest, perhaps, and most awful scene in the history of mankind'.

9 The *History of England* by David Hume appeared in 1754–61, that by Sharon Turner in 1814–23. In 1845, the year of Alison's essay, Turner published *Richard the Third: A Poem*.

10 William Robertson wrote a *History of Scotland during the Reigns of Queen Mary and King James VI* (1759); Patrick Fraser Tytler was the author of a *History of Scotland* (1828–43); Scott's *The Abbot* (1820) deals with Mary's fortunes during her imprisonment in Lochleven Castle and afterward; her 'Last Sacrament' is depicted in v.vii of Schiller's *Maria Stuart* (1800).

11 What Andrew Fletcher of Saltoun actually wrote was: 'I knew a very wise man so much of Sir Chr—'s sentiment, that he believed if a man were permitted to make all the ballads, he need not care who should make the laws of a nation'; *An Account of a Conversation concerning a Right Regulation of Governments for the Common Good of Mankind in a Letter to the Marquis of Montrose, the Earls of Rothes, Roxburg, and Haddington* (1704).

12 The (first) Reform Bill, enacted in the year of Scott's death (1832), enlarged the electorate for Members of Parliament and corrected some inequalities of representation in the House of Commons. For the basis of Alison's objections to the 'dangers' of this piece of legislation, which struck him and like-minded men as truly revolutionary, see the headnote to this essay, p. 58.

13 *Essai sur les fictions* (1795) by Anne Louise Germaine de Staël, translated into German by Goethe the following year.

14 Reference to the test of skill in Bk XXI of the *Odyssey*, where Penelope challenges her suitors to draw the great bow of her presumably dead husband, Odysseus (or Ulysses), promising to marry whichever one of them can use it to shoot an arrow through twelve axes. After all the suitors fail, Odysseus, disguised as a swineherd, succeeds.

15 *The Last of the Barons* (1843) is a novel by Edward Bulwer Lytton. His *The Last Days of Pompeii* was published in 1834.

16 A novel (1837) by G. P. R. James.

17 Scott's *Anne of Geierstein* (1829) is set largely in fifteenth-century Switzerland, *The Surgeon's Daughter* (1827) – published along with *The Highland Widow* and *The Two Drovers* in *Chronicles of the Canongate* – in eighteenth-century India, and *Count Robert of Paris* (1831) in the Eastern Roman Empire ('the Lower Empire') at the time of the arrival of the first crusaders in Constantinople.

18 In Discourse XI Reynolds praises Titian for his 'excellence with regard to colour, and light and shade', but states no such rigid formula as that offered by Alison.

19 Jules-Gabriel Janin, author of the popular *L'âne mort et la femme guillotinée* (1829).

20 G. P. R. James's *Philip Augustus* was published in 1831.

21 Published in 1807.

22 W. Harrison Ainsworth, author of *The Tower of London* (1840), *Old Saint Paul's* (1841), *Windsor Castle* (1843), and other historical novels.

23 James Fenimore Cooper's *The Last of the Mohicans* was published in 1826, *The Prairie* in 1827.

24 Alessandro Manzoni; his *I Promessi Sposi* (1827) was warmly praised by Scott.

25 Probably a reference to the Sorbonne lectures of François Guizot, published in

Histoire générale de la civilisation en Europe (1828) and *Histoire de la civilisation en France* (1829–32).

26 George Sand, whose real name was Lucile-Aurore Dupin, Baroness Dudevant. Alison was probably thinking of novels like her *Mauprat* (1837), as well as Hugo's *Notre-Dame de Paris* (1831), Janin's *L'âne mort et la femme guillotinée*, and *Les Mystères de Paris* (1842–3) by Marie-Joseph (Eugène) Sue.

ANONYMOUS

1 The doctrine here set forth echoes other mid-nineteenth-century statements regarding the exalted function of prose fiction. See, e.g., Bulwer Lytton's preface to the 1845 edition of *Night and Morning*, where he asserts that his novels propose 'to take man from the low passions, and the miserable troubles of life, into a higher region, to beguile weary and selfish pain . . . to raise the passions into sympathy with heroic struggles – and to admit the soul into that serener atmosphere from which it rarely returns to ordinary existence, without some memory or association which ought to enlarge the domain of thought and exalt the motives of action.'

2 Wordsworth, 'Personal Talk', ll. 33–6.

3 Wordsworth, 'Lines Composed a Few Miles Above Tintern Abbey', ll. 47–8.

4 *Hamlet*, I.v.104.

5 Joseph Addison, *Spectator*, No. 58 (7 May 1711). From 'were to be cramped' to the end of the sentence this is more direct quotation than paraphrase.

6 We have been unable to identify the quotation, but it is clearly a reference to the degradation of a noble art into a commercial commodity. The Egyptians regarded the cow as sacred to their goddess Isis, but by the nineteenth century the term 'milch cow' had come to bear the figurative meaning 'a source of regularly-accruing gain or profit' (*OED*).

7 Philip James Bailey, *Festus* (5th edn 1852), p. 339 (scene xxii, ll. 725–6, 736–41).

8 Published 1850–3.

JAMES FITZJAMES STEPHEN

1 Novel by Daniel Defoe, published 1724.

2 Periodical conducted by Sir Richard Steele and Joseph Addison in 1711–12 and revived briefly by Addison in 1714. It was purportedly put out by a small club of fictitious gentlemen, including Sir Roger, a baronet from Worcestershire.

3 Works by Alphonse de Lamartine and Jean-Baptiste Capefigue, published 1847 and 1831–3, respectively.

4 *The Light of Nature Pursued* (1765–78), a philosophical work by Abraham Tucker, who used the pseudonym Edward Search.

5 Published 1849; the author is Félix Bungener.

6 Paul Rabaut (1718–94), French Protestant pastor.

7 Possibly a reference to Lord Chesterfield's letter of 16 October 1847, in which he tells his son: 'Observe carefully what pleases you in others, and probably the same things in you will please others.'

8 Tales by Maria Edgeworth (1767–1849).

9 Characters in novels by William Makepeace Thackeray: *Vanity Fair* (1847–8) and *The History of Pendennis* (1848–50), respectively. Pendennis is also the narrator of *The Newcomes* (1853–5).

10 Novel by Charlotte M. Yonge, published 1853.

11 Weekly periodical started by Charles Dickens in 1850. 'Transported for Life'

appeared in vol. 5 in two parts: 31 July 1852, pp. 455–64; and 7 August 1852, pp. 482–9.

12 Roman woman violated by Sextus, son of Tarquin, king of Rome; the most famous version of her story is Shakespeare's 'The Rape of Lucrece' (1594).

13 The *Römische Geschichte* (1811–12) of Barthold Georg Niebuhr, first translated into English in 1827.

14 Scottish rebels, characters in *Waverley*.

15 Collected accounts of trials for alleged offences against the state, published in several series beginning in 1719. The most famous nineteenth-century publisher of *State Trials* was William Cobbett.

16 Colonel James Gardiner (1688–1745), killed at the battle of Prestonpans, in circumstances described in *Waverley*.

17 Charles Edward Stuart (1720–88), the 'Young Pretender' to the British crown; appears in *Waverley*.

18 Baron of Bradwardine, father of Rose (see below), in *Waverley*.

19 'Judgment of Lord Stowell in *Evans* vs. *Evans*. 1 *Hagg. Cons. Rep.* 36, 37' (Stephen's note).

20 Probably a reference to 'The Convalescent' by Charles Lamb, published July 1825 in the *London Magazine* and 1833 in *The Last Essays of Elia*.

21 Robert Burns wrote the poem sometimes called 'To Mary in Heaven' in 1789; it is usually referred to by its opening words, 'Thou ling'ring star'.

22 Protagonist of Scott's *The Black Dwarf* (1816).

23 Strained, unnatural literary contrivances: e.g., in *Spectator*, No. 351 (12 April 1712), where Addison refers to 'the changing of the Trojan Fleet into Water-Nymphs' as 'the most violent Machine in the whole *Aeneid*'.

24 Protagonist of *Westward Ho!* (1855) by Charles Kingsley.

25 Novel by Alain-René LeSage, published 1715–35.

26 Major Pendennis's unscrupulous servant in *The History of Pendennis*.

27 Alexander Pope, 'An Essay on Man', Bk VI (1734), ll. 121–2, 149–54, 167–72.

28 Travel book, published 1792.

29 Protagonist of Charles Kingsley's *Yeast* (1848).

30 Kingsley's *Alton Locke, Tailor and Poet*, was published in 1850.

31 Fifth-century Alexandria, the setting of Kingsley's novel *Hypatia* (1851); Cyril is the zealous patriarch of the Christian church in that city. 'England in the days of Elizabeth' in the following reference is the setting of *Westward Ho!*

32 George Primrose, son of Dr Primrose, the 'vicar of Wakefield'.

WILLIAM CALDWELL ROSCOE

1 Reviewing Thackeray's *The Newcomes* in the *Quarterly Review* in September 1855, Whitwell Elwin had written: 'The goad which is applied too freely by contemporary criticism to abate the pride, or stimulate the flagging imagination of popular authors, is at any rate not called for in the present instance.'

2 Sir Pitt Crawley, Lord Steyne, Major Dobbin, and George Osborne appear in *Vanity Fair*; Major Pendennis, George Warrington, Laura Bell, and Arthur Pendennis in *The History of Pendennis*; and Colonel Newcome and the other characters named in this passage in *The Newcomes*, which is narrated by Pendennis.

3 For Roscoe's judgement of Daniel Defoe, see his 'De Foe as a Novelist', *National Review*, 3 (October 1856): 380–410; this is reprinted as 'Unideal Fiction: De Foe' in *Poems and Essays*, vol. 2, pp. 222–63.

4 Characters and incidents in novels by Charles Dickens: James Carker and Edith

Dombey in *Dombey and Son* (1846–8); Thomas (Tommy) Traddles in *David Copperfield* (1849–50); the trial of Bardell v. Pickwick in ch. 34 of *The Pickwick Papers* (1837).

5 George Berkeley (1685–1753), philosopher and Bishop of Cloyne, who held that material objects have no independent being but exist only as concepts of the mind.

6 Publishers of a number of Thackeray's books, beginning with *Vanity Fair* and including those that occasioned this essay: *The Newcomes* and the first two volumes of *Miscellanies: Prose and Verse* (1855–6).

7 Possibly a reference to Goethe's statement recorded by Eckermann in the *Gespräche mit Goethe* (1836) that he wrote *Götz von Berlichingen* at the age of twenty-two 'and was astonished, ten years later, to observe the fidelity of my own representation. It is obvious that I could have seen and experienced but a small part of that various picture of life, and could only know how to paint it by presentiment'.

8 In Lecture VI, 'Sterne and Goldsmith', of *The English Humourists of the Eighteenth Century* (1853), Thackeray laments the omnipresence in Sterne of 'a latent corruption – a hint, as of an impure presence', and cites Coleridge's opinion of Sterne's licentiousness in a footnote consisting of a lengthy quotation from vol. I of Coleridge's *Literary Remains* (1836).

9 Published under various titles and editors since 1826, beginning with *A General and Heraldic Dictionary of the Peerage and Baronetage of the United Kingdom*, compiled by John Burke.

10 Friend of the protagonist in *Pendennis*.

11 Thackeray contributed satirical writing to *Fraser's Magazine* in the 1830s and 1840s, but does not appear to have written for *Blackwood's Edinburgh Magazine*.

12 'Sawedwadgeorgeearllitnbulwig' = Sir Edward George Earle Lytton Bulwer, whom Thackeray frequently satirized, as the name is first understood by the footman Yellowplush in 'Mr Yellowplush's Ajew' (*Fraser's Magazine*, August 1838), reprinted in the second volume of *Miscellanies* under review in this essay. After Thackeray's *The Kickleburys on the Rhine* (1850) was reviewed severely in the *Times* on 4 January 1851, he retorted with an 'Essay on Thunder and Small Beer' prefaced to the second edition (1851).

13 *Pendennis*, ch. 11.

14 Both 'The Chronicle of the Drum' and 'Jacob Omnium's Hoss' were reprinted in the first volume of *Miscellanies* under review in this essay. The former was initially published in 1841 in a small volume also containing 'The Second Funeral of Napoleon'; the latter originally appeared in *Punch* on 9 December 1848.

15 *Vanity Fair*, ch. 62.

16 *Pendennis*, ch. 61.

17 Another reference to 'Mr Yellowplush's Ajew', near the end of which Yellowplush's master rebukes him for his impertinence, 'bursting into a most igstrorinary rage'.

18 *The Newcomes*, ch. 23; the italics are Roscoe's.

19 John xviii: 38.

20 *Pendennis*, ch. 75.

21 Joseph Grimaldi (1779–1837), celebrated clown and pantomimist; Charles Mathews (1776–1835), actor best known for his one-man 'At Home' performances.

22 Tennyson, 'The Palace of Art' (1832), ll. 230–2:

> from which mood was born
> Scorn of herself; again, from out of that mood
> Laughter at her self-scorn.

23 John James Ridley, character in *The Newcomes*.
24 *Pendennis*, ch. 56.
25 *Macbeth*, I.vi.1–2.
26 More characters in novels by Thackeray. In addition to those identified in n. 2, Amelia (Sedley) appears in *Vanity Fair*, Helen Pendennis in *Pendennis*, Lady Esmond (probably Rachel Esmond, wife and then widow of Francis Esmond, who became the fourth Viscount Castlewood; she marries Henry Esmond at the end of the novel) in *The History of Henry Esmond* (1852), and Madame de Florac in *The Newcomes*. The Colonel Esmond referred to a few lines later is Henry Esmond.
27 Bitter and bawdy ballad about a murderous chimney-sweep sung by W. G. Ross beginning in the 1840s. It 'became a legend expressive of the corruption and immorality which attached to the fashionable Caves of Harmony' and was characterized by a 'combination of unmitigated realism ... with the power and the intention of shocking' (J. S. Bratton, *The Victorian Popular Ballad*, 1975, p. 97).
28 The Honourable Algernon Percy Deuceace makes his first appearance in 'Dimond Cut Dimond' (*Fraser's Magazine*, February 1838), reprinted in the second volume of the *Miscellanies*; like the rest of *The Memoirs of Mr Charles J.* [for James] *Yellowplush*, it is rendered in the peculiar 'orthography' of that footman. This phonetic spelling also appears in the 'Diary' of the ex-footman C. Jeames de la Pluche that ran in *Punch* between 2 August 1845 and 7 February 1846; this too was reprinted in the second volume of the *Miscellanies*.
29 Such down-to-earth novels as *Georgette* (1820), *Gustave* (1821), *Mon voisin Raymond* (1822), and *L'Amant de la lune* (1847) by a French writer with a large English following.
30 Sir James Simpson, commander of British troops in the Crimea between June and November 1855.
31 Mrs Kewsy = a character in *The Kickleburys on the Rhine*, who also appeared in *The Book of Snobs* (1848; reprinted in the first volume of *Miscellanies*); the Portmans = the credulous vicar of Clavering St Mary's and his gossip-loving wife in *Pendennis*.
32 Character in *Doctor Birch and His Young Friends* (1849).
33 Christopher Marlowe, *Doctor Faustus*, V.i.111–12.

DAVID MASSON

1 Becky Sharp is a character in Thackeray's *Vanity Fair*; Harry Foker and Captain Costigan appear in his *The History of Pendennis*; and Jeames is C. Jeames de la Pluche, the fictitious footman of the *Yellowplush Memoirs*.

GEORGE ELIOT

1 By Henrietta Georgiana Marcia Lascelles, Lady Chatterton; published 1856 (as were all six of the 'silly novels' on which Eliot concentrates her scorn in this essay).
2 Allusion to Ninetta Crummles, 'the infant phenomenon' in Dickens's *The Life and Adventures of Nicholas Nickleby* (1838–9), whose growth has been deliberately stunted by means of 'an unlimited allowance of gin-and-water from infancy' (ch. 23).
3 Georg Friedrich Creuzer (1771–1858), German philologist and archaeologist.

4 Henry St John, Viscount Bolingbroke (1678–1751). According to the *Anecdotes* (1820) of Joseph Spence, this was the answer of Alexander Pope to the question whether or not Bolingbroke knew Hebrew.

5 Author unknown; published 1856.

6 Almack's = assembly rooms in King's Street, St James's, where fashionable balls were held; Scotch second-sight = the power of seeing things invisible to others or foretelling the future, claimed, e.g., by the Scottish minister Dr Cumming (see p. 170 and n. 10 below); Mr Rogers's breakfasts = fashionable gatherings at the house of the poet Samuel Rogers (1763–1855).

7 Author unknown; published 1856.

8 Deists = believers in a God who created the world and then abandoned it; Puseyites = followers of Edward Bouverie Pusey (1800–82), one of the founders of the Tractarian or Oxford movement in the Church of England.

9 Author unknown; published 1856.

10 Dr Cumming = John Cumming (1807–81), minister of the Scottish National Church, Crown Court, Covent Garden; Robert Owen = early English socialist and proponent of the co-operative movement (1771–1858); Spirit-rappers = mediums who claim that they can induce spirits to communicate with them by means of rapping.

11 I.e., Policeman X, a recurring character in Thackeray's work: narrator of such cockney 'Ballads of Policeman X', originally published in *Punch*, as 'The Three Christmas Waits' and 'Jacob Omnium's Hoss' (both 1848); also appears in *The History of Pendennis* and, later, in *The Adventures of Philip* (1861–2).

12 Renowned hero; after Orlando, or Roland, the most famous of Charlemagne's knights.

13 By Caroline Lucy Scott; published 1856.

14 In *Uncle Tom's Cabin* (1851–2) by Harriet Beecher Stowe.

15 Foolish and unattractive girl in love with Nicholas Nickleby in Dickens's novel.

16 Jannes and Jambres = adversaries of Moses (2 Timothy iii: 8); Sennacherib = king of Assyria in the Old Testament (2 Kings, 2 Chronicles, and Isaiah); Demetrius the silversmith = maker of shrines in honour of Diana of the Ephesians (Acts xix: 24–7).

17 William Wordsworth, 'Lines Composed a Few Miles above Tintern Abbey' (1798), l. 91.

18 By Jane Margaret Strickland; published 1856.

19 The Run and Read Library for Railway, Road, and River, published beginning in 1853 by Clarke, Beeton. By the time *Adonijah* appeared as No. 21 three years later, the series had been taken over by Simpkin, Marshall. '*Taste, sprightliness, humour and command of diction, combined with sound principles*, will be the leading qualification of the works admitted to the series', according to Clarke, Beeton's preliminary announcement. (See Michael Sadleir, *XIX Century Fiction*, 1951, vol. 2, p. 70.)

20 Catherine Sinclair (1800–64), novelist and philanthropist.

21 Charles Daubeny (1795–1867), chemist and naturalist; John Stuart Mill (1806–73), philosopher; Frederick Denison Maurice (1805–72), clergyman and religious thinker.

22 Proverbs xiv: 23.

23 We have not been able to identify the fable of Jean de la Fontaine in which this ass appears.

GEORGE HENRY LEWES

1 Charles Edward Mudie (1818–90), founder of the largest circulating library in Victorian England.

2 *Le Comte de Monte-Cristo* (1844–5), thriller by Alexandre Dumas père.
3 In Lewes's 'The Principle of Sincerity', ch. 4 of *The Principles of Success in Literature*, *Fortnightly Review*, 1 (1 August 1865): 697–709.
4 'Among the slight but significant indications of imperfect attention to accuracy, may be mentioned the inadvertency with which the French language is treated on the two occasions when French phrases are used: *bête noir* might be charitably accepted as a misprint, but *au discrétion* tasks even charity' (Lewes's note).

HENRY JAMES

1 *English Criticism of the Novel, 1865–1900* (1965), p. 115.
2 Besant (1836–1901), novelist, writer about social conditions in the East End of London, initiator of the *Survey of London* (1902–12). His lecture on 'The Art of Fiction' was delivered on 24 April 1884.
3 James's 'Anthony Trollope', published in the *Century* in July 1883 (26, n.s. 4: 385–95), was an overview of the work of that prolific novelist, who had died seven months earlier. In that essay James had censured Trollope for taking 'a suicidal satisfaction in reminding the reader that the story he was telling was only, after all, a make-believe' (p. 390), applying this stricture specifically to *Barchester Towers* (1857). 'Anthony Trollope', like 'The Art of Fiction', later came out in James's 1888 collection of critical essays, *Partial Portraits*.
4 'Un Coeur simple', the first of the *Trois Contes* (1877).
5 'Mumu' (1852).
6 Emile Zola, whose *Le Roman expérimental* (1880) was the manifesto of the naturalist movement in fiction.
7 Character in the comedy *Speed the Plough* (1798) by Thomas Morton, synonymous with the strait-laced, disapproving neighbour or, more broadly, puritanical, hyper-respectable society.
8 By Andrew Lang, 30 April 1884, pp. 1–2.
9 Novel published in the same year as 'The Art of Fiction', 1884, by Fortuné Du Boisgobey.
10 The reference is to James's own novella, 'An International Episode' (1878).
11 Controversial tenets of the Dutch Roman Catholic theologian Cornelis Jansen (1585–1638), emphasizing predestination, denying free will, and maintaining that human nature is incapable of good.
12 Another novel published in 1884.

ROBERT LOUIS STEVENSON

1 Besant, in his lecture, 'The Art of Fiction', delivered at the Royal Institute, April 1884; and James, in his article of the same title, September 1884.
2 Phidias, fifth-century BC sculptor; William Hogarth, eighteenth-century English graphic artist; Tommaso Salvini, nineteenth-century Italian actor.
3 This sort of expansion of definition had characterized romance criticism from as early at least as Clara Reeve's *The Progress of Romance* (1785). In general, realists tended to define their genre narrowly and to claim for it a recent origin – hence the term 'novel' – while romancers were anxious to claim a long and broad tradition.
4 Charles Edward Mudie (1818–90), founder and publisher of the large and influential lending library which bore his name.
5 Bulwer Lytton's occult novel, 1842.

6 *Le Paradis perdu de Milton*, 1836.

7 Nineteenth-century Scottish clergyman and writer of miscellany; also an editor of Milton.

8 We have been unable to identify this nineteenth-century prose version of *Paradise Lost*, written, RLS seems to be claiming, by a Scot. Gilfillan is not the author, but perhaps it is a lost or an intended work by Stevenson himself, whose youthful interest in Milton is evidenced by a talk, 'Notes on *Paradise Lost*', which he delivered before the Speculative Society, a student group at the University of Edinburgh, 14 March 1871.

9 Stevenson here enters the second stage of his argument, joining issue with James, and here, once again, his is the quintessential romance position. He is insisting that art, including narrative art, means artifice, abstraction, signification, and that it is not the naive, conventionless imitation of life which the forthright realists represented it as.

10 This final stage of the argument insists once again that fiction is not the simple form which the realist James represents it to be. At the beginning of the Victorian period, Bulwer Lytton, another romancer, had, as we noted, spoken of two classes of philosophical novel: one making its appeal to the intellect, the other to the more emotional and mystical faculties. Stevenson tries here to establish a similar distinction between the intellectual novel of character, such as he believed James wrote, and the kind of fiction he was himself writing at this stage of his career, the adventure novel, which makes its appeal to the reader's irrational nature and to his senses. This position looks forward to Conrad.

11 Stevenson's own *Treasure Island* (1881–2).

12 Picaresque French novel, 1715–35, by Le Sage.

13 Here RLS defines the dramatic differently from earlier critics, who thought of it mainly in terms of the Aristotelean unity of action. For Stevenson, educated as he was by late Victorian acting styles, the dramatic seems to mean something like the operatic.

14 Auguste Maquet (1813–88). His play, from which Reade adapted the novel *White Lies*, was originally entitled *Le Château Grantier*. Reade's translation, which pre-dated the adaptation, was not produced in England until 1867, when it appeared with the title, *The Double Marriage*.

15 In the three years which separated the publication of Parts I and II of this essay, Stevenson and James had become close friends. However, it may not be fair to say that RLS is here shifting the brunt of his attack merely for reasons of friendship. Even in 1884 Howells rather than James was perceived by the romancers as the most outspoken and dangerous apologist for the American school of character at the expense of incident.

16 Character from *The Minister's Charge: Or the Apprenticeship of Lemuel Barker*, 1886.

VERNON LEE

1 At the edge of the village in West Yorkshire where the Brontës lived.

2 Story of the youthful love of Dante for Beatrice, a collection of thirty-one lyrics linked by a prose narrative and commentary, written in or about 1292.

3 Karl Hillebrand, 'About Old and New Novels', *Contemporary Review*, 45 (March 1884): 388–402.

4 Character in *Le Barbier de Séville* (1775) and *Le Mariage de Figaro* (1784), comedies by Pierre-Augustin Caron de Beaumarchais, who reappears in operas by

Rossini and Mozart based on these plays: *Il Barbiere di Siviglia* (1816) and *Le Nozze di Figaro* (1786).

5 Jules Michelet (1798–1874), French historian.

6 Protagonists, respectively, of *La Cousine Bette* (1847) by Honoré de Balzac and *Madame Bovary* (1857) by Gustave Flaubert.

7 Described at the opening of Balzac's *Le Père Goriot* (1834).

8 'Christmas-Eve' (1850), ll. 139–86.

9 *A Modern Instance* (1881) by William Dean Howells. Like Dorothea Brooke's marriage with Edward Casaubon in *Middlemarch*, Marcia Gaylord's marriage to Bartley Hubbard in Howells's novel is a difficult one; neither woman finds widowhood much easier.

10 Published 1882. Lucas Malet was the pseudonym of Mary St Leger Kingsley Harrison. The emphasis here is on the widowhood of Elizabeth Lorimer; in defiance of her conventional aunt, she tries unsuccessfully to lead an independent life after her husband's death, eventually succumbing to fever exacerbated by her feelings of guilt.

11 Characters in *The History of Tom Jones* (1749).

Select booklist

The following is a guide to further reading, not a bibliography of the subject.

PRIMARY SOURCES

Full bibliographical details of the texts in the main body of the book can be found in the headnotes.

A number of modern publications have reprinted significant works of Victorian criticism of the novel. The largest collection, edited by John Charles Olmstead, is the three-volume *A Victorian Art of Fiction: Essays on the Novel in British Periodicals* (New York, 1979), but the Routledge and Kegan Paul Critical Heritage Series volumes on Jane Austen, the Brontës, Wilkie Collins, Conrad, James Fenimore Cooper, Stephen Crane, Defoe, Dickens, George Eliot, Fielding, Gissing, Goldsmith, Hardy, Hawthorne, Henry James, Kipling, Melville, Meredith, Scott, Sterne, Stevenson, Thackeray, Tolstoy, Trollope, and Twain contain many Victorian critical essays and reviews. Critical statements by practising Victorian novelists can be found in Miriam F. Allott's *Novelists on the Novel* (London, 1959), George L. Barnett's *Nineteenth Century British Novelists on the Novel* (New York, 1971), and Myron F. Brightfield's *Victorian England in its Novels, 1840–1870* (Los Angeles, 1968).

SECONDARY MATERIAL

On the individual writers

Bulwer Lytton: There is, as yet, no full biography or edition of the letters, but the following critical books are helpful – Allan Conrad Christensen's *Edward Bulwer-Lytton: The Fiction of New Regions* (Athens, Georgia, 1976) and Edwin M. Eigner's *The Metaphysical Novel in England and America: Dickens, Bulwer, Hawthorne, Melville* (Berkeley and Los Angeles, 1978); and the following doctoral dissertations – Andrew Brown's 'The Metaphysical Novels of Edward Bulwer Lytton' (University of Cambridge, 1979) and William H. Taft III's 'Lytton as a Literary Critic' (Princeton University, 1942).

Moir: The best of the few available sources of information is Albert Frederick Pollard's entry in the *Dictionary of National Biography*, vol. 13 (1894).

Alison: His posthumously published autobiography, *Some Account of My Life and Writings* (2 vols., London, 1883), was edited by his daughter-in-law, Lady Alison.

'Recent Works of Fiction': The history of the *Prospective Review*, in which this essay appeared, is given in the *Wellesley Index to Victorian Periodicals*, vol. 3 (3 vols., Toronto, 1966–79).

Select booklist

Fitzjames Stephen: *The Life of Sir James Fitzjames Stephen* (New York, 1895) was written by his brother, Sir Leslie Stephen. In *Saturday Review, 1855–68* (New York, 1941), M. M. Bevington discusses Fitzjames Stephen's work as a critic, with special reference to his substantial contributions to that periodical.

Roscoe: *Poems and Essays by the Late William Caldwell Roscoe*, ed. R. H. Hutton (2 vols., London, 1860), contains an extensive 'Memoir of the Author' by Hutton, who was Roscoe's brother-in-law.

Masson: Masson's reminiscences, collected by his daughter Flora Masson in *Memories of London in the 'Forties* (London, 1908) and *Memories of Two Cities: Edinburgh and Aberdeen* (London, 1911), are largely anecdotal, containing little information about Masson's life and less about his work as a critic. The most useful general account of Masson's career remains G. Gregory Smith's article in vol. 2 of the Second Supplement to the *Dictionary of National Biography* (London, 1912).

Eliot: The standard life is *George Eliot: A Biography* by Gordon S. Haight (Oxford, 1969), who also edited the *George Eliot Letters* (9 vols., London, 1954–78). The best collection of Eliot's critical writings is *Essays of George Eliot* (London, 1963), which contains a ten-page introduction by the editor, Thomas Pinney. U. C. Knoepflmacher's *George Eliot's Early Novels: The Limits of Realism* (Berkeley, 1968) attempts to show how her own fiction went beyond the theories set forth in these essays, as does George Levine's *The Realistic Imagination: English Fiction from Frankenstein to Lady Chatterley* (Chicago, 1981).

Lewes: Lewes's career is treated in all good biographies of George Eliot, such as Haight's; Anna T. Kitchel's *George Lewes and George Eliot* (New York, 1933) is also still useful. Lewes's critical ideas have been studied by Morris R. Greenhut and Alice R. Kaminsky, most notably in Greenhut's 'George Henry Lewes as a Critic of the Novel' (*Studies in Philology*, 1948) and Kaminsky's 'George Eliot, George Henry Lewes, and the Novel' (*PMLA*, 1956). Also see Kaminsky's edition of *Literary Criticism of George Henry Lewes* (Lincoln, Nebraska, 1964).

James: Leon Edel's monumental study of Henry James is one of the landmarks of twentieth-century literary biography; the subtitles of his five-volume *Henry James* (London, 1953–72) are, respectively, *The Untried Years* (1953), *The Conquest of London* (1962), *The Middle Years* (1962), *The Treacherous Years* (1969), and *The Master* (1972). No doubt the earliest systematic attempt to relate James's practise as a novelist to his theory of fiction was Joseph Warren Beach's *The Method of Henry James* (New Haven, 1918), published only two years after James's death; it remains more readable and more illuminating than most of the scores of book-length works on James spawned during the past three decades. Another book that remains useful despite the passing of more than a half-century since its publication is Morris Roberts's *Henry James's Criticism* (Cambridge, Mass., 1929). Also of interest to the student of James's critical ideas, both for themselves and as they apply to his fiction, are R. P. Blackmur's introduction to *The Art of the Novel* (London, 1934; see headnote in this volume, p. 193) and *The Notebooks of Henry James*, ed. by F. O. Matthiessen and Kenneth B. Murdock (New York, 1947).

Stevenson: Biographies are plentiful and continue to appear, but the best remains J. C. Furnas's *Voyage to Windward: A Life of Robert Louis Stevenson* (New York, 1951). Some helpful critical books are G. K. Chesterton's *Robert Louis Stevenson* (London, 1927), David Daiches' *Robert Louis Stevenson: A Revaluation* (Norfolk, Conn., 1947), Edwin M. Eigner's *Robert Louis Stevenson and Romantic Tradition* (Princeton, 1966), Robert Kiely's *Robert Louis Stevenson and the Fiction of Adventure* (Cambridge, Mass., 1964), and Andrew Noble (ed.), *Robert Louis Stevenson* (London, 1983), a collection of new essays. Roger G. Swearingen's *The Prose Writings of Robert Louis Stevenson: A Guide* (Hamden, Conn., 1980) is an indispensable research tool.

Lee: Peter Gunn's *Vernon Lee: Violet Paget, 1856–1935* (London, 1964) is a thorough examination of the life, the works, and the ideas.

Conrad: There have been many biographies of this colourful figure. (It is becoming increasingly clear that much of the colour was added by the subject himself.) For two decades Jocelyn Baines's *Joseph Conrad: A Critical Biography* (London, 1960) was widely regarded as the best, but it has recently been challenged by Frederick R. Karl's exhaustive *Joseph Conrad: The Three Lives* (New York, 1979) and especially by Zdzislaw Najder's *Joseph Conrad: A Chronicle* (New Brunswick, N.J., 1983). Karl has also examined 'Joseph Conrad's Literary Theory' (*Criticism*, 1960), and Walter F. Wright has brought together author's notes, prefaces, and other relevant statements, including excerpts from the letters, in *Joseph Conrad on Fiction* (Lincoln, Nebraska, 1964). An earlier collection, *Conrad's Prefaces to His Works* (London, 1937), includes less material by Conrad but a longer introduction by the editor, in this case Conrad's friend Edward Garnett. The Norton Critical Edition of *The Nigger of the 'Narcissus'*, ed. Robert Kimbrough (New York, 1979), contains, among other useful items, two essays on the preface to that short novel: one by Ian Watt (originally published in *Novel*, 1974) and the other by John Howard Weston.

MORE GENERAL STUDIES

The essential research tool is the *Wellesley Index to Victorian Periodicals* (3 vols., Toronto, 1966–1979). Two excellent and readable histories covering parts of the period have been published. They are Richard Stang's *The Theory of the Novel in England, 1850–70* (New York, 1959) and Kenneth Graham's *English Criticism of the Novel, 1865–1900* (Oxford, 1965). The earlier part of the period is dealt with in three doctoral dissertations: Carolyn Washburn's 'The History, from 1832 to 1860, of British Criticism of Narrative Prose Fiction' (University of Illinois, 1937), R. M. Schieder's 'Novelists' Theories about the Novel, 1830–1885' (University of Toronto, 1953), and James P. Runzo's 'Aspects of English Criticism of the Novel, 1830–1850' (Indiana University, 1971). Useful doctoral dissertations on the last part of the period are A. B. Wilkenson's 'The Principles and Practices of the Criticism of Fiction in the Quarterlies, Monthlies, and Weeklies, 1850–1860' (University of Cambridge, 1959), Joseph T. Bennett's 'The Critical Reception of the English Novel, 1830–1888' (New York University, 1968), and Lynn C. Bartlett's 'English Criticism of Technique in Fiction, 1880–1900: A Study of Challenge and Response' (Harvard University, 1951).

By the end of the nineteenth century the novel unquestionably had become the most popular and influential of English literary forms. Yet it has not always been clear how the Victorians themselves regarded the nature, aesthetic and moral, of prose fiction. This volume is a collection of twelve 'landmark' essays which chart the development of English theories of fiction during the great age of the novel.

Spanning the whole of the Victorian period, from Bulwer Lytton's 'On Art in Fiction' (1838) to Conrad's Preface to *The Nigger of the 'Narcissus'* (1897), the volume also includes pieces by George Eliot, Henry James, Robert Louis Stevenson, and a number of important critics of the time such as George Moir, Archibald Alison, W. C. Roscoe, Fitzjames Stephen, and David Masson. The editors' introduction surveys the major and contentious issues addressed by novel criticism throughout the period – issues such as realism vs. romance and artistic form vs. moral purpose. Each of the selections that follow is set in its precise historical context by a prefatory essay, and each is fully annotated for the student. There is a helpful bibliography of further reading. The volume as a whole will be an indispensable tool for all serious students of the Victorian novel.

Cambridge English Prose Texts consists of volumes devoted to substantial selections from non-fictional English prose. The series provides students with the opportunity of reading important essays and extracts from larger works which have generally been unavailable in suitable editions.

Cover design by James Butler

Cambridge University Press

GO 0885   ISBN 0-521-27520-2